1985

THE HIGHER SCHOOLING
IN THE UNITED STATES

THE HIGHER SCHOOLING
IN THE UNITED STATES

C. Ashley Ellefson

G.K.HALL &CO.
70 LINCOLN STREET, BOSTON, MASS.

SCHENKMAN PUBLISHING COMPANY
Cambridge, Mass.

Library of Congress Cataloging in Publication Data
Ellefson, C   Ashley.
   The higher schooling in the United States.

   Includes bibliographical references.
   1.   Education, Higher—United States.
I.   Title.
LB2328.E48   378.73   77-7146
ISBN 0-8161-8274-4

For
Beverly Ann

CONTENTS

"He must be prepared, too, for resistance in the world to what he represents. The thinking man is not readily popular. Disinterested criticism is disturbing, for it is criticism which never ceases, and it is stubborn with real questions to which there may be no quick answers. . . . The liberally educated person . . . will be harsh if he has to. . . ."

Mark Van Doren
Liberal Education
(Boston: Beacon Press, 1959)

"The player who trespasses against the rules or ignores them is a 'spoil-sport.' The spoil-sport is not the same as the false player, the cheat; for the latter pretends to be playing the game and, on the face of it, still acknowledges the magic circle. It is curious to note how much more lenient society is to the cheat than to the spoil-sport. This is because the spoil-sport shatters the play-world itself. By withdrawing from the game he reveals the relativity and fragility of the play-world in which he had temporarily shut himself with others. He robs play of its illusion. . . . Therefore he must be cast out, for he threatens the existence of the play-community."

J. Huizinga
Homo Ludens: A Study of the Play-Element in Culture
(Boston: Beacon Press, 1955)

"Well, if you think about teaching enough it will do that to you: she slit her throat."
Line from a dream

This book is an effort to make sense out of the schooling system of the United States. A lot of people criticize that system, but since their criticism does not result in any fundamental change the schools must be doing pretty much what they are supposed to be doing. That is my argument: the schooling system of the United States is not supposed to educate anyone but rather exists to protect the economic, social, and political power of the ruling class by indoctrinating young people so thoroughly that they become incapable of using their minds. They can neither discover anything that the propertied class does not want them to discover nor apply their minds to what little information they do possess.

The function of the schooling system, then, is to guarantee that people do not become educated. The educated person, it seems to me, is one who understands the world and the forces that operate in it and on it. That includes understanding the forces that operate on him. Obviously, therefore, no person is truly educated: there are only degrees of ignorance. Education must be a process rather than a product. The best-educated person is the one who is most at home in the world. In the world, not in society: no one who has read his complete *Memoirs* would consider Casanova, who could charm almost anyone, an educated man.

One of the problems of writing a book such as this is that it might appear to be an attack on specific individuals. It is not. I believe that what I say applies almost universally to the schooling system of the United States. I make a lot of generalizations, and anyone who tells me that I should not generalize I challenge to go through a single day without generalizing. He will be either silent or boring. A generalization is, after all, only a statement of what appears to be generally, not universally, true. Of course there are exceptions to every one of them.

Writing in any case is a very lonely pastime, but writing a book such as this, which some people might take personally, is all the

1

worse. Half the time I have been afraid that it would never be published, and the other half of the time I have been afraid that it would. Sometimes I have been afraid that no one will read it, and often I have been terrified that someone might. Sometimes I am afraid that what I say is not true, but more often I despair because I know that it is.

For me one of the more important results of writing this book is that it has impressed on me the inadequacy of my own education. More and more I resent my schooling. Although I cannot prove it, there seems no doubt that my schooling retarded my education. It did this chiefly in two ways. First, it gave me the wrong answers to the most important questions we can ask. Second, it kept me busy doing useless things so that I would not have time to do worthwhile things. In geography—in college!— we handed in drawings copied directly from textbooks. In history we handed in notebooks copied from textbooks. In a course in Shakespeare we made thick notebooks copied out of the *Variorum*. It was several years before I could read Shakespeare again. Professors had me read books that they had not read themselves.

One of the great embarrassments of my life is that as a young teacher I thought that my students should be doing the same sorts of useless things that I had done in college. I must have supposed that if they hated the work enough it must be good for them. But my greatest single embarrassment is an incident that occurred in a course in American history that I was conducting at Sondrestrom Air Base in Greenland in the fall of 1956. The desegregation decision of 1954 was still very fresh, and in a discussion in that class I repeated that "You cannot legislate morality." A black sergeant—the only black in the course—never came to class again. I do not know whether my ignorance or his having more important things to do on those evenings caused him to drop the course, but I have always supposed that my foolishness had a lot to do with it. In either case I decided later that my education was lacking because *although* I had a master's degree in American history I did not recognize the falsity of that cliché. Now I would say that it was *because* I had the master's degree that I did not recognize its falsity. While it is obvious that most people without degrees accept lies as truth, I think that it is also true that formal schooling delays recognition of lies by those who would otherwise recognize them sooner than they do and in many cases prevents the recognition entirely. It appears to me that exactly *that* is the primary function of schooling: to get people to accept incorrect perceptions—the so-called conventional wisdom—without thinking about them.

But among the terrible teachers were some very good ones. The best teachers, it turns out, were those who gave us reading lists and then left us alone except for testing and grading. And there are still some very good teachers today. They are fighting a very tough battle, and some of them are almost heroic. They know who they are. In academia there is a cliché that states that everyone thinks he is a great teacher, but that is not true. While some teachers are so bad that they do not know they are bad, ordinarily people who cannot teach know it. They get their satisfaction from advancing their careers. They spend most of their time trying to prove to others, and therefore to themselves, how great they are. Teachers who can teach also know it, and they become discouraged because they cannot teach more.

The last thing I want is for this book to be construed as a general attack on either teachers or students. Teachers generally are doing the best they can under impossible circumstances. One can scarcely condemn them for their insecurities and their inadequate educations. The worst that can be said about them is that they have been *too* anxious to do what they have been told to do. It seems characteristic that administrators and other agents and functionaries of the elite are now attacking them for doing the wrong things. Because colleges and universities since approximately 1966 or 1967 have not responded immediately enough to the demands of the propertied class, administrators, in the interest of their propertied-class employers, have conducted a sustained and vicious attack on faculties. It is the administrators who are conducting that attack, not the teachers, who are the real enemies of education.

What I say about teachers should not provide any comfort for administrators with their fondness for what they call faculty-development programs. Faculty-development programs, like the emphasis on flexibility, are designed not to educate anyone but rather to make colleges and universities more immediately responsive to the demands of the propertied class and by impressing teachers with their insecurity make them easier to control. The primary reason why teachers do not teach these days is that they are not allowed to teach, and faculty-development programs are not going to change that. What has happened is that the people who control the schools have made it impossible for teachers to teach, and now they are blaming the teachers for not teaching. Administrators are running wild in their efforts to develop gimmicks to please their propertied-class bosses by harassing teachers. The foundations appear to have plenty of money available for assessing faculties, as the phrase runs, and administrators are overjoyed with any silly scheme that might impress those who run the foundations. Ordinarily these schemes have nothing to do with improving education but rather are designed to advance the careers of the administrators who propose and implement them by proving how much money they can get and how effective they can be in harassing faculties. Until we can get rid of these administrators completely the best thing we could do for education would be to take their pencils, typewriters, and secretaries away from them.

And the students are only what the schools and the other institutions of society have made them. The proper attitude toward them would seem to be sympathy rather than contempt. But we must never forget what students refuse to believe: that the teacher who is toughest on them is often the one who respects them the most.

The person who wants to look at schooling in the United States has some very good books available to him. Among the best are Raymond Callahan's *Education and the Cult of Efficiency* (1962), Michael Katz's *Class, Bureaucracy, and Schools* (1971), and Joel Spring's *Education and the Rise of the Corporate State* (1972). Merle Curti's *The Social Ideas of American Educators* (1935) might be best of all. Others I have included in my footnotes. Quite possibly the best book ever written on the higher schooling is Thorstein Veblen's *The Higher Learning in America* (1918). The best book I have found on educational philosophy or theory is Mark Van Doren's *Liberal Education* (1943). I have not referred to it in my footnotes: only reading it can do it justice.

Van Doren suggests that the college curriculum should consist of the great books, and he lists those used at St. John's College in Annapolis at the time he wrote. He challenges any critic in advance by saying "If such a curriculum . . . seems bare, that is because the beholder does not know the books." (Beacon edition; Boston, 1959, p. 152.) But I do suggest something different. The Great Books Approach might in fact be better than what I suggest. But the difficulty, I think, is that it assumes more knowledge than the high-school graduate possesses. The college student can read the great books and still not know anything about his own society or the history of the world since 1800. Van Doren, of course, would say that I can say that only because I do not know the books. Still until we can improve the education of the high-school graduate I think that the curriculum I have outlined in my last chapter, including the great books as they apply, is where we must begin. Van Doren and I are not as far apart as might first appear: the curriculum that I outline would include many of the books he lists. The difference would be one of approach: I would have the students read the books as part of more conventional courses. At St. John's, as I understand it, the books *are* the courses. If we ever make our schooling system through high school an educational system, high-school graduates should be ready for the great books. They would already know contemporary history, politics, and economics. Surely that is something to aim for.

The librarians at Cortland have been consistently courteous in helping me to find information. But I must mention one person by name. That is Mrs. Eileen Williams, who was characteristically courteous and efficient in locating materials that were not always easily available.

Professor Frank Ray and Mr. Theodore Fenstermacher have read the entire manuscript with critical expertise. I appreciate their taking the time to read it.

In several ways my bride deserves much of the credit for this book. She has discovered information that I would not have found by myself; through our discussions she has helped me to get my ideas straight; she has helped me clarify specific wording; and she has done all of the typing. Most important, she has remained confident that the book is worth doing when I have wondered whether I might just as well be doing something else.

Chapter 1

THE MYTH

One of the favorite pieces of conventional wisdom in the middle of the 1970s is the belief that students entering college are brighter, more sophisticated, more knowledgeable, and more serious than the students of any other generation. The myth is widespread. In an article in *Today's Education* late in 1974, Ewald B. Nyquist, President of the University of the State of New York and New York State Commissioner of Education, asserts that the "students coming out of U.S. high schools today are better informed and more sophisticated than those of any previous generation." The reasons for their superiority, he says, are that "They have started formal schooling at an earlier age, have spent more days in the classroom at each grade level, have taken more advanced high school courses, and have become more knowledgeable by virtue of such outside influences as television and travel."[1] Even a person as perceptive as Stanley Aronowitz can say that workers of the younger generation are the best-educated ever.[2] Melvin Kranzberg of the Georgia Institute of Technology implies that students today are better than ever when he says that "Today's students are keenly aware of the major phenomena affecting the world today and tomorrow: the population explosion, urbanization, food shortages, energy crisis, resource depletion, problems of work and leisure, etc."[3]

The belief in the superiority of contemporary students has become an article of faith of the people who operate American schools. Like a religious tenet, the belief is based on faith and rote

6

repetition. There is no specific objective evidence that it is true, and, as with any other article of religious faith, there is no objective measurement to apply to it.

The people who insist that students today are brighter and better than ever include seven groups. First there are those who are connected with colleges and universities but seldom or never have any intellectual contact with students. This group includes state commissioners of education or superintendents of schools and college presidents, vice-presidents, deans, directors, coordinators, and counsellors. Some of them have been teachers and some have not. Most of those who have been teachers have not tried to teach for many years. The higher the person's position— and therefore the greater the authority with which he speaks— the less intellectual contact he has with students and the longer it has been since he has had *any* regular intellectual contact with them.

The second group that regularly claims that students entering college today are superior to everyone who has ever gone before consists of those who are connected with elementary, junior high, and high schools and who must respond to the massive criticism of what goes on in those schools. This group includes state superintendents of schools or commissioners of education and high-school superintendents, principals, counsellors, and teachers. For their own protection they *have* to claim that high-school graduates today are better than ever.

The third group consists of incompetent, ignorant, and under-educated teachers. That includes many college teachers. The chief characteristic of the American Ph.D. has always been that he is over-schooled and under-educated. He might be more or less well trained, but that is entirely different from being well educated. The primary objects of graduate training have nothing to do with education. The first object is to continue the indoctrination to which the graduate student has already been formally subjected for sixteen years. He reads the accepted literature and has his prejudices reinforced. He gains the subtlety and intellectual respectability that he will need in his role as an apologist for the status quo. He becomes more closed-minded than ever, since ordinarily the only things he reads are those that support the prejudices that have already been imposed on him.

The second object of graduate training is to teach the student the techniques of research in his field. These techniques are designed to guarantee that he will never learn anything important or dangerous. Especially in what are mistakenly called the social sciences and the humanities it is important that he learn to ask the right questions in order that he discover the acceptable answers. Learning to ask the right questions includes learning *not* to ask the wrong ones. If he asks the wrong questions he might learn—and then teach—things that the people who control the schooling system do not want him to teach.[4]

If the graduate student properly absorbs his training he spends his life adding to the literature in support of the status quo. The result is that the letters *Ph.D.* literally do mean "Piled Higher and Deeper." Since these teachers are uninformed and uncritical themselves, it is little wonder that they consider uninformed and uncritical college students informed and critical. The ignorance of these teachers makes the students appear to be brighter and more informed than they actually are, and their insecurity requires them to flatter the students in order to create a base of student support. The teacher's feeling of inadequacy makes it necessary that the students like him or at least appear to respect him. Flattery is the price he pays for their good will.

The fourth group that flatters the contemporary student consists of self-interested politicians who exploited the dissent against the war in Vietnam, who opportunistically supported the right to vote for eighteen-year-olds, and who out of expediency have to appeal to the young people who now do have the right to vote. Fifth are the Marxists and other radicals who look forward to fundamental change in society and who look to the young to bring about that change. They can remain confident that the change will come only as long as they can remain confident that the young understand the society and seriously want to change it. Their idealization of the young and the laboring class often appears to be almost desperate: they allow no criticism of either.[5] The sixth group consists of those who never think about anything they say but simply repeat whatever they hear most often. This group includes young teachers who have been teaching for such a short time that they have had no students to whom they can compare today's students. Finally, the seventh group consists of the students themselves. Having no basis for judgment, having been taught all of their lives that they are the greatest generation ever, and in a position that necessarily prejudices them, they find it convenient to believe whatever is most flattering to them. Naive, frustrated, and often having difficulty doing the quality of work required in college in spite of the deteriorating academic stan-

dards, the young people are desperately anxious to believe anything good that anyone says about them.

It is no accident that the belief in the extraordinary intelligence,
knowledge, and sophistication of the modern student developed
during the height of the protest against the war in Vietnam. Many
people mistook noise for knowledge. Others, able to think only in
clichés themselves, equated the repetition of clichés with deep
thought. Still others, particularly ambitious politicians and insecure professors, saw the opportunity to develop a constituency
among the young and so were shameless in their flattery. Even
Richard Nixon, who probably had no more respect for the young
than he had for anyone else, developed his appeal to one segment
of the young while he exploited the dissent of other young people
in his law-and-order campaign of 1968.

Anyone who wants to be realistic when he considers modern
schooling must keep two things in mind. First, there is just no
way to know how students today compare in intelligence, knowledge, and sophistication with those of earlier generations. There is
no way to make the comparison. Second, regardless of how students today compare with those of past generations there is both
subjective and objective evidence that students entering college
today are less knowledgeable than those who entered ten years
ago. The subjective evidence confronts the college teacher every
time he enters a classroom. Freshmen more and more must say no
when a teacher asks them whether they have ever heard of such-
and-such. Some who admit this dismiss it as unimportant because,
they say, an increasing proportion of high-school graduates are
going to college and therefore those entering college will naturally
include an increasing number who are unprepared. But during the
past ten years the proportion of high-school graduates entering
college has remained fairly stable. In New York State the proportion of high-school graduates entering four-year colleges declined
sharply between 1964 and 1966, increased sharply again in 1967,
increased steadily from 1967 through 1970, and decreased again
between 1970 and 1973. The net result is that in 1973 the proportion of high-school graduates in New York State entering four-
year colleges was 2.2 percent lower than in 1964.[6] Nationally
the proportion of high-school graduates entering college in 1974
was 7.0 percent lower than in 1968.[7]

There is also objective evidence that the students who enter
college today are less informed than those who entered ten years

ago. Between 1963 and 1975 the scores that students achieved on the College Board Exam steadily declined.[8] The reason for the decline is *not* that an increasing number of students take the exam. The number of students taking the test is actually declining.[9] Nor is the reason for the decline that the test is harder or that an increasing number of juniors in high school are taking it.[10] The only legitimate explanation for the decline of the scores is that the high-school seniors who take the exam know a little less every year.

The student entering college today not only is less knowledgeable than the student who entered ten years ago. He is also intellectually less sophisticated. In recent years his facility with language has declined[11] and thus he has become increasingly handicapped in his effort to think in anything but the most simplistic terms. Increasingly, therefore, he seeks the simple answers. Increasingly he has become unable to deal with subtleties, and as he has become less able he has also become less willing even to try. It is too frustrating, too discouraging, and, indeed, too heartbreaking.

The anti-intellectualism of the elementary, junior high, and high schools is the natural and probably inevitable culmination of a fifty-year process that began when the Progressive Educationists invaded the schools. The Progressive Educationists have done all of the wrong things. They have emphasized socialization over education. They have decreased the emphasis on homework in junior high school and high school. Through the development of short courses in high school they have encouraged fragmentation and discouraged analysis of relationships. They have developed experimental courses that often accomplish nothing except to keep potential drop-outs off the streets.

The use of mechanical teaching aids has probably helped cause the decline in knowledge of high-school graduates. From their earliest years in school students have been subjected to these machines, which are designed to save money by substituting machines for the teacher and therefore enabling the teacher to service an increased number of students. They are useful, however, only in helping the student to memorize, and once the novelty of using them wears off they probably are not useful even for that. Few things could be more boring to a hyperactive ten-year-old than having to sit in front of a box or screen. He needs the immediate presence of a teacher.

A very moderate use of the machine might be helpful in teaching the fundamentals of spelling, reading, geography, and math. And no one would deny that these things are important. But the machines cannot teach students to think. Educationists, however, reflecting the legislator's desire to save money and encouraged by the representatives of the companies that make the machines, appear to believe that the machines can do everything that is necessary. Teaching students to think is not one of the things that they consider necessary. They appear to believe that teachers are needed only to run the machines. Thus mechanical teaching devices, having taken over the classrooms of elementary, junior high, and high schools, are now invading the colleges.

The increase in non-academic chores also makes it impossible for the schools to teach as much as they did earlier. The high schools have been increasingly inundated with non-academic functions, such as the teaching of home economics, agriculture, woodworking, machine shop, and driving. These activities distract students, teachers, and administrators from the more important job of collecting information and learning to think about it and could be done much better in separate vocational schools.[12] The increasing emphasis on athletics and other time-consuming frivolities takes time that could be better spent reading or at least learning to read and takes money that could be better spent buying books for the library or hiring additional teachers.[13] Teaching good citizenship and consumerism are simply additional devices for indoctrination and take time that could be better spent in other ways if the real object of the schooling system were to teach young people to use their minds.

Cultural factors have also helped to decrease the amount of learning that goes on in elementary, junior high, and high schools. Violence and the threat of violence make it impossible for either students or teachers to concentrate. The entire political, social, and economic atmosphere of the United States in recent years has increasingly discouraged the hard thinking necessary for challenging patriotic mythology and for arriving at legitimate conclusions. Politicians, newsmen, entertainers, and teachers have all encouraged the automatic response, the view of the world and all of the issues that arise in it as easy to state and simple to solve.

Some schools have given up trying to teach even to the extent that they have been allowed to teach in the past. They have eliminated significant literature and history and have substituted popular magazines for the great novels and plays and histories. In at least one school *Sports Illustrated* has been used to teach English, social studies, and math.[14] How it is used in social studies and math is anybody's guess, but the effect of its use in English can only be to deny the students an important part of their cultural heritage. They will know all about the ephemera of batting averages and pulling guards, but they will have no idea where they fit into either history or society.

As high-school graduates know less, colleges lower their academic standards. Their graduates know less—and therefore can teach less—than those who graduated before them. Thus uninformed and uneducated college graduates send increasingly uninformed and uneducated high-school graduates off to college.*

The very people who talk about the superiority of students today implicitly admit that they are wrong when they talk also about changing education. If it were true that high-school graduates today are more informed, more thoughtful, and more capable than students of any other generation there would be no reason for all of the talk about change. The same system that has produced these wonderfully alert and able people could continue to operate with no substantial change.

But the educationists know that what they say is not true, and they know also that they are under constant criticism. They therefore find it necessary to defend themselves and at the same time to appear co-operative and humble. They defend themselves by repeating over and over again that the students graduating from high school today are better than ever. The implication is that they must be doing an outstanding job, but they never make any effort to prove it. At the same time, though, they make concessions to their critics and appear co-operative and humble by constantly talking about changing the schools. They speak of experiment and innovation and of the development of non-traditional methods of education. They are saying that while they have been doing a wonderful job in the past they are going to do an even more wonderful job in the future.

None of the reasons that Mr. Nyquist lists for the superiority of the student today has any necessary merit. As the belief in the

---

*"School officials in Pinellas County, Florida, gave standardized exams to applicants for teaching posts and found that some scored lower in math and reading than the school system's eighth-graders." *The Progressive*, August 1976, p. 11. Reprinted by permission from *The Progressive*, 408 West Gorham Street, Madison, Wisconsin 53703. Copyright © 1976, The Progressive, Inc.

superiority of the student today has become a dogma, however, the reasons why he is superior have similarly become a catechism ritualistically intoned and carrying increased conviction with each repetition. Mr. Nyquist dutifully recites that catechism and apparently expects everyone to share his faith. But additional years, days, or hours spent in the classroom are no advantage if the years, days, and hours are spent playing meaningless games with ignorant teachers.[15] Advanced courses in high school very often are not advanced at all but rather are gimmicks designed to keep the students interested in something—*any*thing—or at least to keep them quiet. The influence of television is almost always bad rather than good.[16] Advertisements encourage the automatic response and discourage thought. Game shows belabor the irrelevant. Westerns, mysteries, and adventure programs offer a thoughtless, frustrated, and distracted audience simple-minded solutions to silly, and often bizarre, problems. News commentators in five-minute slots must resort to quick answers to problems that they scarcely have time to state. Ten-minute interviews—themselves uncommonly long—barely scratch the surface of issues and must content themselves with superficiality. The half-hour weekly panel interviews are not notorious for their student audiences, and besides that people appear on these programs to propagandize rather than to inform. Even if a reporter did want to question the guest intensively and critically he would not have time to do it, but beyond that he must *not* do it. He must be courteous. The guest is, after all, a guest. If the reporters consistently made their guests uncomfortable with serious questioning not only could they be accused of lacking common hospitality but also the programs would collapse because no one would be willing to be a guest. The propaganda value of the appearance would not be worth the discomfort it would cost, and if the newsmen took their questioning seriously the appearance would have no propaganda value in the first place. Still further, the interviewers have the fairness doctrine to worry about. Any really hard questioning could be construed as taking sides, and the result could be recrimination by the government against the network or the stations that carry the programs.[17]

In spite of all of this, however, a historian of the stature of Paul L. Ward can make the astounding assertion that "The greatly widened diversity of students since 1950, *and through television their widened sensibilities*, force on us [history teachers] a rethinking of the right coverage for each learning process."[18]

The final reason that Mr. Nyquist gives for the increased ability of students today is travel. But there is no evidence that a larger proportion of young people are travelling today than ever before or that they are travelling more. Surely in the 1890s as well as in the 1930s there was a great deal of movement. The 1920s had its lost generation, and the 1950s had its beats. And there is no evidence that those who do travel do learn. Often they travel with people exactly like themselves, go to exactly the same places, see mountains, valleys, cathedrals, and tombs, and come home as intellectually innocent as they were when they left. Far more common than the student who has travelled widely is the one who when she was afraid that she would not be able to miss an exam in order to leave early for Florida for spring vacation pleaded, almost in tears, "I've never been *any*place."

Chapter 2

THE IGNORANCE OF STUDENTS

*W*hat really matters is not how students entering college today compare with students of the past but rather just how much they do know and just how socially and intellectually sophisticated they really are. And whether they are more or less knowledgeable and more or less sophisticated than those of the past a high proportion of them are abysmally uninformed and appallingly unsophisticated. Regardless of how they compare to anyone, that is where they are, and that is where the colleges must begin.[1]

The ignorance of students entering college continues to shock even the teacher who has become accustomed to it.* A great many students who have spent twelve or thirteen years in the schools of New York State have never heard of the Albany Congress or the Stamp Act Congress. They have never heard of the Townshend Acts, the Coercive Acts, John Dickinson, or James Otis. They have never heard of Cotton Mather, and while they might have heard of Anne Hutchinson and Roger Williams, they do not know who they were. They have never heard of the Enlightenment, the Genet Affair, the Hartford Convention, or the Burr Conspiracy. They

---

*Here as always I use "ignorance" to describe a condition, not as a term of contempt. Ignorance is a lack of knowledge; stupidity is the inability to acquire knowledge. Students are not stupid. Ignorance is nothing to be ashamed of provided a person recognizes the condition and tries to correct it. Obviously none of us knows everything he should know: we suffer degrees of ignorance.

have never heard of Pan-Americanism, or Harper's Ferry, or Jim Crow. They have never heard of the Marshall Plan, brink-of-war diplomacy, or the domino theory. They have no idea of what the notion of monolithic Communism is. They have never heard of a judge's charge to a grand jury or to a petit jury, and they do not know what a primary election is. They cannot define perjury. They have never heard of revenue sharing, and they have never heard of the Heroin Hot Line. They have never heard of No-Knock or Preventive Detention.

There are two usual responses to this phenomenal ignorance. The first is to deny that it exists, and the second is to explain it away. Those who deny that it exists argue that the students have more information than they have ever had before but just happen not to know those things that come up in class. But the ignorance is too deep and too general to admit that explanation. Those who explain it away have two arguments. They argue first that the ignorance of American history, politics, and judicial procedure results from the loss of confidence in history, the recent conviction of many people who should know better that history is bunk, the suspicion even among some historians that history is irrelevant.[2] This attitude is an extension of the older belief that in order to matter a course must end in -ology or -onomy. It is impossible to convince these people otherwise: to recognize the importance of history one must study history, and these people refuse to study history because of their conviction that it is not important. One can only answer assertion with another assertion: the person who knows no history knows nothing. That does not mean that everyone must be a professional historian. What it does mean is that history is the only subject about which a person must know something in order to perform the elementary functions of intelligent citizenship.

The implication of the argument that the students' ignorance of history results from a de-emphasis of history is that they have learned something else in its place. If they are highly informed and if they are learning something more important than mere history one would expect them to know something about what is going on in the world. The first thing that one has a right to expect of a person who considers himself well informed is that he knows what is happening around him. But the students today know no more about current events than they know about anything else. They are oblivious of everything important. Their ignorance is abysmal in all areas. They are lost in any world.

The teacher can discover the students' oblivion any time he chooses. In an introductory course in American history at a four-year college in New York State on the day after the elections of 1974 sixty-eight students—mostly freshmen but including some upper-classmen—were asked to identify twenty people who had been consistently in the news. When we counted as correct any answer that includes any correct information, even though it is inadequate or even though the student included incorrect information also, the average score is 6.6 out of twenty, or 33.01 percent. This includes counting as correct the identification of Harold Wilson as the head of England or the former Prime Minister or simply as an English statesman; Earl Butz as a presidential economic advisor; Elliott Richardson as a cabinet member or as attorney general; Pierre Elliott Trudeau as President of Canada or a late President of Canada or simply as prime minister; John Connally as governor of Texas or Secretary of the Treasury; James Hanley as having run "for something this year"; Peter Rodino as House committee chairman or Senator from New Jersey; Barbara Jordan as a Senator from Texas; and Thomas Eagleton as Senator from Maine and vice-presidential candidate in 1972. When we count as correct only those answers that include correct information with no incorrect information the average score is 5.53 out of twenty, or 27.65 percent. Even this score includes counting as correct the identification of William Proxmire as a member of Congress; William Proxmire, Herman Talmadge, and Thomas Eagleton simply as Senators; Earl Butz simply as a cabinet member; John Connally only as a Democrat who turned Republican; Harold Wilson as England's minister and Pierre Elliott Trudeau as Canadian minister; Jeb Magruder and E. Howard Hunt simply as names connected with Watergate; Elliott Richardson only as a man who "quit [his] position after [the] firing of Cox"; Tom Hayden simply as a radical; and Thomas Eagleton simply as "V. P. candidate a while ago."

Answers that were considered inadequate and therefore wrong include the identification of William Proxmire simply as a politician or "something in Washington," E. Howard Hunt simply as a Nixon man or a Nixon aide, Thomas Eagleton as a "Senator or Governor," James Hanley only as coming from New York, and Earl Butz only as a politician.

Thirty-nine of the sixty-eight students had five or fewer answers correct. That means that 57.35 percent of the students had scores of twenty-five percent or lower. Sixty of the sixty-eight students could identify fewer than ten of the people. That means that 88.24 percent of the students had scores of forty-five percent or less. Only 11.76 percent of the students had scores of fifty-five percent or higher, and only two could identify more than twelve of the people. Twelve correct answers gives a score of sixty percent, or a D minus, which means that 97.06 percent of the students had scores of D minus or less. One of the two students who had more than twelve answers correct identified fourteen people, and the other identified fifteen. That is seventy percent, or a C minus, and seventy-five percent, or a C.

Number of Students out of 68

Number Correct	Students having correct answers, barely acceptable answers, and answers with both correct and incorrect information	Running Total	Accurate Answers Only	Running Total
0	—	0	1	1
1	1	1	3	4
2	7	8	9	13
3	9	17	10	23
4	5	22	8	31
5	6	28	8	39
6	11	39	6	45
7	6	45	6	51
8	5	50	6	57
9	6	56	3	60
10	1	57	0	60
11	4	61	3	63
12	2	63	3	66
13	1	64	0	66
14	1	65	1	67
15	0	65	1	68
16	1	66	0	—
17	2	68	0	—
18	0	—	0	—
19	0	—	0	—
20	0	—	0	—

Other significant information emerges from this exercise. On the day after the elections of 1974 eleven of sixty-eight students in New York could not identify the governor-elect of the state, and fifty-six of sixty-eight could not identify the incumbent congressman who was re-elected from the district in which they attended school. Only two of the sixty-eight could identify Ernest Boyer, the chancellor of the State University of New York, and the only other student who tried to identify him made him one of the Chicago Seven. Within a few weeks of the end of the trial of Dennis Banks and Russell Means only four students could identify Banks and only five could identify Means. Fifty-four did not even try to identify Means, and sixty-one did not try to identify Banks. After two consecutive summers filled with Watergate, first with the hearings of the Senate Watergate Committee and then with the impeachment hearings of the House Judiciary Committee, only eight students could identify Herman Talmadge, only seven could identify Barbara Jordan, and only nine could identify Peter Rodino. With Israel constantly in the news only five students could identify the Prime Minister of Israel, and with the coal strike in the news only two students could identify the head of the United Mine Workers.

Analysis of Responses

	No Response	Benefit of Doubt	Accurate	Wrong or Inadequate	Total
William Proxmire	17	7	35	9	68
Dennis Banks	61	0	4	3	68
E. Howard Hunt	16	4	40	8	68
Jeb Magruder	14	2	45	7	68
Herman Talmadge	53	2	8	5	68
Barbara Jordan	52	1	7	8	68
John Connally	13	13	13	29	68
Thomas Eagleton	8	3	47	10	68
Peter Rodino	21	4	9	34	68
Russell Means	54	0	5	9	68
Harold Wilson	24	7	21	16	68
Pierre Elliott Trudeau	13	13	29	13	68
Itzhak Rabin	53	3	5	7	68
Arnold Miller	61	0	2	5	68
Elliott Richardson	24	8	13	23	68
Hugh Carey	8	0	57	3	68
James Hanley	52	2	10	4	68
Ernest Boyer	65	0	2	1	68
Tom Hayden	55	3	5	5	68
Earl Butz	29	1	19	19	68
TOTAL	693	73	376	218	1360

But just as interesting as the small number of students who could identify prominent people are the imaginative identifications that they did give to some of those on the list. One made William Proxmire a Watergate defendant, and three others had him involved in the Watergate scandal. One made him governor of Illinois, and one made him governor of Georgia. One student had Dennis Banks involved in Watergate; one made him a Senator; and one made him an intelligence man. Three made Jeb Magruder a a Senator, and two made him the Watergate prosecutor. One had Herman Talmadge involved in the Watergate conspiracy. Four students made Barbara Jordan a news broadcaster, news correspondent, newswoman, or newspaper reporter, while one made her the first woman governor of Connecticut and one the lieutenant governor of New York. Among a great variety of interesting identifications of John Connally four students made him a former Secretary of State, one Secretary of State, one a very old man still in Congress, one a justice of the Supreme Court, one a commentator, one a Senator on the Watergate Committee, one a candidate for the governorship of New York, one a representative from New York, and one a lieutenant involved in the "Le Mai" massacre. Two students had Thomas Eagleton involved in the Watergate scandal, and one made him a former Vice-President. Two students made Peter Rodino the special Watergate prosecutor; one made him the prosecutor at the Watergate trial; five had him involved in the Watergate scandal; one put him on the Watergate jury; one made him the judge hearing the Watergate case; one made him simply "chairman"; one made him a justice of the Supreme Court, one the chairman of the Supreme Court, one a Nixon advisor, and one Nixon's lawyer. One student made Russell Means the Secretary of the Department of Housing and Urban Development; one made him a Congressman from New York, one a candidate for the Senate from New York State, two a Senator, one a member of the Cabinet, and one a member of the House of Representatives. One had him involved in the Watergate scandal, and one made him a member of the Chicago Five. Four students made Harold Wilson the governor of New York, two a candidate for the governorship of New York, and five the former governor of New York. One made him a Watergate lawyer, one a British ambassador, one a Senator, one a Canadian, and one the new Prime Minister of Canada. Two students made Pierre Elliott Trudeau the French ambassador to the United States; two made him simply the French ambassador, three the French Prime Minister, one the president of France and one the French premier, two the French foreign minister, one a foreign correspondent, and one simply a foreign minister. One student made Itzhak Rabin an Arab, one the head of the Jewish Defense League, one a Russian ambassador, one the head of a Palestinian group, one the ruler of an oil-producing country in the Mid-East, one an Arab oil czar, and one a rabbi who supported Nixon. One student made Arnold Miller an author, one an author and former husband of Marilyn

Monroe, one a golfer, one the vice-presidential candidate with Barry Goldwater, and one a Congressman. Three made Elliott Richardson a defendant in the Watergate case; four simply had him connected with Watergate; one made him a Watergate conspirator; one had him involved in the Watergate trials; one made him Nixon's Watergate lawyer, one a special Watergate investigator, one the prosecutor in the Watergate scandal and one the former Watergate prosecutor, and one a judge in one of the Watergate trials. One made him a former press secretary to Richard Nixon, one a Senator, and one a justice of the Supreme Court. One student made James Hanley one of the Chicago Seven. One made Tom Hayden a nominee to the Supreme Court; one made him a Senator, one a composer, one a news reporter who covered Watergate, one a liberal writer for the New York *Times*, and one a revolutionist married to Joan Baez. One student made Earl Butz head of the Environmental Protection Agency; six made him a Senator, two a justice of the Supreme Court, one an appointee to the Supreme Court, one a congressman, and one a news reporter. One had him connected with Watergate.

As any teacher knows, when he supplies his students with answers in the form of multiple-choice questions they do better. In a multiple-choice exercise consisting of twenty-five items, eighty-four students in the fall of 1975 had a total of 1212 correct answers out of a possible 2100. That is 57.71 percent, compared to the 33.01 percent when the students had to supply their own answers. Yet the average student's ability to identify only 57.71 percent of twenty-five people who have consistently been in the news certainly does not support any contention that high-school graduates today are wonderfully aware of what is going on around them. The fifty-seven freshmen who were involved in the exercise had 751 correct answers out of a possible 1425. That is 52.7 percent. Fifteen sophomores got 206 answers correct out of a possible 375. That is 54.93 percent. Twelve juniors got 211 correct answers out of a possible 300. That is 70.33 percent. There were no seniors in the group. These results might indicate that college students do become more aware of their surroundings as they become older and that the year between the beginning of the sophomore year and the beginning of the junior year is a very critical time, but the juniors' identifying an average of only 17.58 out of twenty-five people still represents no outstanding awareness. Their 70.33 percent is barely a C minus.

Of all of these students only forty-one, or 48.81 percent, could

Number Correct—Number of Students

Number Correct	Students Fr.	So.	Jr.	Total	Running Total	Reverse Running Total
6	1	—	—	1	—	84
7	2	1	—	3	4	83
8	5	1	—	6	10	80
9	2	1	—	3	13	74
10	5	1	—	6	19	71
11	1	2	—	3	22	65
12	2	1	1	4	26	62
13	7	1	—	8	34	58
14	6	1	2	9	43	50
15	9	1	—	10	53	41
16	4	2	2	8	61	31
17	4	—	1	5	66	23
18	—	—	1	1	67	18
19	2	1	1	4	71	17
20	3	—	1	4	75	13
21	—	1	2	3	78	9
22	2	—	—	2	80	6
23	—	—	1	1	81	4
24	2	1	—	3	84	3
TOTAL	57	15	12	84		
% Correct	52.7	54.93	70.33	57.71		

Number and Percent of Students
Number and Percent Correct

Number Correct	Percent Correct	Students	Running Total of Students	Percent of Students	Running Total Percent of Students	Reverse Running Total Percent of Students
6	24	1	—	1.19%	—	100.00%
7	28	3	4	3.57	4.76%	98.81
8	32	6	10	7.14	11.90	95.24
9	36	3	13	3.57	15.48	88.10
10	40	6	19	7.14	22.62	84.52
11	44	3	22	3.57	26.19	77.38
12	48	4	26	4.76	30.95	73.81
13	52	8	34	9.52	40.48	69.05
14	56	9	43	10.71	51.19	59.52
15	60	10	53	11.90	63.10	48.81
16	64	8	61	9.52	72.62	36.90
17	68	5	66	5.95	78.57	27.38
18	72	1	67	1.19	79.76	21.43
19	76	4	71	4.76	84.52	20.24
20	80	4	75	4.76	89.29	15.48
21	84	3	78	3.57	92.86	10.71
22	88	2	80	2.38	95.24	7.14
23	92	1	81	1.19	96.43	4.76
24	96	3	84	3.57	100.00	3.57

identify fifteen or more of the prominent people of whom any intelligent citizen should be aware. That means that only 48.81 percent of these students could achieve a score of at least sixty, or at least a D minus. Only eighteen, or 21.43 percent, could identify eighteen or more of these people and thus achieve a score of at least seventy-two, or at least a C minus. Only thirteen, or 15.48 percent, could identify twenty or more and thus achieve a score of at least eighty, or at least a B minus. Only four students, or 4.76 percent, could identify twenty-three or more of these public figures and thus achieve a score of at least ninety-two, or at least an A minus.

Number and Percent of Students Identifying Specific Items

Item	Number Correct	Percent Correct
Chris Evert	80	95.24
James Hoffa	76	90.48
George Meany	70	83.33
Mike Mansfield	68	80.95
Carl Albert	67	79.76
Anwar Sadat	67	79.76
Joan Little	63	75.00
Indira Gandhi	63	75.00
Samuel Bronfman	58	69.05
Itzhak Rabin	54	64.29
William Douglas	48	57.14
Richard Helms	48	57.14
Pierre Elliott Trudeau	46	54.76
Jim Hunter	46	54.76
Earl Butz	44	52.38
William Proxmire	44	52.38
Bruce Morton	43	51.19
Frank Zarb	41	48.81
Harold Wilson	40	47.62
William Simon	38	45.24
Charles Colson	36	42.86
Elliott Richardson	24	28.57
Morris Udall	18	21.43
William Kunstler	17	20.24
Barbara Jordan	13	15.48

It seems significant that the person with whom the most students were familiar was Chris Evert, a tennis player, and that the person whom the second largest number of students could identify was Jimmy Hoffa, who recently had disappeared. It also seems significant that while forty students could identify Harold Wilson, thirty-six thought that he was President Ford's Chairman of Economic Advisors; twelve thought that he was the former governor of New York State; and three thought that he was the racist

Prime Minister of South Africa. While twenty-four students could identify Elliott Richardson, twenty-four thought that he was one of Nixon's lawyers in the Watergate scandal; twenty-one thought that he was a defendant in the Watergate case; and thirteen thought that he was the former head of the Environmental Protection Agency. Eighteen students could identify Morris Udall, but twenty-six thought that he was a United States Congressman from Maine fighting the effort to build a new oil refinery there; twenty-two thought that he was Secretary of Defense; and sixteen thought that he was the former governor of Alaska and that he was the Secretary of Interior for a while under Nixon. Thirty-six students could identify Charles Colson, but thirty-one identified him as a candidate in the disputed Senatorial election in New Hampshire; eleven made him the Governor of Idaho and Democratic presidential hopeful; and two made him a comedian formerly on the Smothers Brothers Show. Only thirteen could identify Barbara Jordan, while thirty-eight identified her as the President of the National Organization of Women, seventeen as a personality on television, and fifteen as a famous author who writes about relations between blacks and whites. Seventeen students could identify William Kunstler, but thirty-one made him Secretary of Interior, twenty-one President Ford's campaign manager for 1976, and fourteen the Chairman of the United States Commission on Civil Disorders. Eighteen made William Douglas a Senator from Rhode Island much concerned about the environment and protection of the consumer, and sixteen made him Attorney General of the United States. Nineteen made William Proxmire a member of the United States House of Representatives from Michigan who was trying to do something about the auto slump; thirteen made him a Democratic presidential hopeful from Texas; and seven made 'him Governor of Massachusetts. Twenty-two made Itzhak Rabin chairman of the Oil Producing and Exporting Countries; five made him a rabbi who supported Nixon; and one made him a famous violinist. Eleven made Frank Zarb one of the astronauts on the Apollo-Soyuz mission, and thirteen made him President of Exxon. Twenty identified Richard Helms as a former justice of the United States Supreme Court; thirteen made Indira Gandhi the former Prime Minister of Israel; twelve made Samuel Bronfman the judge in the trial of the Chicago Seven; and ten made George Meany the head of Nixon's Wage-Price Board.

Obviously 152 students is not a very broad sampling of students entering college today. But there are some indications that the results of these exercises are fairly representative. First, the results confirm the impression that the teacher gets in class that the students are minimally informed about anything. They cannot identify either people of the past or historical events, and when the teacher tries to relate what has happened in the past to what is happening in the present he discovers that they do not know very much about the present, either. Second, the formal examinations that the teacher gives in courses that include the very recent past reveal the same thing. The students learn very little outside the classroom: what the students include on their exams is what the teacher has covered in class. Third, another exercise administered in a recent semester had results quite similar to the results of these.

This ignorance of high-school graduates indicates that regardless of how they compare with students of the past they are almost entirely oblivious of most of what the very people who flatter them pretend to consider important. It indicates that there is no legitimate reason for that flattery and that the flatterers would do the young people a greater service by telling them that they had better begin to learn things than by continuing to tell them how much they already know and how wonderful they are.

The second argument of the people who explain away the students' ignorance of history and politics is that they are learning something more important than mere information: they are learning how to think. People who accept this explanation argue that although the students are acquiring little knowledge they are becoming more sophisticated intellectually than students have ever been before. But those who believe this are forgetting the fundamental reality that before a person can think he has to have something to think about. Before he can apply his mind to something he has to have something to which he can apply his mind. That something is information. The person who argues that the student can learn to think without learning information is arguing that he can apply his mind in a vacuum.[3]

Even more serious than the students' lack of information is the functional illiteracy of a high proportion of them.[4] There are so many illiterate students that the teacher tends to pass anyone who is literate whether he has learned anything or not. The teacher cannot fail both those who are illiterate *and* those who are ignorant. He cannot fail all of those, even, who are illiterate. The exam therefore often becomes a device for sorting out the worst of the illiterates. Worse yet, many teachers never fail anyone at all. Many departments and many colleges actively discourage the assigning of failing grades.[5]

A great many students are illiterate not only in writing but also in speaking. Since in speaking the words disappear as soon as they are spoken while in writing the solid evidence of the illiteracy continues to exist right there in ball-point blue and white, many people have assumed that these young people speak better than they write. But anyone who has listened to newsmen trying to interview eighteen-year-old high-school graduates and any teacher who has seriously tried to communicate with some of his students in his office without putting words into their mouths knows that their difficulty goes beyond their inability to write. They speak as badly as they write.

But more than that, many cannot read, either. The more ambitious of these spend hours on what should take only a few minutes, mechanically reading word for word while their minds wander back to the semi-nude girls in the dormitory or the handsome guy at the next table, and they remember nothing. Reading is so difficult for them that when they consider courses to take their first question is How many books does the instructor assign? and the second is Does he really expect us to read them?

With good hard work the literate student can at least partially correct his ignorance, but by the time the student enters college it is often too late to correct his inadequacy with words. Thus he is doomed not only to having a difficult time in college but also to finding it difficult for the rest of his life to accumulate knowledge or to understand what little information he does acquire. For language is important both for accumulating information and for relating some information to other information. For the adult the single most important potential source of useful information is print,[6] and therefore the person who cannot read is unlikely to learn very much that matters. Beyond that, we think in words. The person who has no words with which to think or who can create no order for the words he does have lacks the fundamental tool for solving problems. Thinking is, after all, only silent speech.[7] The young person's declining ability to use words[8] re-results in his declining ability to think. Yet any teacher who believes that a student should be literate in order to pass a college course and who actually tries to help students by marking their illiteracies and offering to read rewrites of their essays is penalized rather than encouraged.*[9]

---

*From a memo from the chairman of a department, 10 January 1969: "In the evaluation of student performance, the [personnel] committee felt that, considering standards of performance generally recognized at *** and at many other institutions, you have consistently underestimated student achievement in your survey classes, either through adherence to a standard of achievement not consistent with that generally recognized, or *through requiring performance in areas not generally accepted as indicative of mastery of* ***. This has the unfortunate result of actively discouraging students from enrolling in your courses, lessens your value to the department, and shunts part of the burden of teaching to other members of the department." Italics mine. The italicized phrase refers to the teacher's expectation that American college students should be able to write English. It was in the academic year 1968–1969 that an increasing number of professors began to realize that in the future departments were going to have to compete for students with increased vigor.

Chapter 3

THE DECLINE OF
ACADEMIC STANDARDS:1
Students, Grading, and Teachers

$\mathcal{I}$t is clear that when students enter college they are very badly informed and intellectually unsophisticated. The available evidence also indicates that regardless of how freshmen in the middle of the 1970s compare with those of earlier generations they are less knowledgeable than freshmen were ten years ago. And as badly informed as students are when they enter college, they are also learning less and less while they are there.[1]

There are several reasons why academic standards of American colleges have deteriorated. First, because of the ignorance and lack of sophistication of students college teachers are required to teach on an increasingly elementary level. Students cannot grasp what earlier students could grasp. Since they possess almost no ability to see subtleties their teachers must spend an increased amount of time on what they do cover. Starting at a more elementary level than they did earlier, they must also proceed at a slower pace than they did earlier. Starting with the elementary, they often do not get beyond it.

Teachers also proceed at a slower pace than they did earlier because they constantly have to learn to teach all over again. Probably the most important things that experience teaches the teacher are to anticipate questions that might arise and to discover how to answer those questions in ways that the students can understand. As a result of the students' ignorance and lack of sophistication the questions that arise in class are increasingly elementary and naive. The teacher has never had to answer them before. He knows the answers, but he has to discover a wording that the students can understand. The same ignorance and lack of sophistication that causes the students to raise the questions to begin with makes it impossible for them to understand answers that earlier students could have understood. The teacher therefore has to search around for a wording, and that takes time. Not only does the average student not get very far but the brighter student is held back.

Because college students begin at a more elementary level than they did earlier and because teachers must proceed at a slower pace than before, fewer and fewer students are striking off to learn on their own. The gathering of knowledge is cumulative, and the explosion of enthusiasm that comes when the student finally realizes that learning is fun even though it is difficult is coming later and later or never at all. The number of students who enjoy learning so much that they study even when they do not have to has never been very large, but it is getting smaller all the time. Students are increasingly dependent on what the teacher feeds to them in the classroom.

Not only are students less prepared to learn than students were ten years ago but they are also less *willing* to learn. Students have always resisted the work required for learning, but they are resisting it more than ever. They resent more than ever the external discipline that learning imposes upon them. By the time they reach college they have already been subjected to that external discipline for twelve or thirteen years, and if during that time they have learned nothing else they have learned that from that discipline they have gained almost nothing. They are intelligent enough to see that most of the time they have spent on assignments in school has been wasted on busywork. They have not done much, but most of what they have done has been useless. They realize that they would be exactly as well off if they had spent more of their time on the street corner or playing baseball. They resent having spent so much of their time in unenjoyable and meaningless ways when they could have spent it in more enjoyable but meaningless ways. When they go to college they assume that their work there will be more important, but after a couple of weeks they discover that most of that work is busywork, too. The resentment of busywork, combined with the contemporary emphasis on spontaneity and the belief that personal commitment is a positive evil, has made students less patient than ever before with anything requiring self-discipline.

Far more serious than the students' resistance to the self-discipline required for learning, however, is their resistance to the learning itself. They resist learning for three reasons. First, having been told for almost ten years that they are the most informed, most intelligent, most perceptive, and most serious generation in the whole history of the United States if not of the entire world, they see no reason why they should learn anything more. Even if they do believe that it would be nice to know more than they do know they see no reason why they should work very hard at it. If the leisurely pace that they have followed through high school has resulted in their being the best-educated generation ever, surely proceding at that slow pace or even slowing down a little will result in their learning far more than they will ever have to know. If they are the best-educated generation ever they must already know far more than they will ever need to know. Earlier generations, after all, got by knowing less than they do already. They are already far ahead of everyone who ever went before.

Students resist learning in the second place because they have no doubt that everything they think is right. Their intuition tells them that they already know the whole truth. They believe; therefore they know. In their emphasis on intuition they are proudly anti-intellectual. They readily dismiss anything with which they are not already familiar. When a teacher presents a view of history or of economics that does not agree with what they think they know he often hears students say "I know that you don't really believe that." or "You were just giving us the other side." Of course they do not believe that there is any legitimate other side. They do not realize that what they believe is intuition is actually the prejudices that have been foisted upon them during their earlier years of schooling.

Students resist learning in the third place because learning is frightening. Learning might upset the contentment with things as they are that their earlier schooling has imposed upon them. Not only are they convinced that their intuition is correct, but whenever a reality threatens to disturb their illusions they become desperately determined to prove it. The only way to do that is to avoid learning anything. "I have to get away from history for a while," the student tells the teacher. "I can't stand it any longer.

It is too disturbing." And so he does literally try to escape history by continuing to nourish his illusions.

So the students are uninformed, and many are determined to remain that way. One of the more obvious illustrations of this is the noise they call music. Their zeal for oblivion is the only satisfactory explanation of the popularity of that noise. Much of it is characterized by high volume, a heavy beat, indecipherable words, and when the words are decipherable by a simple-minded repetition and an emphasis on mechanical sex.

The high volume and the heavy beat drown out the rest of the world. They drown out any thought about the noise itself. Anyone who has heard this noise has discovered that while he hears it he cannot concentrate on anything at all. Only one word— Boom! Boom! Boom!—repeats itself endlessly in his mind. While such noise is thumping in his ears he cannot concentrate well enough to do even simple mechanical tasks.

The reason that this noise is popular is that it does drown out the world. It allows the person who is hearing it to spend many hours at a time with his mind completely blank. He does not even have to make the effort of listening. The young people have gone one step beyond their schooling: while in school they have been taught not to think about anything important, they have decided that they will not think about anything at all.

To maintain this mental blankness it is desirable that any words in the noise be indecipherable. Words that are understandable convey images, and minds with images are not blank. Songs with understandable words require some thought. Even the silliest of the traditional popular or country-western songs do tell stories that require some mental effort. Not much, but some. Even the nonsense songs evoke images and require some mental effort to learn or even to follow. And the best folk songs not only tell serious stories but also convey the harshest and most poignant reality. It is no accident that the popularity of folk music lasted only a short time and that the most popular of the folk people often hid the sadness of the songs in a jingly rhythm.

The indecipherable words of rock impose no images and require no mental effort. People can sit by the hour, not listening but simply engulfed in the noise. This is not simply temporary relaxation: for many it is almost an occupation.

When the words of this noise are decipherable they often consist only of a repetition of the same phrase over and over again.

"Cain't" pause "git anuf uv yer luv," repeated endlessly over and over. The object is to convey no image, to allow the young person to think about absolutely nothing or, if he does think of something, to enable him to think about sex for the sake of sex. It enables him to avoid commitment even in his imagination. For the person who cannot get enough of your love is not really talking about love, or even of romance. He is talking about plain old biological sex. He cannot screw you enough.

Of course if one analyzes the words of the traditional popular songs he discovers that they are more about sex than about romance or love also. Surely they are bad enough in perverting reality. Usually they are terribly silly, and surely they are intellectually harmful as a steady diet. But ordinarily they have only that one bad quality—the silly perversion of reality. They do not have the other mind-destroying qualities—the high volume, the heavy beat, the indecipherable words, and the simple-minded repetition—of rock noise. They enable the listener to escape from the real world into an unreal one. They do not, as rock noise does, enable the hearer to escape into entirely thoughtless oblivion.

The decline in academic standards in American colleges thus results from three factors related to the abilities and attitudes of students: the declining abilities of high-school graduates, the increased resistance of the students to the discipline required for learning, and the increased resistance of students to learning itself. Since students are less capable of and less interested in learning than they were earlier there has developed pressure on faculties to grade easier simply to maintain enrollments, and that easier grading has become not only a reflection of declining academic standards but also a cause of the further decline of those standards.

Several factors in addition to the changing intellectual qualities of students caused the change in grading practices and therefore the decline of academic standards. One of these is the war in Vietnam. During that war a great many male students entered college only to escape the draft. Many were entirely uninterested in anything but barely staying in college, and many were incapable of doing the quality of work that the colleges required. As their difficulty of staying in college increased their frustrations also increased. Their protests against the war intensified. They often turned their protests against the colleges because the colleges were the immediate sources of their frustrations. They had to stay in

school: their very lives might depend on it. Girls joined the protests because it was chic and because they wanted their men to
stay around. Thus joined to the conscientious opposition to the
war was the protest of those whose only objection to it was that
they—or in the case of girls their boyfriends—would be the ones
who would have to fight it if they could not stay in school. Faced
with the occupying of buildings, administrators collapsed, and
faced with the possible destruction of their libraries and the
records of their research, professors collapsed.[2] Everyone began to
hunt for ways to please the students, and lowering academic
standards was the most obvious way. Assigning less work and grading easier were the most immediately available ways of lowering
academic standards.

Joined with those professors and administrators who collapsed
under the pressure of angry students were those professors whose
decision to lower their standards was a political one. They decided
not to co-operate with the government. Since a student's grades
were the sole determinant of whether he would be drafted the
teacher knew that every time he gave a young man a low grade he
was helping to place him in a position in which he might be
maimed or killed. Even a C might not help the student who was
on the borderline and who had other teachers who still assigned a
D or a failure for D or failing work. Some teachers therefore
began to grade very high because they believed that by grading
high and therefore helping to keep all of the young men in school
they were refusing to help decide who would go to Vietnam. What
they either failed to realize or refused to see is that they were still
helping to decide, since every time they helped a student avoid the
draft by staying in college they were helping to force someone
else, who was not in college and whom these teachers did not know,
into the military and to Vietnam.

As teachers gave some bad students higher grades than they
deserved in order to keep them out of the army they had to give
other bad students higher grades than they deserved in order to
be fair. Better students also received higher grades than they deserved in order to distinguish them from the worst students, and
so on all the way up the line.

Other teachers decided to grade high because of their social and
economic attitudes. Toward the end of the 1960s there developed
among a fair number of teachers, especially the young and the
radical, the notion that the system of higher schooling is nothing
more than an undemocratic extension of an undemocratic class

structure in the United States and that students do poorly in college not because of any lack of ability or intelligence or the willingness to work hard but rather because of the lack of an opportunity earlier to develop their abilities and to acquire the knowledge that should be basic to entrance into college. Believing that the students should not be penalized for their having been deprived of opportunity earlier these teachers began to pass everyone. More than that, they began to give a high proportion of high grades, since the same lack of opportunity that made it difficult for some to do college work made it difficult for others to get high grades, and these teachers believed that the student should no more be deprived of the highest grade because of his lack of opportunity than he should be failed out of college because of his lack of opportunity. These teachers believed that by grading high they were being democratic. They believed that they were helping incapable students to overcome their lack of earlier opportunity. What they either did not realize or refused to see is that they were doing much harm and little good. They were making it possible for all students to get by learning less and were therefore helping to turn out uneducated people with college degrees. They were turning out people who had no respect for learning because they had never experienced learning, who had no respect for education because they had no idea of how education can broaden one's alternatives and help one to understand the universe and his place in it.

Many of the young teachers who graded high for social and economic reasons called themselves socialists. They argued that the capitalistic system exploits the poor and the uneducated and that therefore it is necessary to educate the exploited so that they can understand the exploitation and therefore refuse any longer to accept it. They argued further that educating those students who do not come from the exploited class will enable them also to understand the exploitation and will cause them to refuse to accept it even though they benefit from it. These radical teachers were among the first to quit trying to educate. They often argued that what is important is not how much knowledge or critical ability the student acquires but where his heart is. When they did emphasize the necessity of understanding they often equated understanding with the recitation of leftist slogans. Since the leftist slogans expressed all necessary truth, there was no need for the students to learn anything else. Anyone who could recite the slogans got good grades.

Thus these young radicals, who often claimed to be the only

open-minded people on the campus, were doing exactly what they accused their enemies of doing. They were indoctrinating rather than educating, and they believed that the student's right to a college degree depended on the extent to which he had absorbed— or pretended to have absorbed—the indoctrination. Thus again these young radicals were doing more harm than good. By teaching the exploited student slogans rather than knowledge they added nothing to his understanding of the exploitation and therefore added nothing to his ability to resist it without violence. They added nothing to the more prosperous student's understanding of it either, and therefore they did nothing to help him recognize why he should resist it also. More than that, by failing to provide a foundation of knowledge on the basis of which the student could evaluate other things he heard, and further by encouraging the student to be satisfied with slogans rather than knowledge, he helped to make the student more rather than less susceptible to slogans in the future. He thus helped to defeat his own objective. When it comes down to a battle of slogans in the United States, the capitalists will win every time.

While many teachers began to grade high simply because they collapsed under the pressure of students or for political or social and economic reasons, others based their high grading on what they called their educational philosophy. They believed that the grading system actually discourages learning.[3] They believed that the student's having to be conscious of grades destroys his enthusiasm for learning and that working for grades he has to do busywork that teaches him nothing. They assumed that busywork is anything that the student does not choose to do himself. By eliminating the pressure of grades, they thought, and by thus eliminating busywork, they would emancipate the student who really wants to learn. They assumed that almost every student really does want to learn. Therefore they made it known that they would grade very high. Sometimes they guaranteed whole classes A's or A pluses. Others allowed the students to grade themselves. That also resulted in a very high proportion of very high grades. Some students shamelessly gave themselves grades that they knew they did not deserve, while others actually believed that they had learned a great deal. The first group, which consisted of people who did not know and who knew that they did not know but took the high grades anyway, is probably less dangerous than the second, which consisted of people who did not know but who did not know that they did not know.

In order to appeal to students and to make what they called

learning more palatable by reducing the pressure of grades still other teachers adopted the so-called contract system, by which the teacher assigns a specific amount of work for a specific grade and allows the student to choose the grade for which he wants to work. While teachers present this device as a means of de-emphasizing grades it actually increases the emphasis on grades: the student works *only* for the grade he chooses. The contract system inevitably contributes to the decline of academic standards because it emphasizes quantity of work over quality of work. If the student does the required amount of work, regardless of how well or how badly he does it, he must get the grade the teacher has promised him. As soon as the teacher begins to evaluate the quality of work and to insist that it be of a minimum quality before he will accept it he is destroying the object of the contract system. He is taking control of the grade out of the student's hands. He is involving himself in the decision about the work the student will do and the grade he will receive. He is putting pressure on the student again, and the entire object of the contract system is to take the pressure off.

The pass-fail system also resulted from the effort to release the student from the pressure of grades and has contributed to the decline of academic standards. The rationalization of this system is that the student might want to learn something in an area in which he could not do good work and that he would be more likely to take a course in that area if he did not have to worry about getting a low grade. If the student receives only a pass or a fail, the theory runs, he will take the course, do the best he can, learn something, and not suffer as a result of competing with majors and others who have more ability in the subject than he has himself. But that is not the way pass-fail works. Instead the student considers his pass-fail course a free load, does almost no work, attends class irregularly or not at all, and depends on what little information he does pick up in the little work he does do and the few classes he does attend to get him his D and therefore his pass.[4] The result, though, is that sometimes the student who plans to get a pass gets a fail. The result of that in turn is that soon the students demanded the pass-no-credit system instead of the pass-fail system. Under that plan the student who does almost no work, learns almost nothing, and does not receive a pass at least does not suffer the usual consequences of a failure. The course does not go on his record at all and therefore damages neither his dignity, his grade-point average, nor the beauty of his transcript. The student's only loss is the credit that he otherwise would have received, and his only penalty is the necessity of taking an over-load or attending summer school or graduating a semester or two late.

Still another device for manipulating grade-point averages up-ward and therefore for lowering academic standards is the sys-tem of plus-but-no-minus. The process of adopting this system often followed the same pattern. Schools had five grades: A, B, C, D, and E or F, with no pluses or minuses. Students decided that these grades were not exact enough, since the best B student might be much better than the worst B student. Especially the C was a catch-all: it included students who were doing better than average work as well as those who were doing barely acceptable work. The students decided that they wanted a system of grading that would distinguish more exactly among qualities of work. The plus-and-minus system appeared to be the answer.

To their great disappointment, however, students discovered three things. First, they discovered that they got minuses as well as pluses. The student who earlier would have had a B sometimes got a B minus, and the student who earlier would have had a C sometimes got a C minus. Therefore some of them saw their grade-point averages go down rather than up. Second, students discovered that the teacher could give the student who was high in a category the plus grade in that category rather than the next higher grade. While under the old system the teacher might give the high C student a B in order to distinguish him from the average or low C student, under the new system he could make the distinction by giving him a C plus. Once again many students saw their grade-point averages go down rather than up. Third, they discovered that teachers gave the borderline student the low plus rather than the high minus. While under the old system the teacher might give a student a B because he was not quite a C, with the pluses and minuses he could give him either a B minus or a C plus. Some got the B minus, but a good many got the C plus. In either case the student did not get the B. Once again some students saw their grade-point averages go down rather than up. They might not have bothered to analyze just why it was happening, but they could see that it was happening. They could hardly have missed it: some of them were having a harder time than ever staying in school. They could see that all of those minuses were helping to make life difficult for them.

Faced with their declining grade-point averages, the students had two alternatives. They could work harder. That alternative, however, occurred to only a few, and only a few of those actually adopted it. The second alternative was not only much easier but also much more fun. They agitated for dropping the minuses and retaining the pluses, and in some places they succeeded. Thus while the student who deserves a minus receives a higher grade than he deserves, the student who deserves a plus does not receive a lower grade than he deserves. The result is higher grade-point averages all around.

Those people who believe that the student learns more without the pressure of grades are ignoring one harsh fact. Because most of the students who enter college have had no experience in learning they do not learn because learning is important or fun. The only thing that makes them work is the pressure of grades, the danger of failing out of college or of graduating with a grade-point average that will keep them out of graduate school or law school or medical school. For the ignorance of college students has not resulted in any decline in their aspirations. They still want to become doctors and lawyers and college professors.

All of the devices for removing the pressure of grades have helped to lower academic standards. With high grades easier to get students worked less,[5] and an increasing number did work that by any legitimate standard was failing work. Teachers who did try to maintain legitimate academic standards found it impossible. Students who did not have to work in most of their courses considered it unjust that they should have to work in *any* of them. And so they did not. The teacher could either hold out or give in. He could give low grades to those who deserved them and face the consequences. The first consequence was a decline in his enrollments and therefore in the student-teacher ratio of his department. The further results were the denial of promotions and salary increases, ostracism by other members of his department, and other pressures both subtle and not-so-subtle either to grade higher or to resign. One of the favorite pressures was for the chairman of a department to make it clear that he would listen sympathetically to the complaints of students and in that way to encourage a whole parade of students with complaints about imagined injustices perpetrated by the difficult teacher.

It was not only his colleagues who put pressure on the serious teacher. Students did it also. They not only avoided the more difficult classes but also encouraged others to avoid them. Stories became so exaggerated that even good students, who did want to learn and were willing to work, believed that they would have no chance of passing these courses. Students complained to deans and chairmen of departments that the difficult teachers were arrogant, unfriendly, and unapproachable and that they graded unfairly. They harassed teachers and tried to humiliate them. They made anonymous phone calls at night and either talked nonsense or hung up as soon as the teacher answered the phone. After the bars closed they stopped on the sidewalks outside teachers' homes and talked loudly for hours. They turned up campus loudspeakers aimed at classrooms where difficult teachers were giving exams. They insulted teachers outside the teachers' offices knowing that the teachers would overhear them. They wrote nasty messages on announcements that teachers put on bulletin boards, and they sent vulgar poems and pornographic drawings through the mail to teachers they did not like. They wrote letters attacking teachers to the letters-to-the-editor columns of campus newspapers. In the days when beards were still unusual they shouted Jesus Christ and Moses from windows of dormitories at difficult teachers with beards. They dropped balloons or prophylactics filled with water on teachers using sidewalks near dormitories.

The students who did take the difficult courses also put pressure on the teacher. They became sullen after he returned the first exam and then tried to argue with him in his office. Even when a teacher grades high, returning exams is unpleasant, since there are always students who believe that they deserve higher grades than they get. But at the time of steadily declining academic standards, for the teacher who lagged behind and tried to maintain legitimate standards returning exams was positively excruciating. The students grinned, groaned, frowned, sighed, shook their heads, and laughed outright. For the rest of the semester they were sullen. They cut class, and when they did come to class they refused to respond or even to pay attention. Entire classes reacted this way, since almost everyone believed that he deserved a higher grade than he got and since the social pressure of the rest of the class forced those few students who did get high grades or who were satisfied with what they got to react in the same way or not react at all. The students made it clear that they considered the teacher some kind of a nut who, because he was out of his mind, obviously had nothing worth saying in class. They made it clear that he was talking to the walls. In his office they became belligerent.

Faced with all of this harassment even the teacher who was most determined to maintain legitimate academic standards usually gave in. He made assignments easier and graded higher.[6] He gave up trying to teach.

The serious teacher continues to face a dilemma that in the present circumstances is insoluble. If he assigns an appropriate amount of work the student will refuse to do it because he has not yet learned to distinguish scholarship from busywork, because he resents the external discipline that the assignments impose on him, because he is positively afraid of learning, and because he soon learns that most teachers do not assign much work, that most teachers who do assign a fair amount of work do not expect their students to do it, and that it is easier to take those courses than to take those that are challenging. The serious teacher knows that if he assigns an appropriate amount of work he will not get many students. At the same time, though, he knows that if he does not assign a considerable amount of work the students will never acquire enough information or intellectual sophistication to develop confidence in their own minds and therefore will never break out of the habit of memorizing unrelated facts and of believing what they are told to believe. He knows that they will never recover the curiosity of their pre-school years.

In addition to the decreasing abilities of students, the increased resistance of students to learning, and the higher grading practices of teachers there is a fourth reason for the decline of academic standards in American colleges. That is the increasing ignorance of professors. While the college teacher has always been uneducated, his intellectual condition during the past ten or fifteen years has deteriorated. During the rapid expansion of colleges and universities during the 1960s there were more teaching positions than people to fill them. Three things happened as a result. First, graduate programs expanded to meet the demand, and therefore an increased number of unprepared, incapable, and uninterested students entered graduate programs. For economic and practical reasons graduate departments could not fail out all of those who deserved to fail out, and therefore an increased number of uneducated people did get their doctorates and did become teachers. Beyond that, the large number of graduate students, as well as the graduate school's traditional function of continuing the indoctrination of students rather than of educating them, made it impossible to educate those who could have been educated.[7] While graduate students who can think for themselves rather than simply absorb indoctrination and who therefore can become something other than agents of indoctrination themselves are always a minority, during these years the minority became smaller than ever. Second, many colleges hired people whom they knew were only minimally qualified to teach even though they had completed their doctorates, and while these colleges pretended to hope to replace them with more highly qualified people the continuing shortage of teachers made it possible for administrators to implement better than ever before their desire to hire only those people who they know either cannot or will not teach. Thus they were able to rehire and finally to grant tenure to many who are unable or unwilling to teach. Even under the best of circumstances only a small proportion of teachers ever think. The proportion became smaller than ever. Third, the shortage of people with doctorates caused many colleges to hire people who had not completed the doctorate, and in response to glib promises about completing the degree colleges did grant tenure to many who would never do it, some of whom had only the vaguest intention of doing it to begin with and who in fact might not be capable of doing it. While most of these people would have gained nothing intellectually from completing the doctorate, some would have.

Another reason for the decline in the quality of the teacher is the existence of affirmative action programs.[8] In spite of the claims that sex and minority status are only the last of the criteria and that the woman or the member of a minority is hired only if his qualifications are equal to those of the white male applicants, the truth is that in order to hire a white male the people who do the hiring have to prove to people who have no qualifications for judging that his qualifications are superior to those of a woman or a member of a minority. These people can see when an applicant is a woman or a member of a minority, but they cannot always see when a white male is the superior candidate for a job. Thus the people who do the hiring are likely to hire the less qualified woman or member of a minority because when they do that they do not have to prove anything to anyone. They can avoid the difficulty of having to prove that they did hire the most qualified candidate.

The object of the people who enforce the affirmative action programs is less to provide an opportunity for the woman or the member of a minority than to blunt protest by draining potential dissident leaders from these groups and by creating the impression that opportunities actually do exist for them. The object is to adopt the course that will disturb the status quo the least. The white male who cannot get a job is, of course, upset, but his dissatisfaction is not at all dangerous. He has no constituency. Blacks and women do have.

In encouraging the hiring of less qualified people the affirmative action programs have the additional advantage of guaranteeing that the least possible learning will occur in the classroom. Dependent on their sources, the less qualified people will be able only to indoctrinate. The more qualified person who did not get the job might actually have tried to teach.[9]

Chapter 4

THE DECLINE OF
ACADEMIC STANDARDS: 2
Academic Organization and Policy

*W*hile the decreased abilities of high-school graduates, the increased resistance of students to learning, the higher grading practices of teachers, and the increasing ignorance of professors have all combined to cause a decline in academic standards of American colleges and universities, changes in academic organization and policy have accelerated the decline.

One of these changes is the increasing proportion of non-teaching personnel on college campuses and the increasing influence they have on academic decisions. Very often they are badly educated themselves and therefore have no idea of what an education is. Occasionally one of them is so innocent that he can list *reading* as one of his interests,[1] as though that is unusual on a college campus. Among these people, unfortunately, all too often it is. Very often they have gone into student personnel or other non-academic fields because they have had difficulty with academic courses themselves, and therefore they are sympathetic toward students who have difficulty with required courses or with teachers who try to teach anything beyond platitudes. They also see students only in non-academic situations—girls who have trouble with their boyfriends or are afraid that they are pregnant, or both, and guys who are in trouble for something they did while they were drunk or who are afraid that their girlfriends are pregnant, or both—and therefore even the best-educated of them have no way of recognizing the students' ignorance and intellectual indifference. They know that the students are pretty badly messed up and that they know little about how to straighten out their own lives, but they seldom connect the students' personal problems to their general ignorance about everything, to their having failed ever to think seriously about themselves or anything else. Thus when they vote on academic policy they are at a triple disadvantage: they do not know what an education is; they do not know anything about the intellectual qualities of the students who are supposed to be educated; and they have sympathy for the students rather than respect for the potential of their minds.[2]

Another of the structural reasons for the decline of academic standards is the presence of students on faculty committees. They have already infiltrated curriculum committees, and therefore the serious teacher has to contend not only with teachers who are not serious and with the influence of non-academic personnel on academic policy but also with the brash ignorance of eighteen-year-olds who have no way of knowing what an education is because they have never been exposed to one.[3] These students, who should be in school because they want to learn, are encouraged to believe that they know *what* they should learn. They talk always about learning, but their efforts are invariably directed toward not learning. Every single curricular demand of students has been a demand to make college less strenuous and more fun. It is students who demand the elimination of such requirements as foreign language, physical education, and basic studies or liberal arts in the freshman and sophomore years, the adoption of the pass-fail system, the pass-no-credit system, and the plus-but-no-minus system, the adoption of course-teacher evaluations, and the flood of "relevant" courses. Almost never has there been a student protest about a course because it was too slight. Never yet has there been a rally around a teacher because he is perceptive rather than popular.

Another committee that students sit on is a recent development and should not exist at all. This is the committee to review protested grades. Its existence not only violates the teacher's professional obligations but also increases the difficulty of establishing legitimate academic standards. Not only is the committee dangerous, but it is also unnecessary. No sane teacher would ever claim that he never gives a student a lower grade than he deserves, but no serious teacher would ever do it deliberately. And if the teacher sometimes grades too low, he often grades too high. Thus the student who occasionally receives a lower grade than he deserves does not really suffer. That low grade is more than balanced by grades that are higher than he deserves.

But students are not satisfied with that. They want all of the advantages of receiving higher grades than they deserve without the risk of ever receiving lower grades than they deserve. Therefore in some colleges, administrators, seeing an opportunity to humiliate members of the faculty and to broaden the breach between faculty and students, have permitted the establishment of committees to review any grade that a student wants to protest. Teachers do serve on the committees with students, but many teachers are so insecure that they will do anything that administrators and students want them to do.

A still further structural reason for the decline of academic standards in colleges and universities is the increasing use of student evaluations of faculty. There was a time when a teacher's retention, tenure, and promotion depended on the respect of his colleagues, whom the administrators already—for good reasons or bad—respected. But in recent years, especially as turmoil on campuses and illiterate graduates in teaching positions in elementary, junior high, and high schools convinced regents, trustees, and legislators that college faculties were not doing their job, administrators began to demand objective evidence of effective teaching. It was politically popular as well as academically expedient for them to accept the students' assumption that only the students can properly evaluate the teacher since they are the only people who regularly watch him perform. And so the course-teacher evaluation has become so institutionalized that it can be scored through the Educational Testing Service at Princeton. What the evaluations do not show, however, is that a teacher gets a good rating for the same reasons that he has large classes: because he is easy and sympathetic.[4]

Very often students honestly believe that the easiest and most sympathetic teacher is also the best teacher. His easiness and friendliness help to convince them that they are learning a great deal. By making his assignments easy the teacher who wants a good rating can convince students that learning is easy; by grading high he tells them that they have learned all they are required to learn and therefore that they know all they need to know; and by drinking with them in their hang-outs three or four times a week he tells them that he is one of them and therefore that they are his intellectual equals. Since he is a professor he must be pretty smart, and therefore they must be pretty smart also.

The truth is that course-teacher evaluations are a gigantic fraud. In the first place the students are not competent to judge good teaching. Especially freshmen—in whose introductory courses the course-teacher evaluations are probably most widely used—have no basis for judging good teaching. Presumably everyone learns something—though there are those who would doubt even that— but the student cannot evaluate a course until he has some way of knowing what he *should* have learned in it. Even upper-classmen often equate entertainment with education. Often the student measures what he has learned by the grade he receives. If he receives an A he must have learned what he was supposed to learn, while if he receives a C there must be things that he should have learned but did not. Therefore if the student is entertained and receives a high grade he tends to overrate the teacher,[5] while if he is not entertained or if he receives a low grade the most comforting thing he can do is blame the teacher.

In the second place students are not *willing* to judge teachers accurately. The student wants to help the teacher whom he likes personally. If the teacher appears to be trying to teach well— and few things are easier for the teacher than to convince students he is trying hard—and if he is friendly and generous with his grades they will be friendly and generous with their evaluations. Sometimes the teacher actually asks his students to be generous because he needs a good evaluation for tenure, promotion, or an increase in salary. The implication is that the students will get something in return. That something is high grades. It is the teacher who refuses to give them high grades whom they will penalize.

In the third place, learning requires an intellectual effort that students often are unwilling to exert. An understanding of the serious teacher requires students not only to concentrate on what he says in class but also to accumulate information and to think about it while they are not in class. The teacher who is the most profound they often criticize because, they say, he cannot communicate with them or because he deliberately talks over their heads or because what he says is irrelevant. Of course it often *is* irrelevant, not because of the teacher's lack of knowledge or ability but because the students have nothing in their heads to which what the teacher says *could* relate. Often they have nothing important in their heads at all, and often they are unwilling to put anything there. What the teacher does in class, after all, is far less important than what the student does outside class. No one can teach the student who will not work.

Fourth, there is the simple reality that good teaching cannot be quantified. Good teaching is measured by the impact that the teacher has on his students' ability to use their minds, not on the answers to such elementary questions as whether he is organized or interesting or whether he made his objectives clear, whether he is readily available to talk to students, or whether he makes helpful comments on exams. Those things are important, but a person can do all of those things and still be a horrible teacher. But those are things that students can judge by the end of their first semester with him. What influence he has had on their ability to think they will not know until years later if ever at all. In most cases, of course, the teacher's influence will have been bad, but the student will never be able to think well enough to realize it. Even when a teacher has helped students to think for themselves the effect ordinarily is only temporary, since the serious teacher's influence cannot balance the oversimplifications of politicians, television, the press, and the majority of teachers.

Finally there are those other three simple realities. The first is that teachers whose ratings are too low to do them any good can easily enough destroy the bad ones and fill out some of their own. The second is that the judgments of faculty and students carry no weight anyway. The only evaluation that really matters is the one the cost accountants make. Increasingly in academia it is the cost accountants who count.[6] The question is not how much influence the teacher has on his students' ability to think but how many students he has. No course-teacher evaluation is required to determine that. Finally, teaching is not one of the teacher's functions. Anyone who actually tries to help his students develop a critical ability is likely to be penalized rather than rewarded by students and administrators alike.

Positively evil as the course-teacher evaluations are, many teachers do accept them even though they have heard students say such things as "He's a nice man and a *wonderful teacher*, but I haven't learned a thing in his course." And administrators, who usually have no idea themselves of what education or good teaching is, who have not been inside a classroom for years if ever at all, who have no intellectual contact with students, and who therefore are the logical people to evaluate teaching and successful education, demand quantifiable evidence. The course-teacher evaluation is one result.

From the standpoint of academic administrators, allowing students to sit on faculty committees, establishing committees to review grades, and using course-teacher evaluations have had several favorable results. First, these devices have caused the teacher deliberately to give students—especially politically active students—higher grades than they deserve in order to receive good evaluations and to avoid the humiliation of having the review committee review any of them. Thus they have helped administrators to reduce academic standards, to guarantee that learning will not occur, and to keep the dormitories full. Second, they have provided administrators with ammunition to use against teachers they want to get rid of. The administrators can ignore the unfavorable evaluations of people they like while they can belabor the unfavorable evaluations of those they do not like. Third, by destroying teachers' morale these devices have made them easier to control. By impressing upon the teacher his lack of a voice in determining what comprises adequate academic work they have helped to destroy his feeling of professionalism and have increased his feeling of insecurity.

Fourth, these devices have divided faculties and students. While students and teachers should be natural allies against anti-intellectual administrators, administrators and students have become allies against teachers. Administrators use the students to help control teachers, and the students are flattered with their apparent importance. Students—especially the politicians among them—have become more arrogant toward teachers than ever, since they review the teacher's grades and organize the evaluations. They see the teacher as a powerless functionary dependent upon their own good will. The teacher sees the students co-operating with administrators to humiliate and to control him.

During the past few years, therefore, relations between faculties and students have deteriorated to a point that often is best described as mutual contempt. Many students neither like nor respect their teachers, and many teachers neither like nor respect their students. Because these devices have confirmed the students' notion that they are intellectually equal or superior to teachers they feel less and less necessity of having any faculty at all. Because they have confirmed also the teachers' suspicion that no one respects them and that everyone is against them they are willing to spend less time than they did earlier with students. Students want faculty advisors for their organizations less often than they did earlier, but when they do want them they have more trouble getting serious advisors than they formerly had. Students are less welcome in offices of the faculty than they formerly were. There is increased difficulty getting teachers to attend graduation. The changed attitude has also affected teaching: the teacher sometimes decides that since the students neither recognize nor appreciate good teaching he is foolish to spend a lot of time on it. And he decides that if he grades high enough none of the students will pester him in his office.

Of course there are exceptions to this. Some teachers spend more time with students than teachers ever spent formerly. But that association does not imply respect. The teachers who spend time with students do it increasingly on the students' terms— in the students' hang-outs. They are often the teachers who are the most insecure and who therefore are trying to build up a clientele among students. They are often young teachers for whom the loneliness of professionalism is a vast change from the wide acquaintances of graduate school, who therefore are seeking company, and who in both age and knowledge are closer to the students than to older teachers. The teachers who spend time with students might be breathless middle-aged men whose wives have reached the stage of motherly dumpiness and for whose imaginations the nineteen-year-old girls in their tight pants provide a delightful inspiration and whom the flattering attentions of those same nineteen-year-old girls make feel young again three times a week.

A further structural reason for the decline of academic standards is the rapid expansion of community colleges.[7] Students who go to the community college are often those who cannot get into a four-year college. Once the community college exists it seems always to want to expand, and therefore it often has to seek students actively, advertising just as any other organization that has something to sell and appealing to people who have neither the ability nor the interest to enable them to get anything out of college. Mobile registration units dredge the shopping centers to find housewives who have only vaguely considered going to college. Advertisements on television and in newspapers make college courses appear indispensable and easily acquired keys to automatic success and immediate happiness. For these reasons the students in the community colleges are often even less prepared for college and have even less time to study than those in the four-year colleges. But the teachers move them along, giving high grades for the same reasons that the teachers in the four-year colleges do. Even less prepared to begin with than the freshmen who enter the four-year colleges, the students in the two-year colleges ordinarily learn even less during their two years there than those attending the four-year colleges learn during their first two years.

All of the evidence indicates that the average academic standard in the community college is lower that the average standard in the four-year college. High-school graduates who cannot get themselves admitted to four-year colleges are admitted to two-year colleges. Students who fail out of four-year colleges during the freshman year often go to community colleges to start all over. Students who fail specific courses in the four-year colleges often take the courses in two-year colleges and get the credit transferred. Admissions directors of four-year colleges have done studies that show that during his first semester at a four-year college the student who has transferred from a community college can expect to achieve a grade-point average several tenths of a point below the cumulative average that he achieved at the community college.[8]

One would expect, then, that in order to assure itself that the students who transfer to it are able to do acceptable work the four-year college would admit only those students who have been able to do something better than passing work at the two-year college. The existence of the two-year college would not necessarily result in lower academic standards in the four-year college if the four-year college could retain control over what students it accepts and what it does with them after it accepts them. But there is an increasing insistence that anyone who graduates from a two-year college be admitted to a four-year college.[9] Therefore students who can barely do passing work in the two-year college are admitted to the four-year college, and since the teachers there can no more fail all of the students who deserve to fail in upper-level courses than they can in the introductory courses for freshmen and sophomores they have to lower their standards to accommodate those transfer students.

The conventional wisdom states that since the grade-point average of the student who transfers from a two-year college ordinarily drops a few tenths of a point during his first semester at the four-year college but then returns to approximately what it was at the junior college the transfer student does have the ability to do good work and needs only the one semester of experience to learn to apply that ability. The further conclusion is that after his first semester at the four-year college the transfer student does work of as high a quality as the student who started out in the four-year college does.

Maybe he does. It is clear that most of the students who start out in the four-year college are none too good either. It is clear also that some of those who transfer are better than some of those who start out in the four-year college. It is also clear that students are finding it easier than ever before to maintain grade-point averages that are higher than ever before. And it is clear also that one of the reasons for the ease of getting good grades is the presence every semester of some unqualified transfer students. They often get the low grades, and in order to distinguish the students who deserve low grades but who do better work than the unqualified transfer students the teacher gives them higher grades than they deserve.

Even if after his difficult first semester the transfer student does do work equal to that of the student who has started out in the four-year college we dare not conclude that he is doing work of high quality. Very few students are doing work of high quality. If the student who transfers from a community college eventually gets grades equal to those of students who did not transfer it might be because he arrives at a plateau at which he does the same mediocre work that most of the other students do but receives superior grades for that mediocre work just as they do. The admission of an increased number of transfer students has occurred, after all, at a time when academic standards have been falling.What appears to have happened is that as teachers lowered standards to accommodate the transfer students it became easier for anyone to get a B. And since students work not for excellence but rather to achieve some previously selected approximate grade-point average[10] many students who under the lowered standard could achieve higher grade-point averages work less and still achieve the grade-point averages that they have selected. The student who under the earlier standards would have worked for his C plus could now get an A minus but is content with his B. The gentleman's C has become the gentleman's B. The transfer student gets his B or his A, and the student who could do better work either has no place else to go—there is nothing higher than an A plus—or else does not want to go there. So he gets his B or his A also. Thus the transfer student's doing work approximately equal to that of the non-transfer student might result not from the transfer student's increasing the quality of his work to meet the quality of work of the non-transfer student but rather from the non-transfer student's lowering the quality of his work to meet the quality of work of the transfer student.

Another explanation for the apparent fact that transfer students from two-year colleges achieve grade-point averages as high as those of students who start out in the four-year college is that with the general raising of grades teachers can distinguish less than they could earlier among qualities of work. In many colleges the failure and the D have been all but eliminated, and in some colleges the C also is quite uncommon. If every student is going to get at least a B minus in every course there is obviously little room for differentiating the best students from the worst. Obviously the worst students are going to end up with grade-point averages almost as high as those of any students except the very best.

The demands of the two-year college did not end with the automatic admission of its graduate to a four-year college. The next demand was that the four-year college accept all of his credits from the community college in order that he would be admitted with full junior standing. Since the courses in which he received grades of D counted toward his graduation from the two-year college the four-year college is supposed to accept them toward his graduation from the four-year college. The argument is that since the D grades of the student who spends all four years at the four-year college count toward his graduation it is discriminatory not to accept toward the transfer student's graduation the D grades that he received at the two-year college. That argument would make sense if the standards at the community colleges were somewhere nearly equivalent even to the deteriorated standards of the four-year colleges. But the standards at the community colleges have deteriorated just as rapidly as those of the four-year colleges. They started out lower and they have fallen at least as fast. The D that the student receives in the two-year college is often the equivalent of a failure at the four-year college. And often, it appears, the C at the community college would be a failure at the four-year college. But the four-year college is forced not only to accept transfer students who are unable or unprepared to do legitimate college work but also to accept toward graduation courses in which the students have learned almost nothing and sometimes nothing at all.

A still further structural cause of the decline in academic standards is the granting of automatic credit for living. In some states adults can take examinations for credit without ever attending college. Students who are in college wonder why they should have to work for their credits when the state is giving away credit to others for nothing. Teachers have no convincing answer and therefore are tempted again to lower academic standards. Teachers who believe in having no academic standards in the first place are reinforced in their determination to give high grades that reflect little or no learning.

Credit by examination is one of the symptoms of the loss of confidence in academic education. The implication is that the university can do nothing that life cannot do, and the logical conclusion is that periodically everyone should be granted another degree. Logically the person who lives, say, to the age of forty should automatically receive a bachelor's degree; at fifty he should receive a master's degree; and if he is fortunate enough to live until he is seventy he should receive a Ph.D., an M.D., a D.D.S., an LL.D., or any other available degree. But surely the Ph.D. should be the preferred one. Since colloquially and often actually *Ph.D.* stands for "Piled Higher and Deeper" there is no logical reason why a person outside an institution cannot pile it as high and as deep as a person inside one.[11]

The automatic credit for living is also a symptom of the exaggerated emphasis in the United States on college credit as opposed to real education. No one ever asks What does he know? but rather How much credit does he have? That condition in turn is the result of the American's discomfort with anything that cannot be measured in numerical terms. There exists the feeling that anything that cannot be quantified does not exist at all.

Finally, credit by examination reflects the educationists' and the academic administrators' emotional insecurity. Because they have no understanding of or confidence in education and because they are financially dependent on the taxpayers they seek to increase their importance to the community. Rather than trying to impress upon the community the importance of education—a task that they are intellectually unqualified to perform—they award credits for nothing in order to make people appreciate what they are doing and to make the taxpayers more willing than they otherwise would be to furnish financial support for their institutions. Therefore they prop up their egos and their economic positions at the same time.

Another structural reason for the decline in academic standards is the expansion of extension courses on television. These courses are designed for people who are either too indifferent or too distracted to take serious courses outside their own homes. While they do no doubt result in some learning sometimes, there is no way to assure that the learning is sufficient to justify the credit that the student receives.

Probably the most common device for awarding people credit without leaving the kitchen is Sunrise Semester. It consists of formal courses in which the instructors lecture or, as in a course in music, combine lecture with performance. There are three things wrong with it. First, the courses are offered early in the morning, when the people for whom they are intended can watch them and when time on television is available at relatively low rates. Often they come at six-thirty in the morning. This is the time when people are more distracted than they will be at any other time during the day. The housewife, still not fully awake herself, has to worry about getting the coffee ready, getting her husband and children out of bed, getting breakfast, and getting her husband off to work and her children off to school. The man who takes a course on Sunrise Semester has to think about getting himself off to work and what he will be doing for the rest of the day. There is simply no way that the average person who takes a course through Sunrise Semester can consistently concentrate on it.

Under these conditions the only thing that could keep students from being distracted is a lecture that is so exciting that no one would want to miss any of it and would therefore arrange his chores to fit the program. But the second fundamental fault of courses on television is that they are boring. Most professors are boring in any case, and putting them on television only makes them worse. There are three primary reasons for this. First, the mere realization that he is on television distracts the professor. He might be nervous and therefore not able to think as well as he otherwise would be, but even when he is not nervous he is self-conscious. He is, after all, the star of the show. Beyond that he has to be more concerned with time than he is in the classroom.

Second, the teacher on television does not know who might be watching him, and therefore he has to be careful what he says. Making a factual error is more serious on television than in the classroom, where he can correct it the next day. Making a joke in order to wake up his students might appear frivolous on television while in the classroom it is a legitimate device that many teachers use. Similarly, saying something outrageous just to get the attention of his students is something that the professor on television dare not do. For all of these reasons the professor on television tends to give very straight-laced lectures and to say nothing that he cannot immediately footnote.

The knowledge that anyone at all might be watching him has an especially deleterious effect on the American history teacher. Most American history teachers believe nothing that is not entirely acceptable to most Americans, but the teacher on television must be sure that he does not say anything that is not acceptable even to the most reactionary American. If there is a chance that an F.B.I. or C.I.A. agent is watching him he must be sure that he says nothing to which that agent might object. Thus teaching American history on television encourages the professor to tailor his presentation to assuage his terror, and the result is not history but a perversion of history. Beyond that, the professor who does dare to say something unacceptable to the F.B.I. or the C.I.A. will never get a chance to say it. "Educational" television needs public support, and the surest way to lose that support is to hire a professor who says things that the F.B.I., the C.I.A., the state legislators, or the local sheriff considers un-American.

The third reason why courses on television are particularly boring is that the professor does not have the immediate presence of students to reinforce his enthusiasm. Every serious teacher knows how difficult it is to maintain his enthusiasm before an unresponsive class. Having no class at all is all the worse. For all he knows, the professor might be talking to the walls. Alone in the studio with the camera and the technicians he is indeed talking to the walls. Even in those rare instances in which he does begin with some enthusiasm his lecture almost inevitably degenerates into a mere recitation of words or a reading of notes.

The third fundamental fault of the courses on Sunrise Semester is that the professors who offer them recognize that the students have little or no interest in or time for reading and therefore assign little or no reading. When reading is required it ordinarily consists of only one book for the entire semester, and the serious teacher is constantly impressed with the regularity with which the announcer informs the students that there will be no reading to accompany the next lecture. Thus students who are too distracted to get much out of the lecture get very little anyplace else, either.

Recently there has developed the practice of granting credit for watching programs that are designed primarily as entertainment. These are ordinarily presented on the non-commercial networks and often do appear during prime time. They do therefore avoid some of the pitfalls of Sunrise Semester. But they have pitfalls of their own. They come at the end of the day when everyone is tired. They come on weekends when people are engaged in social activities. They are designed for college students who at night and on weekends like to be in bed with their friends and for whom the action under the blankets is far more immediately fascinating than the action on the screen. Thus the evening program, like the Sunrise Semester, becomes a device designed not to educate anyone but rather to generate credits. As in the case of Sunrise Semester, no one except the student ever knows how many programs he missed and what he was actually doing when he was supposed to be watching.

Evening courses in extension programs have many of the same faults that courses on television have. The classes meet for long periods late in the day, when people are already too tired to concentrate. Between classes the students, often working full-time, have neither the time nor the energy to read. Often the evening classes, like the courses on television, become nothing more than devices for generating credits.

Other structural causes of the deteriorating academic standards are local programs and policies of individual colleges and universities. One of these is the Educational Opportunity Program, which is designed to provide minorities especially but also others who have been deprived of previous educational opportunity a chance to go to college. Since these people cannot meet the standard criteria for admission they take light loads and receive special tutoring. The assumption is that they are bright enough to meet the requirements for graduation, although their previous educational deprivation makes it necessary for them to spend five years in college rather than four.

While that is a very pleasant theory, however, the reality is different. These students are expected in five years not only to acquire the learning that the ordinary student should acquire in four but also to make up for twelve or thirteen years of educational deprivation. Of course that is impossible if the college retains any legitimate standards for graduation.[12] Because the student's weaknesses are so fundamental when he enters the program it is doubtful that in five years—or even in a lifetime—he can acquire the learning and the intellectual sophistication that he should have acquired before he left high school. Much less can he acquire the knowledge and the intellectual sophistication that the college graduate should have. While the best of these students do do legitimate college work, many of them, like many of the students who do not come from minorities and who have not been so obviously educationally deprived, are able to graduate only because of the reduced academic standards of the colleges. A high proportion of them also either drop out or fail out. The presence of these unprepared students has the same influence in further lowering academic standards that the presence of other unprepared and uninterested students has. Some teachers try to avoid the alternatives of failing a high proportion of the students in the Educational Opportunity Program or lowering academic standards for everyone by having separate standards for the students in the special program. The same quality of work that would get the ordinary student a D gets the special student a C.

While the Educational Opportunity Program contributes little to the knowledge or the intellectual sophistication of many of its students, it does serve some very important functions. First, it salves the consciences of white liberals who when these programs were established during the 1960s were feeling very guilty about what Americans had been doing to Negroes for three hundred and fifty years. The white liberals could establish these programs, forget about them, and get on with their own lives. Second, by providing college degrees for selected members of minorities this program provides the illusion of opportunity and therefore helps to blunt black protest. Third, by providing an opportunity for some members of minorities to go to college it drains off the most able, who might otherwise become leaders of protest, and by absorbing those potential leaders into white society it again helps to blunt black protest. Fourth, by providing the illusion of opportunity it blunts the demand for educational opportunity for minorities and other dispossessed people where it would really mean something—in the elementary, junior high, and high schools. The Educational Opportunity Program is not the threat to middle-class whites that real educational opportunity for blacks and other deprived people would be. It affects only a tiny proportion of the minorities and the laboring class, and most of those will provide little competition for the better-trained middle-class whites.

Another policy that speeds the deterioration of academic standards is sometimes called a Special Talents Program. It provides that the student who has some special talent can be admitted to the college even though he cannot meet the normal standards of admission. Thus an apparently less able student takes the place of a student of apparently greater ability. While administrators speak of a variety of special talents such as music, acting, and art, and while they speak of the advantage to the college population of having a more heterogeneous student body than mere emphasis on academic ability would provide, the Special Talents Program is designed ordinarily to allow the admission of athletes who have nothing in their favor except their athletic ability.[13]

Still another policy that encourages the deterioration of academic standards is the effort to maintain a student body of approximately half men and half women. Some colleges receive far more applications for admission from one sex than from the other. In order to get an even split in their student bodies they admit less qualified students than they would admit if they accepted only those who are most qualified regardless of whether they are male or female. While this policy might encourage romance it is a violation of the doctrine of equality of opportunity.

Both the Special Talents Program and the fifty-fifty policy are probably unconstitutional. If they are not they should be, since they deny opportunity to more able people in favor of less able people. They do not have even the doubtful justification that the less able people have been denied opportunity earlier, as the students admitted under the Educational Opportunity Program have been.

Finally, there is the policy of open admission. Under that policy anyone who wants to go to college can. Once the college admits a student it is committed to giving him a degree. It cannot fail out all of those who should fail out, and thus it must lower its standards to accommodate the students who are not capable of doing legitimate work.

Chapter 5

THE DECLINE OF
ACADEMIC STANDARDS: 3
Adjustment of Teachers, Departments, and
Institutions to the Threat of Retrenchment

*A*t the same time that the inadequacy of students, higher grading, the decreased competence of teachers, and structural and pro-
cedural changes have resulted in the lowering of academic standards, colleges have consciously and deliberately lowered standards
in response to the threat of retrenchment. During the 1960s
colleges expanded their faculties and facilities to meet the needs of
increasing enrollments, but in the 1970s many colleges found that
they had expanded too much. Enrollments no longer expanded
and even declined. With the end of the draft young men who
previously would have gone to college lost interest in it. As a result
of the protests, violence, and drugs on campuses during the late
sixties and early seventies many parents who had intended to send
their children to college decided that college was not a very good
place for them after all. With inflation families who earlier would
have sent their children to college no longer could. With increasing
expenses for administrators, welfare, roads, and lavish plazas in
capital cities the states have less money for schooling than they
had earlier, and therefore they increased tuition and thereby
eliminated other potential students. Upset at the disturbances on
campuses late in the 1960s state legislatures punished the colleges
by halting the expansion of faculties, by retrenching, and by
threatening to retrench, and again they punished students by raising tuition.

Inflation together with expansion and then retrenchment and

the threat of retrenchment has had three adverse effects on academic standards. First, the decreased interest in going to college and the increased cost of a college career has made it difficult for many colleges to keep their dormitories and classrooms full. Since every empty room costs money there is increased pressure to keep every student in school and to attract additional students. The obvious way to do this is to lower academic standards in order to admit those who formerly would not have been admitted and to keep in school those who under the earlier standards would have failed out.

Second, as a result of expansion and then inflation the living conditions of students have deteriorated and make it increasingly difficult for them to study even when they want to. In an effort to make dormitories pay some colleges force certain students— as freshmen and sophomores—to live on campus, where frivolity and noise make studying impossible. Because of increasing economic hardship students who previously would have lived in apartments or in rooms in private homes now choose to live in dormitories, and there they have the same difficulty that other students have studying there. Students who live off campus live in the same crowded conditions. The owners of scarce off-campus housing often exploit students by charging so much for apartments that four or more must live in an apartment scarcely big enough for two. Again students find it almost impossible to study. Going to the library does no good, since college libraries serve primarily a social rather than an academic function. Thus many who could have succeeded in college even under the earlier higher academic standards now succeed only because of the lowered standards.

The third adverse effect of the expansion and then retrenchment is that no teacher wants to be retrenched and no department wants to be the one that loses a line. Thus the teacher who is threatened assigns little work and grades high in order to get students and therefore to increase or at least to maintain the student-teacher ratio of his department and to build a base of student support. Even people whose jobs are not immediately threatened put pressure on each other to grade high. The loss of a line would result in decreased prestige for the department in an atmosphere in which the relative prestige of departments depends almost entirely on size. The loss of one or more lines might result in a loss of apparent power for the department in the governance of the college. This fear exists even though colleges are being governed increasingly from the top and departments have a steadily decreasing influence on what goes on in them.[1] As the influence of faculties decreases departments guard more intently than ever what little influence does remain to them. The only way they can do that is to maintain their numbers.

Beyond that, there is a loyalty within departments. No one wants to see one of his colleagues retrenched out of a job. Finally, once retrenchment starts no one knows where it will end. It might not stop with the loss of one position: anyone's job might be threatened. No one wants to be retrenched himself, and therefore anyone who tries to maintain academic standards even at the expense of the student-teacher ratio of his department is considered a disloyal maverick who is dangerous to everyone in the department. He is anti-social.*

As the threat of retrenchment intensifies there is an increased competition for students not only through light assignments and easy grading but also through the development of courses deliberately designed for uninformed and unenthusiastic students. These new courses became necessary because the pass-fail and pass-no-credit systems did not accomplish the primary object for which they were designed. That objective was to get more students—called non-majors—into the courses of each department. Each department hoped that its courses would be the most appealing to students who were selecting electives for which they would have to do little or no work. But through these devices no department increased very much the number of students it serviced, since most of the students were quite indifferent about what they took as long as they did not have to do any work or attend many classes. Thus the pass-fail and pass-no-credit students were distributed among many departments, and therefore each department was left pretty much where it had been in the first place except that its standards had deteriorated.

Each department therefore had to invent some other device for attracting students. While looking for popular devices, however, the teachers did not talk about attracting students. They spoke instead of devising courses that would enable them to serve the college and the students better. The only way they could improve their service was to get more students. They convinced themselves

---

*On one occasion when a departmental personnel committee was interviewing one of the tougher graders in the department a member of the committee who had less seniority than the person being interviewed said,"I would hate to be retrenched because someone else graded too hard."

that they were being innovative and realistic rather than desperate and cynical. What were called the innovative departments created a whole proliferation of courses designed to be relevant—that is, to have an immediate even though transitory appeal to students. It was no longer sufficient that a course was easy: now it also had to be immediately and constantly fascinating.

The very demand for relevance is another indication of the emptiness of the minds of students. In order for something to be relevant it has to relate to something else. In order to be relevant to a student a course has to relate to something he already has in his head. But since a large proportion of students have precious little in their heads, the teacher's job when he taught a traditional course was to put something into their heads so that they would know something to which he could relate additional information. The teacher's hope was that eventually some students would begin to gather information on their own and see relationships for themselves. But with the development of relevant courses the teachers gave up that hope. They decided to appeal to what little was already in the students' minds. Therefore many of the new courses are so elementary that any information the student gathers is what he should have got automatically by reading books, newspapers, and news magazines and by watching television news and documentaries. Many of the teachers of the innovative and relevant courses make no pretense of trying to increase the students' information but speak only of developing understandings. While the development of understandings is important, what very often happens is that understanding is equated with the repetition of clichés and the superficial discussion of what little information—and misinformation—the students already have. These courses often consist of nothing more than what students call rapping. They are often bull sessions regularly scheduled. That is exactly what the students like about them.

By agreeing to develop relevant courses college faculties are allowing students to decide what will be taught.[2] This is a perversion of the whole object of education, which should be to acquaint the student with the wisdom of the past. Scholars and teachers, who are supposed to be the best-educated people in the society, are the logical people to help acquaint the young with that wisdom. Very often they have done an inadequate job, but many of them have at least tried. Now, when ignorance and popularity reign as the highest ideals, these teachers, having to contend with the influence of people for whom knowledge has never been important and who believe that it should not be important for anyone else, either, have discovered that if they want to teach at all they have to compete for students. To do that they have to accept the standards of the most ignorant. As Ray's Law states, bad courses drive good courses out of existence.[3] *

Often the new and relevant course might be not only hopelessly elementary but also entirely irrelevant to anything important. Possibly the classic example of this type of course is the literature of sport. In this course the students can become acquainted with such weighty literary masterpieces as Jim Bouton's *Ball Four* and Jerry Kramer's *Instant Replay*. They might read Gary Shaw's *Meat on the Hoof* and Peter Gent's *North Dallas Forty*, Dave Meggyesy's *Out of Their League* and Don DeLillo's *End Zone*, Roger Kahn's *The Boys of Summer* and Robert Coover's *The Universal Baseball Association, Inc., J. Henry Waugh, Prop.* As a concession to respectability the teacher might also assign James Dickey's *Deliverance*, Alan Sillitoe's *The Loneliness of the Long Distance Runner*, or Bernard Malamud's *The Natural*. The teacher who assigns them, though, must not expect most of his students to read anything that serious.

Most of the books that students read in a course such as this are the sort of junk that students used to read in their spare time or not at all and that teachers who were seriously interested in literature positively discouraged them from reading because of the illiteracy and simple-mindedness of the authors. But in the age of television *any* reading has come to be considered an intellectual —or at least a collegiate—activity, and therefore teachers are delighted to get their students to read anything at all, including, often, comic books. And students adamantly refuse to read unless they get college credit for it. Once they graduate they will see no reason to do any more reading because no one is giving them any credit for their effort.[4]

Despite the teacher's delight in getting his students finally to read a hundred consecutive pages there is a good chance that he is doing positive harm rather than good. Including trashy books in a college course bestows on them a respectability that they do

---

*Stated by Professor Frank Ray of the History Department at Cortland. Hildebrand's Law: "The number of courses offered by an academic department is inversely proportional to the intellectual distinction of the faculty and the amount of basic knowledge in the field." Quoted in James D. Koerner, *Who Controls American Education? A Guide for Laymen* (Boston: Beacon Press, 1968), p. 179.

not deserve. Instead of having no real impression of great literature except that he knows that he does not know what it is but does not like it anyway, the student as a result of taking a course such as the literature of sport will still have no impression of what great literature is but will believe that he does know what it is and that he does like it. If Shakespeare is taught in one course and Jerry Kramer in another, Kramer must be as significant as Shakespeare. The student, looking at the two from a different angle, might say that Shakespeare must be as significant as Kramer even though he likes Kramer a lot better than he likes Shakespeare.

The result of a course such as the literature of sport is a general deterioration of taste. Taste is an appreciation of what is perceptive and of what makes the reader more perceptive. Taste in literature is determined not only by what people read but also by what they think is good, and it is far better to have students refuse to read Shakespeare but believe that he might be worthwhile for others to read—or even for themselves if they could only get interested in him—than to have them refuse to read Shakespeare and believe that he is no more worth reading—for themselves or for others—than Jerry Kramer is.

Another popular new course, which could be useful but tends instead only to reinforce the arrogance of the students who take it, is contemporary history. This might be called America in the 1960s or America in the Sixties and Seventies, or it might go under a more jazzy title such as Very Recent History. Usually this Very Recent History is American history. Surely American history since 1960 is worth studying, but often the object of this course is to illustrate that the 1960s were in fact somehow different from any other period in American history. One of the characteristics of the 1960s was protest, and the study of the protests of the 1960s in isolation from those of other eras reinforces the student's belief that protest was something new then and that therefore the students of those years and since are indeed more alert, aware, serious, sensitive, moral, ethical, humane, and knowledgeable than students of any other time.

There are other courses that could be worthwhile. There is a whole spate of new courses on or including movies. Some of these could be more legitimate than others, but their common characteristic is that they require little or no reading. Since many students cannot read they hate to read, and since they neither can nor will read the teacher designs courses that will allow them to get their college degrees without reading. The film is the source.

While the film could be the basis for reading and discussion and thus for the student's actually learning something, the same reason why the courses exist in the first place makes it impossible to teach anything in them. They must be popular. Therefore they must be easy. They must draw students who cannot read or will not read. The department creates them to begin with in order to increase its student-teacher ratio. As soon as the assignments go beyond the actual watching of the film and then rapping for a while about it, with perhaps a little haphazard reading now and then for the most serious students, the courses will become unpopular and therefore defeat the very purpose for which they are created.

One of the results of the fading popularity of academic subjects has been to create an identity crisis among academics. Having students read Jerry Kramer reveals the identity crisis among teachers of literature, but historians also have lost contact with history. Historians, in fact, appear to be particularly prone to this mental disease. The teacher who is suffering from an identity crisis has to find an identity, and often he does this by trying to achieve popularity. To do that he might teach a course that stands history on its head by starting at the present and working backward.[5] Such a teacher should not be surprised when his students conclude that World War II resulted from the failure of the United Nations or that the Civil War resulted from the South's resistance to Reconstruction. Teaching history that way is probably worse than teaching no history at all.

But especially popular as a treatment for the historian's identity crisis is his effort to get others to understand and appreciate him. He gives up trying to get students to understand history and tries to get them to understand historians instead. At the University of Tennessee the "freshman-level course in United States history seeks to show the student *how* history is made by historians, principally by taking them step-by-step through the historians' craft."[6] The new curriculum that was introduced in history at Franklin and Marshall College in 1966 was "an attempt to close the gap between what historians do and what they teach."[7] In 1968 Carleton College replaced its survey of Western Civilization with "one-term topical seminars," which are "Collectively entitled the Introduction to Historical Inquiry."[8] Surely that is an appropriately meaningless title.

One of the earliest experimental courses in history was "The Wisconsin Laboratory Course in American History." The "emphasis was upon the operations that historians can perform to 'make sense' out of data. . . ." The teachers "found it increasingly valuable to ask students to examine precisely how they proceeded from what they read to what they wrote and how they formulated the judgments and concepts which they brought to the materials." The teachers "found that when . . . [the students] had done this for themselves they became much more sensitive to the uses and abuses of sources by historians who wrote from the same materials." The teachers were "able to trace the developing skill of a substantial number of students in handling original source materials." [9]

Now all of that is very nice. Students *should* recognize the difficulty of making sense out of the past. They *should* become aware of the historian's abuse of the past. They *should* learn to analyze what they read. But programs such as this reveal also that many historians themselves are uncomfortable with the past and are comfortable only when they are playing with their own tools. They are less interested in teaching history than in teaching about historians. Having lost confidence in their ability to teach history— or even to understand it—they suffer identity crises. They try to recover their identities by seeking the understanding—and therefore the approval—of students. Soon students will understand all about historians but nothing about history. But the historians will not care. Just as many teachers of literature have lost confidence in literature, many historians have lost confidence in history.

While these new courses are always presented as devices to increase the student's understanding of history, sometimes their designers inadvertently reveal their real purpose. A news story about a course in American history through films at California State University at Northridge reports that students "are learning American history in a fun way." The last paragraph of the story gives the course away. "The course has gained such popularity that it boosted the sagging enrollment in the history department." [10] Boosting sagging enrollment, of course, was the object, and in order to accomplish that the emphasis must be on fun rather than learning. At Stanford University "the abolition of the History of Western Civilization program . . . left the department without a basic European survey *and without a means of attracting freshmen to departmental offerings.*" [11] When West Georgia College introduced family history it was trying to make the students aware "of their own roots and heritage," but historians there were also trying to "recruit more history majors." [12] Such majors will define history as antiquarianism or genealogy.

There is only an occasional protest against this huckstering of history. [13] Indeed, the thrust of explanations of the huckstering is that it is all very proper, and the hucksters rally to each other's support against their critics. [14] Historians have been very honest about what they are doing because they cannot conceive that they have anything to hide. They are, after all, only trying to save their jobs. They are only trying to protect their own economic security.

While historians are developing these unusual and innovative courses to protect their jobs their efforts might well have exactly the opposite effect. With the increased popularity of role-playing [15] as a device for making history fun academic administrators might decide that history departments can be eliminated altogether because all history can be taught in the drama department. When the teacher of the innovative exercise claims that he learns as much in it as the students do [16] he might convince academic administrators that no teachers are needed at all. They can put students or inexpensive laymen in charge. The students in the new course at the University of Tennessee do, after all, meet in small groups *without* teachers. [17]

The admission that the teacher learns as much as the students in a course might provide a clue about what is really wrong with history courses and why students do not take them unless they include exciting gimmicks. Often the teachers are ignorant. Possibly the solution is for graduate departments to teach their students more history rather than to help them seek out gimmicks for making pseudo-history popular.*

Not only have colleges placed a premium on relevant courses, but they have also developed entirely new fields of relevant studies. Of course Black Studies and Women's Studies are the most obvious of these, but there is no limit to what colleges can do once they start down the garden path of relevance. No doubt conven-

---

*The people who develop new courses often criticize traditional courses for faults that have nothing to do with the courses but result rather from the incompetence of the professors who teach them. If a teacher concentrates only on military campaigns, causes of wars, and what presidents have done (" 'Pop History' Viewed as Valid Discipline," *The News* (State University of New York), October 1976, p. 8), it is probably because he does not really understand history, and putting him into a new and jazzy course is not going to improve his understanding. The solution, again, would seem to be to improve the education of the professors before they ever begin teaching.

tional courses have concentrated on the influence of white males in history and in the process may have underestimated the importance of women and minorities, but the solution would appear to be to integrate the women and the minorities rather than to isolate them. Often the effect of the special courses and courses of study is to tear the subjects from their context and thus to misrepresent history in a way different from the misrepresentations of the past but nevertheless to continue to misrepresent it. Black teachers who have been accused of misrepresenting historical facts have been known to reply that "whites have had their lies; why shouldn't we ours" or that their misrepresentations are no worse than what whites have been doing for years.

To teach Black History or Women's History is to teach about exploitation. That is all to the good: it is important that people understand that exploitation has existed and continues to exist. But anyone who teaches history properly teaches about exploitation even though he might seldom mention either blacks or women. If he teaches history properly he will give his students a context into which they can fit the exploitation of women and blacks and anyone else even though he does not deal with those specific groups. Concentrating on one or two exploited groups, on the other hand, is likely to create the impression that they are the only people who have been exploited. It is likely to give the student an even falser view of history than he would have got if those groups had never been mentioned at all.[18]

One has only to leaf through any college catalogue to discover the large number of "innovative" courses. Departments compete with each other for relevance. Blacks and women, of course, are especially popular. The catalogue of the Borough of Manhattan Community College for 1975-1976 lists "The Roles of Women in a Changing World" under anthropology, "History of Women" under history, "Psychology of Women" under psychology, and "Women in Dramatic Literature" under theater.[19] But blacks and women are not the only new subjects of study. The catalogue for Alfred University for 1974-1975 lists courses titled "The Problem of Death," "People in History," "Witchcraft Now and Then," and "The Ethics of Revolution."[20] Almost any college catalogue reveals the same sorts of relevant courses.[21]

While departments have tried to outdo each other in the creation of relevant courses, the new courses would do them no good if students did not know about them. Therefore departments advertise in any way they can. They announce them in their classes; they send mimeographed flyers around to all members of the faculty; they place eye-catching announcements on bulletin boards; they place advertisements in campus newspapers; and when they want to convince themselves that they are subtle they plant news stories in campus newspapers. But members of the faculty advertise their courses most effectively by the personal campaigning they carry on while they drink with students in student hang-outs. College courses are treated like any other commodities that someone has to sell.

Closely related to the emphasis on relevant courses is the emphasis on innovation in methods of teaching. Every year the teacher has to report his innovations. If he does discover something that works he dare not do it two years in succession, since that would not be innovative, and his increases in salary depend at least partly on his innovative ability. The teacher who discovers a successful method of teaching and sticks to it, as for example learning as much as he can and then telling his students what he has learned, is penalized. The teacher who knows almost nothing but flounders around first with this innovation and then with that one trying to teach his students something that he has not yet learned himself is rewarded. The teacher who is constantly innovating, whether out of his own inclination or insecurity or because of pressure from administrators, is not likely to teach very much.

Another way that faculties have found to lower academic standards in order to protect themselves is to increase the credit the student receives for a course without increasing the work he has to do in it. Since every department is judged by its student load it is necessary for each department to generate the highest possible number of student-credit hours each semester. A very simple way of immediately increasing the credit hours a department generates is to increase the number of credits it allows for a course. It can make all two-hour courses three-hour courses and make an occasional three-hour course a four-hour course without changing anything else except possibly the number of hours the class meets during the semester. It is no accident that in the past ten years two-hour courses have all but disappeared from college catalogues. This change might slightly increase the amount of work for the teacher, since he might have to meet the class an extra hour each week, but that additional hour is not very wearying. The serious teacher might think that since the student receives fifty percent more credit for a course he should teach fifty percent more than he did before. But most teachers do not feel that way. The object, after all, is not to teach more but only to generate more credits.

Therefore the increased credit the student receives ordinarily does not increase the teacher's work in preparation, either. Even if the teacher does increase the amount of work he does himself, he must not increase the amount of work for the student, since that would defeat the object of guaranteeing additional credit for no additional work. The student does not even have to attend more classes during the semester than he did for fewer credits. Attending classes is not taken very seriously these days.

An indication of the deteriorating academic standards as well as a cause of the deterioration is this declining emphasis on attending classes. When courses were solid and did require the student to accumulate some knowledge in order to pass them and to exhibit some perception in order to receive high grades he did attend classes regularly. Recognizing that students entering college are immature and that they often require rules to help them adjust to their new independence colleges often required attendance and penalized students who had excessive cuts. Especially the college discouraged students from leaving early on vacations. There was often either a written or unwritten rule that the student could cut one class for each credit he received—for a three-hour course no more than three cuts during the semester—and that a cut either immediately before or after a vacation counted as two. Students did sometimes cut more than three classes in a three-hour course, and they did sometimes leave early on vacation, especially when they went to Florida in the spring. But there were relatively few of those.

Very often, however, requiring attendance was not necessary. The teacher might tell his students that their object was to learn something and that he did not care how they went about it. If they could learn without attending class they could do that. Some students did choose not to come to class very often. Those who still learned passed, and sometimes did very well, while those who did not learn failed.

In the past ten years, however, the change has been complete. As students became convinced that they already know as much as they need to know and that therefore college should be a four-year lark they discovered also that attending classes often interferes as much as reading does with their real purpose in being there. As they became more vocal during the late 1960s they convinced many administrators and teachers that they were so mature and so serious that they should not be required to attend classes. Violence and the threat of violence convinced others that it was inexpedient to require attendance even though it still might be desirable. Those who want to continue requiring attendance cannot because they are not allowed to. Now students miss a third or a half of their classes even in what they consider their tough courses, and they miss more than that in others. Students not only leave early on vacations but irresponsible students organize whole busloads to leave the campus almost a week early. If the vacation begins at the end of classes on Tuesday the buses often begin to leave on the previous Thursday. Ordinarily students do not stay away from campus beyond the end of the vacation, since long before the vacation ends they and their parents are so sick of each other that both are glad to have them get back on time.

Because of the deterioration of academic standards students can get through courses without attending classes, just as they can without reading. While earlier students who did not attend classes either learned on their own or failed, now they do not attend classes, do not learn on their own, and pass. The increased cutting of classes, however, not only reflects the deteriorating standards but also has helped to speed the deterioration. Always there have been students who could not pass their courses, and always there have been those who could barely pass them. Often the students who most need to attend class in order to do even barely passing work do most of the cutting. The result is that not only do the hopeless failures do failing work but also that those who with a lot of work and regular class attendance could do barely passing work now do failing work. Since teachers cannot fail all of the students who deserve to fail they have had to lower their standards in order to pass those who under the earlier standards would fail. Because they pass in spite of their cuts the students believe that they can safely miss even more classes. Other students see them pass and decide that they can cut also. Students who are on the borderline even under the reduced standards begin to cut classes and do unacceptable work. Since the teacher still cannot fail all of the students who deserve to fail he has to reduce his standards still further. And on and on it goes. Because students who do failing work receive passing grades, the teacher in order to be fair must give the student who does barely acceptable work a higher grade than he deserves, and so on, again, all the way up the line.

Still another reason for the decline in academic standards during the past ten years is the elimination of many or all required courses. This results in the first place from an exaggerated emphasis on utilitarianism, since the requirements that are dropped first are usually those courses that the student cannot immediately use in his major. The history major, the theory runs, needs no math or science, and no one but a foreign language teacher needs a foreign language. The theory does not answer the question of why, if no one needs to know foreign languages except the foreign language teacher, we should continue to teach foreign languages at all.

The elimination of required courses results in the second place from the theory that the main reason students do badly is that they are forced to take courses that they do not want to take, about which they know nothing, and in which they have no facility. This theory holds that students are desperate to learn but that they are desperate to learn only what they want to learn or what they are good at. Faced with courses that do not grab them, as the saying goes, they are only desperate.

Students who take only courses that they want to take are supposed to learn more for two reasons. First, it is on the courses that they do not want to take that they have to spend most of their time, since those are the ones that are most difficult for them. Thus they have little or no time for those in which they could otherwise do well. Second, the misery that results from their concern about the courses that they do not want to take destroys their enthusiasm entirely, and therefore even when they have time to study what they like best they cannot do well because they are unhappy about and preoccupied with those courses that they would not have chosen if they had had a choice.

This theory ignores one very important reality. That is that a very high proportion of today's college students do not want to study anything at all, since they believe that they have better things to do and that since they are already the best-educated generation ever there is little need for them to learn more. If they do have to study they will study as little as possible, and they do not care very much what they study so long as they must study only a little. Whatever they can study least they like best. Thus the elimination of requirements has indeed resulted in the student's taking those courses he likes best, but he likes best not those courses in which he might learn the most but rather those courses in which he will have to learn the least. He takes those courses in which the teachers require the least work, and other teachers have to lower their requirements also in order to compete for students.

Chapter 6

THE DECLINE OF
ACADEMIC STANDARDS : 4
The Multiple-Choice Exercise, Manipulating
Essay Exams, and the Personal Interview

*I*t is clear that the chief characteristic of the American college is frivolity. The amount of learning going on in it is very small. Some teachers see this and fight it; some see it and accept it; but the majority either refuse to face it at all or deny that they have any responsibility for it. Some teachers have been able to convince themselves that if academic standards are declining they are not contributing to that decline. But most have convinced themselves that standards are not declining, that important learning is indeed going on, and that they are contributing to that learning.

The teacher who wants to convince himself that important learning is going on in the college has several devices available to him. One of the most popular is the multiple-choice exercise. Faced with the illiteracy of many students and the laziness of most of the rest, the teacher quits giving essay exams and administers the multiple-choice exercise instead. Of course the multiple-choice exercise is inadequate for testing what college students should know and what they should be able to do. It measures the relative amount of information the student has, but because he can sometimes guess answers it does not measure in any exact fashion the total amount of information he possesses. And in college surely the student should be tested not only on the amount of information he has but also on his ability to relate some information to other information. He should be tested on his ability to make sense out of the information he has.

Not only is the multiple-choice exercise inadequate as a testing device but it is also positively harmful as a teaching device. It is harmful in two ways. First, no learning occurs while the student mechanically marks the narrow slots on his answer sheet. Writing an essay, on the other hand, is a valuable experience. It allows the student not only to discover what information he has but also to experiment in putting that information together. It is not unknown for the light to dawn in the student's head while he is in the middle of writing his essay. Beyond that, the essay allows and even encourages the student to relate information and understandings that he has acquired outside a course to what he has acquired inside it. This ability to sort out and see connections in the mass of information and misinformation that bombards the student every day of his life should, after all, be one of the primary objectives of education. On the multiple-choice exercise, however, the teacher dare not include anything that has not been covered either in the classroom or in the readings that he specifically assigns. Thus the multiple-choice exercise positively retards learning.

The multiple-choice exercise does positive harm in the second place by giving the student an entirely wrong idea of what learning is all about. It gives him the mistaken impression that learning consists of nothing more than accumulating a myriad of facts all isolated from each other. He sees no value in it, and he develops a contempt for what he thinks is learning.

In spite of its inadequacy for testing and its destructiveness in teaching, however, for the teacher the multiple-choice exercise does have several advantages over the essay exam. First, since the student has only to mark slots on his answer sheet the teacher is not confronted with his illiteracy. He avoids the agony of reading a pile of illiterate and semi-literate essays. Second, the teacher can easily grade the multiple-choice exercise on a curve and therefore have whatever proportion of high grades he wants. What he calls a curve is more often a triangle, with the B as the apex. Third, by substituting easier questions for those that the most students miss the teacher can assure himself of a high proportion of high scores and thereby justify his high proportion of high grades. Fourth, by sending the answer sheets to the people who run the computers the teacher can avoid checking them. All he has to do is develop his triangle out of the scores once he gets them. Fifth, the teacher can adopt the illusion that he is not assigning grades but that the grades are determined only by the scores that the students achieve. Thus he avoids the agony of admitting that he is making judgments.

But the greatest advantage of the multiple-choice exercise is its usefulness in indoctrination. By teaching the student that there is a correct answer for every question that arises and that his job is only to find it the multiple-choice exercise discourages him from thinking for himself. By asking which of several answers is *most* correct the teacher can guarantee that the student will either agree with him or suffer. The student, not wanting to suffer, will either believe what he is supposed to believe or pretend to, and what he pretends to believe he eventually will believe.[1]

The multiple-choice exercise also has some advantages for the student. First, marking the slots on the answer sheet is itself much less fatiguing than writing an essay is. Second, in marking the slots rather than writing an essay the student does not reveal his illiteracy. Third, the multiple-choice exercise removes the pressure to study. The student knows that the teacher who uses it wants to grade high, and therefore he expects to benefit from the teacher's generosity. He also knows that in many cases when he does not know the correct answer the alternative answers will give him some hints and that therefore he will be able to figure it out. Finally, he knows that sometimes even when he has no clue about the correct answer he will be able to guess it.

The teacher who resorts to the multiple-choice exercise as a substitute for the essay is often self-conscious about it. Because he is insecure about the value of the multiple-choice exercise he often includes a short essay with it, and his most common justification of its use is that the students who do best on it also do best on the essay.* Naturally they do, but that does not prove anything. The teacher, in fact, has got his thinking backward. He should say that the student who can write the best essay also does the best

---

*A second justification of the use of the multiple-choice exercise is that the teacher can test more broadly with it than with an essay exam because he has more questions to work with. But that argument has three faults. First, a wide-ranging device that does not test what is most important in the student and that positively retards learning is hardly worthy of praise. Second, the teacher can make his essay exam as broad or as narrow as he wants to. Third, many multiple-choice exercises are no broader than the narrowest essay exams are. The teachers concentrate on a few issues. A few years ago I checked several multiple-choice exercises in order to determine the validity of the teachers' claims that they tested more broadly than essay exams do. On one final exam in the survey of American history ninety-three out of 105 questions concerned the pre-Civil War South, slavery, abolition, Lincoln, and the Civil War, and many of the remaining questions were related to the same issues. On another, forty-nine out of fifty questions had to do with the Civil War and Reconstruction. Other exams were similar.

job on the multiple-choice exercise. The student who can write a good essay can do both, while the student who can pass a multiple-choice exercise can often do only that. And often he can do that only because the teacher can manipulate the points of his triangle. After a teacher has manipulated his triangle for a while he tends to conclude that there is no such thing as a D or an E student. Sometimes he does not even have a triangle but rather only a straight line from A to B, and in that case he concludes that there is no such thing as a C student. For a while there were—and possibly still are—teachers who did not have even a line from A to B but only a dot at A: they believed that there is no such thing as a B student. Everyone got an A.

Those teachers who are still either too serious or too proud to resort to the multiple-choice exercise have ways of manipulating their essay exams. One is the take-home exam. The teacher who assigns a take-home exam knows that a high proportion of his students will plagiarize their essays directly out of printed sources. They might be cheating, or they might be plagiarizing without knowing that they are doing anything wrong. For two reasons the teacher does not check on the plagiarism. First, he cannot. There is just too much of it for him to trace it all. Second, he does not want to. He wants his students to get high grades, and therefore he would rather grade the work that they copy than work that they might do themselves. Naturally since he is grading the work of professionals he comes out with a high proportion of high grades, though even some of these should fail. This system seems unfair to students who do their own work, but they have, after all, an equal opportunity to plagiarize. If they do less well than the others, they have only their own honesty to blame.

A second device that teachers use to enable them to give high grades on essays is to give the students the questions in advance and sometimes to allow them to use notes when they write their essays in class. If the student uses notes he can almost plagiarize, while if he does not use notes his memorization often results in something very close to plagiarism. A third device is to give the students examples of past exams with the explicit or implicit assurance that their questions will come from those exams. This requires the student to memorize several essays rather than only one or two.

The objects of all of these devices are of course to eliminate the teacher's discomfort in reading inadequate and illiterate essays and to enable him to grade high with an only partially blackened conscience. But these devices are not foolproof. Some students stubbornly insist on doing their own work. Some of these do well, while others do not. The teacher still has to read disasters. Second, even with all of these advantages some students do not try to do well. They do not copy, but they make only the slightest effort to do a good job. They take advantage of their knowledge that the teacher wants to grade high. Again the teacher has to read disastrous essays. Third, some students cannot even plagiarize correctly.

The result is that not all teachers adopt these devices. The teacher who is too serious or too proud to resort to the multiple-choice exercise but who cannot bear to read plagiarized, inadequate, and often illiterate essays sometimes adopts another device. He substitutes personal interviews for written exercises and exams. The first advantage of the personal interview is that while the student is usually as inarticulate in speaking as he is in writing —and often even more so—his incapacity with language is not as obvious in his speaking as it is in his writing. Spoken words disappear into the air, while written words remain as discomforting evidence. Once the sounds of the interview cease reverberating through his office the teacher can convince himself that the student is really not so bad after all.

The second advantage of the personal interview is that often the teacher by hinting and probing can cause the student to say pretty much what he wants him to say. Then he can exaggerate the student's part in the conversation and de-emphasize his own.

The irony is that every one of these last five devices is a useful one for teaching. The take-home exam, giving out questions in advance, allowing students to use notes while they write their essays, and showing students past exams all can take the pressure of guessing the questions off the student and can encourage him to concentrate on learning rather than on memorizing facts that will only enable him to pass the exam. The personal interview not only can acquaint the student with the teacher's mind—and hopefully give him something to which he can aspire—but also can, through the teacher's hinting and probing, allow him to arrive at thoughtful conclusions, often for the first time in his life. But ordinarily these devices are not adopted as teaching devices. Ordinarily the teacher adopts them in order to grade higher, and any learning that results from their use is purely coincidental.

Another device that teachers adopt in order to guarantee high grades is not a good teaching device. This is the open-book exam.

It does take the pressure of guessing off the student. It does enable him to come to the exam without studying. It assures him that the teacher wants to grade high. But it also means that the teacher is teaching straight from the book. The open-book-open-note exam is only slightly better. Like the multiple-choice exercise, both of these devices discourage the student from thinking. Both encourage him to believe that it is not necessary for him to think. Both encourage him to believe that what he learns in each separately titled course is entirely unrelated to anything that he might discover outside that course. Both reinforce his belief that there is already an answer for every question and that his job is not to figure it out but only to find it. Both encourage him to accept someone else's answer as his own. Both encourage him to accept authoritarianism.

Chapter 7

THE FUNCTIONS OF
ACADEMIC INSTITUTIONS

*W*hile academic institutions are doing very little educating, they are serving exactly the functions that the people who control society want them to serve. They are not serving these functions perfectly, but they are doing very well at them.

Educating students is not one of those functions. Anyone who seriously studies the American schooling system knows that it does precious little educating.[1] The development of the students' minds has never been one of the objectives of the schooling system.[2] Nor is technical training very important. While the schools do concentrate on such non-academic chores as driver education and home economics they do not provide people with even the most basic tools that would enable them to live confidently in a complex society. In the middle of 1975 eighty-six million Americans could not compute the gasoline mileage of their cars. Fifty-two million could not determine whether they were qualified for jobs listed in classified ads, and forty-eight million could not figure out how much change they should receive after making a purchase in a store. Thirty-nine million could not find the deduction for social security on the stubs of their paychecks.[3] Only one percent of American seventeen-year-olds could balance a check book.[4]

The most important function that the schooling system does serve is to ruin people's minds. This is accomplished by subjecting young people to an indoctrination that is so thorough that it will destroy their ability to think for themselves. The main feature

79

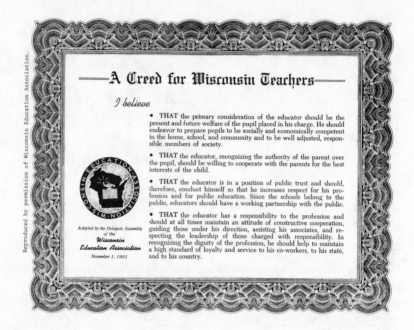

——A Creed for Wisconsin Teachers——

I believe

• THAT the primary consideration of the educator should be the present and future welfare of the pupil placed in his charge. He should endeavor to prepare pupils to be socially and economically competent in the home, school, and community and to be well adjusted, responsible members of society.

• THAT the educator, recognizing the authority of the parent over the pupil, should be willing to cooperate with the parents for the best interests of the child.

• THAT the educator is in a position of public trust and should, therefore, conduct himself so that he increases respect for his profession and for public education. Since the schools belong to the public, educators should have a working partnership with the public.

• THAT the educator has a responsibility to the profession and should at all times maintain an attitude of constructive cooperation, guiding those under his direction, assisting his associates, and respecting the leadership of those charged with responsibility. In recognizing the dignity of the profession, he should help to maintain a high standard of loyalty and service to his co-workers, to his state, and to his country.

Adopted by the Delegate Assembly of the
Wisconsin Education Association
November 1, 1951

It seems significant that in this Creed nothing is said about teaching anybody anything.

of this indoctrination is the creation of an appropriate Americanism.[5] An appropriate Americanism, as defined by the people who control the schools, requires that young people not only accept but also glorify the economic, social, and political status quo.[6] It requires respect for and awe of property, which really means respect for and awe of the rich. It requires solemn worship of what is called free enterprise: students drink deep of the propaganda from their earliest years.[7] Most of all it requires that people never doubt the truth of what the economic, social, and political leaders of the country tell them. It requires the acceptance of the deliberate falsification of the real world.[8] Teachers reward or penalize students on the basis of how completely they believe the distortions and how thoroughly they accept the indoctrination.[9]

It is no accident that public schooling—the common school—developed in the United States primarily between 1820 and 1860, a period of immigration and social upheaval,[10] * and that com-

*Part of the upheaval of this earlier period was the extension of the

pulsory attendance developed between 1870 and World War I, another period of immigration and social upheaval.[11] In each case the primary objective of the people who established the schools and then required attendance was not to provide educational opportunity for the children of immigrants and the poor but was rather to protect the propertied interests from "foreign" ideologies and therefore to protect the status quo.[12] Acceptance of the status quo requires docility, and in the schools there has always been a high premium on docility of both teachers and students.[13] This docility is often called motivation.[14] Any educational opportunity or opening of young people's minds that resulted from the establishing of the public school system was both accidental and undesired.

While this indoctrination is often called socialization,[15] that term lends too much dignity to the process that actually occurs. Socialization is directed toward making people sociable. That does not mean that the socialized person has become an extrovert; it means rather that he has developed a social awareness. Socialization develops in people a feeling of community and responsibility. Indoctrination in American schools does exactly the opposite. It teaches the student to get along, but only for the sake of whatever profit he can get for himself from his cooperation. It divides him from his class. It is designed to cause him to identify with the rich—with those who have made it—rather than with the rest of the population. It teaches him to want to get out of the class into which he was born rather than to rise with that class.[16] Since an important part of the indoctrination is to instill in the student a spirit of competition, it creates in him a feeling of irresponsibility. That irresponsibility is often called individualism.

If indoctrination is successful it will destroy the child's mind[17] and turn him into an automaton.[18] The first step in this process is to destroy his curiosity. Everyone is familiar with the six-year-old

---

franchise. If members of the lower economic classes were going to vote, it was important to the elite to guarantee that they would not vote for candidates who would question the class structure of the country. Schooling would guarantee that the new voters would think only within the confines that the elite established for them in the schools.

It is probably no accident that what the elite called laissez faire also was adopted during the fifty years or so following 1820. If the lower economic classes were going to have an influence in the government it was important to the elite to guarantee that the government could not do anything to threaten the propertied interests. What the schools did not accomplish, the doctrine of laissez faire would.

who refuses to accept unsatisfactory answers but rather persists in his probing until the adult to whom he is talking becomes so frustrated that he refuses to answer at all. The school smothers this enthusiasm with dullness. The second step is to provide an automatic response to any question that arises. This the school accomplishes by drilling the response until it becomes second nature to the child. The drilling is repeated endlessly.[19] The responses to various questions may be contradictory, but the repetition of the acceptable responses is designed to prevent the student from seeing those contradictions. The object is to reinforce the walls of the water-tight compartments of his mind, to guarantee that one part of his mind will never see what another part of his mind is doing.[20] The third step is to destroy the child's confidence, so that if he ever should doubt the validity of the unsatisfactory responses that the school has imposed on him he will believe that his doubts result from his own ignorance rather than from the inadequacy—and often the positive inaccuracy—of those answers. The school must convince him that even if he should someday doubt the validity of the answers it has foisted on him he will never be able to find more satisfactory ones himself.

The function of the school, then, is to drill the automatic response until the student begins to believe it, then becomes desperately convinced that it is a satisfactory answer, and finally believes that the answer is his own. Almost always the school succeeds in accomplishing that objective. The student has to make sense out of the world, and he is taught to accept the sense that the school imposes on him rather than the sense that comes from his own probing mind. Eventually he quits probing. When that happens the school knows it has succeeded.

In this respect all schools are reform schools. They are established to re-form the characters of the people who attend them.[21] They are designed to transform curious, energetic, exuberant, and optimistic six-year-olds into dull, unenthusiastic, lazy, pessimistic, and complacent eighteen-year-olds.[22]

In most cases twelve or thirteen years of schooling is enough to ruin the student's mind. The college student's fear of learning anything at all and his stubborn dependence on what he thinks of as his intuition is a sign that elementary, junior high, and high schools are doing a very good job of indoctrinating young people. By the time they graduate from high school the young people's minds are closed to anything that they have not already been told.

The reward of attending college exists for those with whom the system has succeeded best. They can be trusted, and therefore they are given the chance to achieve a middle-class or even upper-middle-class status in return for becoming apologists for the system.

But college exists also for a second group. These are the students whom the schools in the first twelve or thirteen years have not succeeded in taming but who are bright enough that they could be useful to the propertied class if they would only consent to be tamed. They are dangerous, but not quite dangerous enough to be sent to prison, and so the functionaries of the propertied class send them to college instead. The expectation is that as they get four years older they will see the desirability of achieving middle-class status where they have not seen it before and that therefore the college will succeed with them where the kindergarten and elementary, junior high, and high schools have not. Usually it does.[23]

While academic administrators never explicitly admit that the function of the schools is to ruin people's minds, they do constantly implicitly admit that that is their function. They do this especially in three ways. First, academic administrators in elementary, junior high, and high schools constantly advise teachers not to discuss controversial issues. Since there are very few issues on which there is universal agreement the administrators are actually telling the teachers that they must take the proper position on each issue. That position is the position of the people who control the local public opinion. The teacher's job is to provide the student with a predetermined position. Second, academic administrators advise teachers to present both sides of every issue. This is administrative code language for informing a teacher that he has been too objective in presenting both sides of an issue and that he has not strongly enough supported the appropriate position. To the academic administrator, presenting both sides of an issue means showing why the unacceptable position or system— as for example socialism or communism—is unacceptable and why the acceptable position or system—as for example capitalism—is acceptable. This they call objectivity. The teacher's job again is to provide the student with a predetermined position.

The third way in which academic administrators admit that the function of the schools is to indoctrinate students so thoroughly that they will never try to think for themselves is less common but more obvious than the other two. This is their saying something such as "Yes, that is a very interesting and challenging idea, but high-school students are not ready for it yet." What the administrator is really saying here is that high-school students have not yet been thoroughly enough indoctrinated—their minds have not yet been sufficiently closed—to make it safe to expose them to ideas unacceptable to the propertied class. By the time they get to college they are ordinarily so thoroughly brainwashed that no teacher will be able to dent their prejudices. That is why there can be a greater degree of academic freedom in colleges than in high schools. By the time the student gets to college his mind is already ruined. Nothing any teacher says will have any effect on him.

The same administrator who tells a teacher that high-school students are not ready for the ideas that he has presented has been known to tell the same teacher that he is too bright to teach in high school but should be teaching in college instead. Once again he is telling the teacher that the things he is saying are too dangerous for students whose minds have not yet been effectively closed. He is telling the teacher that since he can still think for himself he does not belong in high school but rather in college, where the students will have more power of resistance.

If ruining people's minds is to continue it is necessary for those in whose interest the minds are ruined to gain and maintain the support of the victims of the brainwashing. They must never allow the students to realize what is happening to them but must convince them that they are actually benefiting from the system. They use two chief devices to accomplish this. First, they flatter the young people. They tell the young people that they are the most alert, serious, compassionate, intelligent, and knowledgeable generation in the entire history of the United States. Second, they use slogans, myths, and clichés that glorify both the society in general and the schooling system in particular. "The free society" and "equality of opportunity" are two of the favorites. In large letters at the front of the auditorium at graduation each year there is a motto to perpetuate the myth: "Let each become all he is capable of being." College development foundations have slogans that are almost religious: "Through Thee We Enter Larger Life." Of course those sentiments have no connection at all with what actually happens to students either in school or after.

The second function of the schooling system is to drain potential leaders out of their natural groups and make them loyal to the propertied elite.[24] A chance to go to college and then to acquire middle-class status as a lackey of the rich is held out as a reward for good behavior not only to favored members of minority groups but also to the brighter members of the laboring class. Nelson Rockefeller made this objective clear in an incident that was reported on television as part of the background of the hearings on his confirmation as vice-president. As almost everyone knows, while Rockefeller was governor of New York he vastly expanded the State University of New York. No one knows exactly why he did this. Some have suggested that he wanted to create an enduring physical monument to himself—one that nobody could miss—just as those same people suggest that his motive in creating the Mall in Albany was to create an enduring physical monument to himself—one that nobody could miss—in the state capital. Some suggest that he was interested in the immediate political prestige that would result from his making the State University of New York the largest in the nation. Still others have suggested that in the construction and banking industries Rockefeller had friends who would profit nicely from the expansion of the University. Some have suggested that by wasting a lot of money on construction he was deliberately trying to place the state in an unsound financial position and thus create an excuse for cutting back on welfare payments and for putting pressure on labor unions to accept lower wages and pensions and other benefits as well as reduced employment and less favorable working conditions. Some have even suggested that he was interested in improving higher schooling in the state.

But whether or not any or all of these motives were in Rockefeller's mind when he encouraged the expansion of the State University he did have another motive that he made entirely clear. That was to acquire for his class the loyalty of the students who could attend the expanded State University. When at one of the units of the state system a student criticized Rockefeller for providing a boondoggle for the bankers who bought the bonds that the state sold to expand the University his response was that if those bankers had not been willing to buy those bonds that student would not be in school at all. The implication was clear: that student's opportunity to go to college should result in his being loyal not to the people who were being taxed to pay off the bonds and to provide the bankers with their guaranteed interest but rather to the bankers who bought the bonds. There was no hint that the State University could have been expanded without the bankers. There was no hint that the money could have been raised in any other way.

The third function of the schooling system is to train workers for American industry and its branches—the local, state, and national governments—and then to certify them as safe and quiescent.[25] It teaches them the skills and creates in them the attitudes that will make them productive workers. Like the parts of a machine, they must be interchangeable.[26] Among the most important traits that the schools try to establish in the student is persistence in accomplishing things that others tell him to do and that are of no importance to himself. Since that is what he will be doing for the rest of his life, it is important that he learn it while he is still young. This persistence requires docility, pacificity, and conformity.[27] The chief device that the school uses to develop and to test the student's persistence is the boring and meaningless required course in which the successful student accomplishes nothing except to prove his persistence and his willingness to accept whatever eccentric demands are made on him. These courses are not boring and meaningless by accident: they are designed that way. If they were interesting and if the student learned anything in them he would not prove his persistence by remaining in them.

There is a widespread lack of understanding of the importance of the schools' creating functionaries for business. To some people who should know better it is astonishing that the government will subsidize vocational training but not education designed to raise the cultural level of society or the political sophistication of its citizens.[28] Actually such a condition is not astonishing at all. The last thing that the people who control the American economic and political system—and therefore the schooling system[29]—want is an educated population. Education might result in the development of critical minds, and that is a possibility too dangerous to risk. The last thing that the propertied class wants is a population that would be able to make independent judgments on public issues. Education might also result in a decreased emphasis on the accumulation of material goods. The last thing that the propertied class wants is a population for whom the music of Mozart is more important than the buying and selling of cars.[30] The first thing it wants, on the other hand, is an ignorant proletariat that will produce goods, do the dirty work of the rich, purchase commodities as far as they are able, fight wars, and believe the propaganda of the elite.[31] It is to the positive advantage of the propertied class to keep people ignorant.[32]

The schooling system indoctrinates young people, siphons potential leaders away from their own natural groups and makes them loyal to the propertied class, and trains people to become functionaries of industry and government and to be good consumers by teaching them what are called the middle-class virtues. The most important of these virtues is patriotism, or a thoughtless support not of one's country but of the leaders—especially the economic leaders—of the country. The economic elite are in fact identified *as* the country. The second middle-class virtue is respect for motherhood, which of course means respect not only for mothers but for all of one's elders. Proper respect for motherhood requires that one never have any ideas of his own but rather willingly, wholly, and thoughtlessly adopt the precepts of the older generation. It means the adoption of received wisdom intact. The third middle-class virtue is respect not for God but rather for organized religion, provided always that those religions are mainstream and not ex-treme. This too is a conservative virtue, since the way that a main-stream religion becomes main-stream is to support the interests of the propertied class against the interests of the dispossessed.

The fourth middle-class virtue is work. This virtue is developed in the first place to allay the resentment that the poor or the middle-class might otherwise feel toward the rich. In the emphasis on work the implication is that it was through good hard work—and not through lying, cheating, and murder—that the rich got their wealth and that if a person does not become wealthy it is because he is either not ambitious enough or not smart enough. Second, the virtue of work encourages production. This is the effect of the perversion of the Protestant ethic of work. Work is presented as virtuous in itself. No matter how much a person hates his job, he is supposed to feel good when he is busy.[33] Accepting misery, in fact, is itself a virtue. Working hard enables the workers to produce those things through the sale of which the rich accumulate their riches. It is because people are willing to work that they produce the wealth that the rich continue to appropriate for their own use.

But the work ethic also encourages consumption: if one works hard enough he can have all of those things he sees advertised on television. If workers were suddenly to decide that there is no virtue in work or that the things they buy with their labor are not worth the effort the rich would no longer have anyone either to produce or to buy the products that create their profits. That is why the propertied class hates Hippies so much. Hippies make a virtue out of idleness and non-consumption. There is no money in *that* for anyone.*

Indoctrinating young people into the capitalistic religion, draining potential leaders away from their natural groups, and training people to do the grueling and dirty work of the propertied class and to buy the things that produce its profit make teachers the primary arm of the propertied class.[34] Since the decline of the church the teachers have been the most essential apologists for the status quo.[35] There are signs that they will be replaced by television, but at the moment they are still absolutely vital to the propertied interests. As a reward for their service to the propertied class they receive middle-class status.

The people who complain about teachers' being overpaid ought to remember this. Teachers do an important job, and they deserve to be well paid for it. They deserve a few thousand dollars a year just for accepting the indignity of subservience, and beyond that they surely deserve something for their effectiveness in destroying

---

*It is for this reason also that the propertied class hates the drug culture so much. Police spend their time pursuing and prosecuting people who use drugs rather than criminals because the drug culture is so much more dangerous to the propertied class than the burglar or bank robber or murderer is. Although burglary, robbery, and murder are potential threats to every individual, they actually affect only a small number of people, and very few of these are members of the propertied class. The use of drugs, on the other hand, does threaten the propertied class because it represents a rejection of the entire ethic of the society. If the drug culture became widespread profits would decrease because the users of drugs, like the Hippies, get their satisfaction from something other than the production and consumption of economic goods.

The same explanation applies to the question of why the propertied class condemns drugs but not alcohol. The use of drugs represents a rejection of the work ethic, while the use of alcohol reinforces it. People use drugs to help them escape from what they consider the corrupt values of a corrupt society, while people use alcohol in order to help them accept those values. A person can get through his day's work if he can have a martini at ten, a couple more with his lunch, and three or four more before dinner, while the person who stays high on marijuana feels no need for a job.

There are signs that this is changing. The decriminalization of the use of marijuana appears to result at least in part from the recognition of the propertied class that marijuana can serve the same function for younger workers that alcohol serves for older ones. It can help them to accept their lives and therefore the social ethic, and therefore it can become as useful to the propertied class in maintaining the status quo as alcohol is already.

young people's minds and in making them the loyal worshippers of the propertied class.

If teachers are to continue suitably to perform their appropriate tasks it is important either that they be unable to think or that they dare not think. They must not be educated themselves but only trained. Their courses of study are called teacher-*training* programs, not teacher-*education* programs. In these programs they learn the proper responses to various stimuli, just as trained dogs and trained seals do. Their job will be to train their own students to respond the same way to the same stimuli. If the person who has gone through this training program still shows signs of thinking for himself the functionaries of the propertied class frighten such tendencies out of him by threatening to take his middle-class status away from him.

Because the schooling system never fully succeeds in satisfactorily indoctrinating all students and because even the student who appears to be satisfactorily indoctrinated by the age of eighteen might begin to use his mind again if the indoctrination is not constantly reinforced the brainwashing must continue throughout his life. The adult as well as the student is constantly bombarded with ceremonies designed to deaden thought and create the conditioned response of patriotic emotion.[36] Not only is the Pledge of Allegiance repeated every day in school, but the National Anthem is played before every athletic event. Invocations at college football games, with "America" played softly in the background, are designed to make everything American seem holy and godly and everything un-American—as for example a just distribution of wealth—unholy and devilish. American flags one hundred and ninety feet long are unrolled while bands again play "America" softly in the background and while pathetic young ladies make heart-rending efforts to twirl batons and other ungainly girls go through grotesque gyrations that the broadcasters politely refrain from identifying. Politicians speak in words designed to evoke the conditioned response but also to reinforce the conditioning. Officials appear daily in interviews on television news programs. Holidays glorify war and the country as it is. Advertisers connect their products with the flag or with the American colors, while pacifists or opponents of the war in Vietnam were punished or threatened with punishment for connecting the American flag with peace. Weekly services in church reinforce patriotism and the connection between God and country.

The success of the schools in training young people for business and industry is also often less than complete. In conducting this training the school must follow a very narrow line. It must teach the student to read and write well enough to follow instructions and to fill out forms but not well enough to understand or to express—or even to have an interest in—unpalatable notions. It must develop in him a willingness to consider his employer's competitors devious without developing in him the ability to see the deviousness of the identical practices of his own employer. It must develop in him the certainty that the pronouncements of other countries and other economic and political systems are propaganda but not the ability to recognize the propaganda in the identical pronouncements of Americans and capitalists. It must create in him the certainty that anyone who disagrees with him is not thinking for himself but not the ability to recognize that he is not thinking for himself.

Determined not to teach too much, the school often teaches too little. The high-school and college graduate often cannot read well enough to follow simple instructions or write well enough to fill out simple forms. He often cannot add, subtract, multiply, and divide well enough to conduct simple transactions. Thus a schooling system that was never designed to educate anyone but rather to produce thoughtless workers and consumers does not provide young people with the training necessary even to drones.* When the economic and political elite periodically discover this they demand that the high schools and colleges teach more—but,

---

*The people who control society are trying to get training on the cheap. In a highly technological and otherwise complicated society it should not be surprising if one of the greatest expenditures of time and money were for educating and training the young. But as long as those who control society consider it necessary to provide the rich with guaranteed profits with such things as what are euphemistically called national defense and the exploration of space there will not be sufficient money for training, much less for educating, the young. The rich will provide more money for training—money from the pockets of the middle and lower economic classes—only when the lack of training of the young begins to handicap the rich in their pursuit of profits.

The movement to test the "competencies" of high-school students is evidence that the rich believe that this is happening now. They want to be sure that high-school graduates can compare prices, read theater schedules and recipes, and understand such things as classified ads, telephone bills, qualifications for the Navy, applications for jobs, bus schedules, directions for taking medicine or operating an appliance, street maps, doctors' bills, and articles in newspapers. Mary Fiess, " 'Competency Tests' Will Be Mandatory in January," Cortland *Standard*, 18 October 1976, p. 1. There could be no

of course, only a little more.[37] What they mean is that the high schools and colleges should train more. And their protests are not very vigorous: they know that the development of the proper social and economic attitudes is far more important than technical training—even the ability to read and write—is.[38] It is when it appears that the students have not adequately absorbed the appropriate social and economic attitudes that the members of the propertied class really get upset.

When the economic and political elite discover that students have not been adequately indoctrinated or trained their obvious response is to blame the teachers. It is therefore no surprise that it was in the late sixties and the early seventies that teachers came

---

greater indictment of the people who control the schools and no greater condemnation of the system that they have created than that they limit the aspirations of the young to learning the things that will make them more functional for business. All of the things that the competencies test would be accomplished automatically in any adequate educational system.

The immediate object of the people pushing the competency tests is to get something for nothing. They want more efficient workers at no extra cost. The object of introducing the competency tests is, after all, to provide the schools with an additional "incentive" to teach students these things. Ibid. There is no sign that those who control the schools are going to provide them with additional resources. And incentive without resources is useless.

Obviously, therefore, a large number of students will fail the competency tests. If they do not it will prove that the attacks of the elite on teachers were unfounded. When the students fail and continue to fail, the elite, still refusing to provide the resources necessary to correct the deficiencies, will have additional ammunition to use against the teachers and will thus be able to make them all the more insecure. Thus the introduction of the competency tests will have the effect—and might have been intended from the beginning to have the effect—of intimidating teachers and therefore of making them easier to control. Finally, when things get bad enough and teachers become sufficiently obedient, the elite will provide additional resources for the schools, but only enough to guarantee that graduates will be adequately trained to make them useful to the propertied class.

It is only when the lack of training threatens its own position and profits that the elite become willing to improve the schooling system of the country. The latest emphasis on improving training did not come, after all, until after the Russians successfully fired their Sputnik in 1957. The elite in the United States were afraid that economically they were about to lose out to the Russians. With the success of the American space program that fear subsided and therefore the support for schooling could be reduced again. At the same time that that fear was subsiding violence on campuses convinced the elite that college students are as dangerous as the Russians, and that perception intensified their determination to limit college to students who would be appropriately appreciative of their opportunity.

under increasingly intense attack. During the height of the American involvement in Vietnam they found it impossible to keep their students quiescent because the events outside the classroom made the lies inside the classroom so obvious that even some American students could not avoid recognizing the lies. Most students remained convinced that the United States is always right, but the propertied class was not satisfied with that. It wanted unanimity. It wanted universal approval of a policy of rapine, destruction, and death.

During the late 1960s and the early 1970s the failure of teachers to drain potential leaders away from their natural groups also became obvious. Blacks remained loyal to blacks, and Indians to Indians. To the propertied class it became clear that the schools were not doing their job. Either they were not turning the young people into thoughtless automatons, or else they were allowing the thoughtless automatons to follow the wrong leaders.

Because those who had an opportunity to attend college were either so impercipient that they could not recognize their true benefactors or so ungrateful that they refused to exhibit a lifelong loyalty to them the economic and political elite felt betrayed, and they decided that both teachers and students must smart for their failures. They decided to punish teachers with retrenchment and students with increased tuition.

But it was not enough simply to punish teachers and students for their past failures. It was also necessary to develop techniques to guarantee that such a failure would never occur again. Speedily those who control the schooling system sought devices to guarantee that students would be more quiescent in the future than they had been in the past. The gimmick that has increased in popularity in the middle of the 1970s is "competency-based teacher evaluation." No one knows exactly what it is, but its emphasis is on developing skills. Thus again training is emphasized over education.[39]

Competency-based teacher evaluation combined with the increasing use of television and the political attacks on the media—whether they are the attacks of a vice-president on the networks or the jailing of reporters for not revealing their sources—provide a clue of what is to come. The prospective teacher will not be certified until he has demonstrated his competencies, which will include such things as the ability to operate a movie projector, slide projector, and tape recorder. The teacher will become a technician who operates the machines that transmit the materials prepared by a central office.

This system would have two advantages over the present one. First, it would require far fewer teachers, since one technician at a central panel would be able to operate each student's separate machine. Eventually "educational" television could be adapted to the system and through the use of network programming make even fewer teachers necessary. Or the machine could be programmed in many cases to eliminate the need for a teacher altogether. Second, in several ways the new system would provide an even more effective indoctrination than the present system does. The students would get a universal brainwashing without the influence of the idiosyncracies of the individual teacher.[40] The system would eliminate the teacher's personality and interpretation. It would be much easier to supervise than the present system is: it would be much easier to keep track of what is going on on a limited number of television channels than in thousands of classrooms. In order to keep the children's attention the producers of the television shows could use tricks that are beyond the skill and means of even the most expert teacher.[41] Finally, the new system would make it unnecessary to teach the young people the very dangerous ability to read.[42]

The intimidation of commercial television networks and stations would guarantee that what students see there will not destroy the credibility of what they see in the classroom.

If the people who operate the schools do not correct their shortcomings the need for schools might vanish entirely.* The potentially appreciative members of the lower economic classes can be drained off through the use of non-academic criteria, and the indoctrination can be accomplished through an intensified

*Anyone who believes that the schools are not expendable need only observe what is happening in Detroit and other major cities in the United States. The school system of Detroit is almost bankrupt (CBS Morning News, 10 September 1976), and the people who run it are talking about operating the schools for half days only and, if the news reports are correct, have eliminated such programs as music and most athletics. No one would expect the public schooling system to be abandoned all at once, but it appears likely that it will be reduced gradually until eliminating it entirely will be only a short step. In November of 1976 a group of educationists recommended that high-school students spend only two to four hours in class each day and spend the rest of their time learning to cope with the world. CBS Morning News, 8 November 1976. For cope read adjust to.

use of the non-academic media. Television outside the classroom is just as effective as television inside the classroom in accomplishing the objectives of the propertied class, and young people can be subjected to the mindlessness of television outside the schools for many more hours each day than they can be subjected to the mindlessness of the schools.

What probably will happen eventually is that students will attend school only four days a week and be required to watch television all day on the fifth. They will not have to watch any specific programs: most of what appears on television is already effective in ruining minds. Gradually the number of days the young people spend in school can be decreased and the number they are required to spend watching television at home increased until eventually the public schools disappear altogether.[43]

Already the indoctrination of television supplements the indoctrination of the schools.* But if television is to continue that function—even if it never does replace the schools entirely—it is

---

*Teachers are making a mistake in underestimating the extent to which television has already taken over their function of indoctrinating people. Not only the scripted programs but also the talk shows, news shows, news commentators, and ads bolster the status quo. The scripted programs, talk shows, and news reports are more or less subtle, while ads and news commentators are direct in the misrepresentations. The Bicentennial Year has brought an epidemic of ads that misrepresent history and has illustrated the potential of watching ads as a substitute for attending school. Even more effective are the news commentators. They carry the aura of learning, thoughtfulness, and sincerity, while even the most unsophisticated Americans distrust ads. The distrust of ads for commerical products might make them somewhat suspect also in their perversion of history and contemporary reality. Ads therefore rely on repetition, while commentators rely on reputation. One often wonders whether such people as Eric Sevareid and Howard K. Smith really believe the things they say or whether they believe that their job is to keep the public optimistic and calm. Howard K. Smith's ability to say such things as "Discrimination against women is like prejudice against every class of human—too inconsequential to make a Federal cause out of." (Quoted in Betty Medsger, "On a Million-Dollar Misunderstanding," *The Progressive*, August, 1976, p. 20), makes it clear that he is only an apologist for the status quo. With an unemployment rate in the United States of approximately 7.9 percent by the administration's own figures, Eric Sevareid's ability to say that only a minor fraction of the American work force is unemployed (CBS Evening News, 7 September 1976) represents a complacency and an arrogance that in any humane society would be appalling. The droning of such people as Bruce Morton and Dan Rather is less objectionable than the pontifications of Smith and Sevareid only because they do not have the stature of the older men. Quote from *The Progressive* reprinted by permission. Copyright © 1976, The Progressive, Inc.

necessary that the television networks and stations be frightened into a submission at least as complete as that of the schools. Therefore it is no accident that Spiro Agnew's attack on the television networks and then the other attacks on the media began very soon after the attacks on the schools began.

In order properly to indoctrinate students as well as to train them to work well for industry and to be good consumers the schools must accomplish a fourth function. This is the creation of insecurities.[44] The object is to destroy the student's confidence in himself and in his own mind. The ultimate object is not only to get him to accept a low economic status but also to believe that he cannot understand what is going on in the world. The object is to get him to believe that although things are not what they are supposed to be and that although those who control the economic and political life of the country do not appear to be doing what they say they are doing he probably does not understand what is happening and that they must know what they are doing or they would not hold the positions they hold. If a person is going to feel this insecurity throughout his life it is important that he knows little, but it is equally important that he knows he knows little. He must be insecure enough to be willing to spend his life in a routine and menial job without aspiring to anything better and without ever trying to figure things out.

At the moment of his graduation from high school or college the young person does know little, but he does not always know how little he knows. He has been told for years that he is a member of the brightest generation ever, and with one part of his mind he believes it. But sometimes he does have doubts. Sometimes he wonders why it is that if he knows so much he has so little confidence. He wonders why if he is so smart he did not get better grades, especially since he is aware that high grades have become increasingly easy to get in recent years. He realizes that there is a whole wide world out there, and he realizes that about all he has done with his life so far is play football and fool around. And he is scared to death.

Once he finds a job he has his inadequacies confirmed. He knows that he can barely do it—if he can do it at all—but he hopes that as time goes on he will become more competent at it. Experience, however, does not improve his competence but rather confirms his inadequacy. His confidence ebbs even further, and his insecurity increases. He will be frightened all of his life. He is not likely to do or say anything that his employer does not approve.

There is little chance that he will ever be a danger to the propertied class. He will work hard and keep his mouth shut in order to surround himself with the material possessions with which he will try to convince himself that he is as good as anyone else.

But not all students recognize their inadequacies when they graduate from college. For them college has been fairly easy. They have got fairly good grades. They have done well on the Law Boards or on the Graduate Record Exam. They have been big wheels on campus. They are glib and confident. They are convinced that no one ever spoke a truer word than those who say that they are members of the brightest and best-educated generation ever. They are convinced not only that they are among the elite but that they are the elite of the elite. They are convinced that they can conquer the world.

For these exuberant young people the propertied class has further treatment. It sends them off to professional school or graduate school, where the competition is greater, where the work is harder even though academic standards have declined there as well as in undergraduate colleges, and where professors can give more individual attention to indoctrinating,[45] intimidating, awing, belittling, and humiliating them.[46] They discover that if they want to conquer the world they first of all have to get along, and then they discover that it takes all of their energy just to get along. They lose confidence in themselves and so concentrate on developing their earning power. They learn that if they want to sell themselves they must be sure that someone will want to buy them, and gradually they lose confidence even in their earning power. They decide to do what they must do.

If anyone escapes from professional school or graduate school still believing in his own mind and ability—and indeed in his own personality—his first job will smash his illusions. That process is known as on-the-job training. He will submit or get fired. If he gets fired he will not want to get fired again.

The object of creating this insecurity in young people is not only to destroy their confidence in their own minds but also to destroy their confidence that they might be able to change the things that appear to them to be wrong. The object is to create in them a deep despair. First they must despair of ever understanding the world, and then they must despair of ever doing anything about anything anyway. The despair about ever changing anything guarantees that even those who continue to have confidence that they do understand the world and do see through the myths that the schooling system has tried to impose on them will be passive and quiescent. It guarantees that they will continue to believe that indeed they cannot fight city hall and therefore that they will not even try.*

If indoctrination, weaning potential leaders away from the groups to which they have a natural loyalty, training people for business and industry, and creating insecurities were the only objects of schooling it would not be necessary to send so many people to college or even through four years of high school. While the high schools and the colleges do provide a centralized and extremely efficient system of indoctrination, the same thing could be accomplished through a more intense use of the media that are available to all people. Potential leaders could be alienated from their natural groups by a more careful selection of those who would be offered a chance to join the white middle class, and workers could be adequately trained by a more intense indoctrination during the earlier years of schooling. People who have never been to college could surely be made to feel just as insecure as those who have. People who have had only two years of high school could surely be made to feel just as insecure as those who have had four.

But a fifth function of college and the last two years of high school is to hold down the level of unemployment.[47] If all of the students who either do not want to be in school or are gaining nothing there that they could not get equally well someplace else were suddenly turned loose to look for jobs the unemployment rate would soar. It is necessary therefore to keep as many of them

---

*Of course the schooling that creates insecurities in students is even more effective in creating insecurities in those who do not go to school, since they have not accomplished even the basic requirement of the rulers of society. The process in the case of those who drop out is similar to but speedier than that of those who graduate from high school or college. These youngsters might start school with less confidence than those who graduate, or they might simply lose their confidence faster. Or both. In any case they start school at the age of five or six with at least a little hope, and when they lose that hope and feel sufficiently insecure they drop out. Many more could drop out than do without hurting the propertied class. All that is necessary is that enough people continue to graduate from high school so that the high-school diploma continues to be considered the minimum requirement for even a minimal success in life—so that those who do not have it will not expect even that minimal success—and that enough people continue to graduate from college so that the college degree continues to be considered the minimum requirement for moderate success—so that those who do not have it will not expect anything beyond the minimal success.

off the streets as possible. Since the object is not to educate anyone but only to keep him in school it is necessary only to keep
him occupied at something he will tolerate doing and that has
some value as indoctrination. Thus the great emphasis on athletics
and other anti-intellectual activities.[48] Except for athletics all of
the activities designed to entertain and indoctrinate must be
carried out at the lowest possible expense:* schools are judged by
their cost per unit of production—their cost per graduate—just as
any other economic enterprise is judged. The school is, after all,
just another factory.[49]

A sixth function of the college is to train athletes for the
professional leagues. This is a subsidy for the rich and the middle
class, since if the professional teams had to develop their own
talent the increased expense would result in higher prices for the
tickets to their games. The poor, who pay more than their share of
the taxes to support the schools that train the athletes,[50] cannot
afford the tickets in any case.

It is not because the schools have been distracted into these
non-educational and anti-intellectual functions that they do not
educate. These functions are not distractions. They are the real
functions of the school. The fact that the schools do not educate anyone does not result from their failure. It results from their
success. They accomplish what they are supposed to accomplish.
The schools have never been designed to educate anyone. It is
only when someone escapes from the schooling system without
having his mind completely ruined that the system has failed. In
accomplishing those functions that they are supposed to accomplish the schools have been a resounding success. In accomplishing their primary task—ruining people's minds—they have been a
sensational success.[51]

The young people are the ones who pay, and they will pay all
of their lives. All of the real functions of the schools are accomplished at the expense of the student. Through his years of school-

---

*It is significant that during the past five years or so there has been in-
creasing pressure to make fuller use of academic facilities. There is pressure to
use them more hours each day and more days each year. Yet states and cities
have no hesitiation about building multi-million-dollar auditoriums and
stadiums that will be used for only a few hours each year. More than that,
they happily supply the police to direct traffic outside and to patrol inside
when the structures are in use. For the upper-middle and upper classes who
use these facilities nothing is too good. For the lower-middle and lower
classes who attend the public schools nothing is too bad.

ing he sees alternatives being closed off rather than opened up, and by the time he finishes high school or college his life is pretty well planned for him and he has learned to accept the limitations placed on him. His acceptance is not reconciliation or wisdom but rather despair. He does not like what he sees before him but he feels powerless to do anything about it. One of the functions of the school is to *make* him feel powerless. The specific job that he will fill is not always obvious to him but his choice is very narrow or entirely non-existent. Ordinarily he does not select a job but rather the job selects him. Lonely and insecure young men and women do not choose husbands and wives but rather come together in their alienation and allow their insecurities to magnify each other.

Yet the schools do not succeed completely. As successful as the elementary, junior high, and high schools have been, they have never yet completely ruined young people's minds. Considering what they have suffered through for twelve years, an amazing number of young people enter college still willing and able to learn. They are not stupid. Most of them are capable of learning. They do continue to think. Their doubts remain. "You mean that if something does not make sense to me," the more daring student has asked in class, "it might be because it really does not make sense rather than because I am too stupid to understand it?" When that happens, the serious teacher breathes "Eureka!" The college adds another course in American institutions.

It is precisely because the elementary, junior high, and high schools do not succeed in completely ruining students' minds that colleges are necessary. Most high-school graduates have not been turned into completely conditioned robots. They are well on the way, but most of them are not there yet. In spite of having been subjected for eighteen years to social institutions designed to destroy their minds, they do still retain some of their intelligence. The colleges exist to destroy that remaining intelligence.

Many students enter college not only able to learn but also anxious to learn. It is only after they discover that college is only an extension of high school that they give up. If they do happen to have a good course it cannot compete with the bad ones. The disillusionment of the bad ones makes it difficult for them to work on the good one, and they quickly quit trying to learn. "Why should I stay around," the teacher who still talks to students often hears the perceptive student say, "when in three years I've had only one good course? I hoped that when I got to be a junior and could concentrate on my major the busywork would end, but the advanced courses are just like the introductory ones." Most of these students hang on in order to graduate, but it is no accident that many of the most mature ones drop out. And their dropping out is easy to understand when one hears a European history teacher who has assigned Erasmus's *The Praise of Folly*, apparently without ever having read it, report that he refused to discuss it with a student because it is not very important anyway.

The problem, then, is not that the young people entering college are stupid. They are *not* stupid. The problem is not that they are unable to learn. They *are* able to learn. The problem is not even that they do not want to learn. Many do want to learn. The problem is that by the time they graduate from high school they are so far behind in their learning that they will never catch up. The years that they have lost are gone. Their conditioned responses have such a strong hold on them that the effort to develop a critical ability will take many years longer than it would have taken if they had started earlier. And this great task they must undertake at an age when they have been taught that their education should be coming to an end rather than only beginning. They see that they will never catch up, and they do not have the heart to undertake an effort at which they know they cannot succeed anyway. They see that even partially to catch up they would have to work harder than they ever thought they were capable of working and that the process would mean the development of terrifying uncertainties at a time when they have just spent twelve or thirteen years trying to become certain. They are unwilling to work that hard and to suffer those uncertainties. It is much easier simply not to think at all. Lacking educated and thoughtful teachers whom they can emulate, battered by a society that discounts and even positively discredits learning, realizing that aspiring to anything beyond a mediocre knowledge might be a positive disadvantage to them,[52] and recognizing that what will determine their future economic prosperity is not how much they know but how well they are able to get along, they see no reason why they should suffer the agony of lonely hours in the library when they could be enjoying charming company in someone else's bed. And it is very difficult to fault them for that. If the fornication does not add to their happiness it does at least for the time being moderate their despair.

But in the end they suffer. Their schooling has provided them with no alternatives. It has provided them with no alternative ways of living. It has provided them with no alternative ways of earning their living: they take what jobs they can get and hate them but keep them. It has provided them with no alternative ways of using what leisure they have. They do what they did in school: drink, watch television, and dally about. But most basic of all their schooling has provided them with no alternative ways of thinking. They do what they did in school: they believe what they are told to believe. They have no understanding of their place in the world or of the forces that brought them there, and they lack the information, the critical ability, and the energy to figure it out. From the time they entered school—indeed, from the time they were born—their lives have been outside their own control.

Chapter 8

CULPABILITY*

$\mathcal{I}$t is always tempting to explain the lack of learning in the schools by emphasizing the inadequacy of the students.[1] The students are ignorant, it is true, and they are lazy, and they are arrogant. But it is the schools that have made them so. They have been taught that they are well informed, ambitious, and humble. They are only what the rulers of the society want them to be. They are the almost perfect products of what to the rulers of society is an almost perfect system. It is not their fault that they learn little.

Those who deserve the most credit for the absence of learning

---

*I would not argue that the people who co-operate in ruining minds always know what they are doing. They have been subjected to the same schooling that they are imposing upon the young, and while many of them recognize that the schools are not educating they usually credit that to the failure of the schools rather than to their success. These people are not deliberately conspiring to ruin minds. In most cases their own minds have been ruined and therefore the system continues on its own momentum.

But the direction of the momentum does sometimes change slightly, and these changes are the result of the conscious decisions of the elite or their functionaries. We are in such a period of change in the middle of the 1970s. Of course even in such a period those who control the schools do not ask themselves specifically how they can better ruin minds. Rather they see that the schools are not doing what they are supposed to do, and they ask themselves therefore how they can make the schools more adequately serve their appropriate function—how, that is, they can be made to serve society better. In asking that question, of course, the elite and their functionaries identify *themselves* as the society.

in the schools and therefore for the vast and increasing ignorance of the American public are the members of the propertied class. The propertied class controls the schools as well as all of the other institutions of society, and anyone else connected with the schools is either its agent, its functionary, or its enemy.[2]

A propertied class has two essential characteristics. First, it must control enough wealth to control the economic and therefore the political and social life of the nation. Second, it must reproduce itself. The wealthiest families in the United States do meet both of these criteria.[3] These are the Rockefellers, the du Ponts, the Kennedys, the Harrimans, and the few others who control such vast wealth that the decisions they make affect the lives of all of the rest of us. They are the beautiful people,[4] the rich and the super-rich.[5]

If the propertied class wants to continue to be a propertied class it has to convince the public that there is no such thing. It does this by teaching myths.[6] It teaches first that while it is obvious that some people are very wealthy their wealth does not give them any control over the economic, social, and political system. One of the few hilarious incidents in the United States during the entire sad year of 1974 was the spectacle of Nelson Rockefeller trying to convince the Senate Rules Committee and the House Judiciary Committee that in spite of its immense wealth his family has no economic or political influence.[7] Second, the propertied class teaches that the rich do not reproduce themselves but that anyone can become wealthy. It does this through the myths of equal opportunity and social mobility. It teaches that the reward of riches is available to anyone who has the ambition, the energy, and the intelligence to seek it and that the person who tries can readily move out of the class into which he was born and become a member of even the very richest class,[8] which the rich continue to deny is a class even while they praise it. The rich never suggest that while there has always been a limited social mobility in the United States that social mobility has been vastly exaggerated in the propaganda of American institutions.[9]

If the propertied class wants to remain a propertied class it also has to convince the public that its wealth is justified, that it is not only proper but also necessary that great differences in wealth exist. It does this first by teaching that some people must be fabulously wealthy in order to guarantee the investment that keeps the capitalistic system going. It never suggests that there is any better way to provide the money for investment or that far from doing the population a favor by investing its money the propertied class is actually exploiting the public. Second, it teaches again that great wealth is the reward for superior ambition, energy, and intelligence and that therefore the rich do deserve the rewards they have reaped. It never suggests that the rich got their wealth to begin with not because of any superior ambition, energy, or intelligence but rather because of a public policy that has provided and continues to provide boondoggles for a few favored families. Third, it teaches that it is only the potential reward of great riches that gives people the initiative and energy to do anything at all.

At the same time that they try to convince the public that there is no such thing as a propertied class but that it is essential that great differences in wealth exist, the rich also teach that the poor are actually better off than the rich.[10] Not only are the poor better off than the rich on earth, but they also have a better chance of getting into heaven.

The agents and the functionaries of the propertied class deserve the immediate credit for the condition of the schools. Among the most important of these are the regents or trustees of universities and colleges. Members of these boards are either members of the propertied class themselves or people who have a long record of loyalty to it and to the status quo.[11] Their job is to ride herd on academic administrators and faculties. They take action to eliminate any real or imagined threat to the status quo.[12] They make the rules by which the schools operate day to day, and these rules reflect the attitudes of the propertied class. They very seldom believe that the function of the schooling system is to provide a liberal education. They believe that its function is to protect the status quo and that faculties exist to say what they are told to say. In 1970, fifty-three percent of the trustees of American schools believed that it is reasonable to require faculty members to take a loyalty oath; seventy percent believed that only administrators and trustees should take part in the selection of a new president of a college or university; sixty-four percent believed that only administrators and trustees should have a voice in decisions on tenure; sixty-three percent believed that faculties should not have a major voice in the appointment of deans; and twenty-seven percent believed that faculty members should not have a right to express their opinions freely.[13]

While trustees and regents ordinarily come from the propertied class and are therefore its agents, state legislators seldom come from the propertied class and are therefore its functionaries. They are dependent on the propertied class for its continued favor. They are usually very minor politicians who will never achieve any higher office or acquire any more prestige than they have while they sit in the assemblies. Their intelligence and abilities are limited, and their education, though it might include college and even law school, is wanting. They are not liberally educated. They reflect the values of the propertied class, and for the appearance of power they gladly follow its orders. They write into law the rules that the propertied class demands. While they appear to be the seat of authority, they are actually only the voice through which the real authority speaks. For them as for their bosses the schooling system is the structure through which the values of the propertied class are maintained. In their view as in the view of their bosses the schooling system deserves support only as long as it does satisfactorily perform that function. When it fails to do the bidding of the powerful, the legislators punish it by withholding funds, raising tuition, and retrenching.

The school board performs the same function in relation to local schools as regents and trustees perform in relation to colleges and universities. Its job is to guarantee that the local school does nothing that might threaten the position of the propertied interests. Members of the propertied class itself seldom sit on the school board. It is not prestigious enough for them. They know, however, that there are plenty of candidates whose loyalty is unquestioned. These ordinarily are professional and business people who while they are not filthily rich are prosperous enough that they worship the system that has made them so.[14] Since the school board is elected there is no absolute reason why a less prosperous person could not become a member, but there are practical reasons that ordinarily keep him from it. First, in order to get elected to anything notoriety is necessary. Next to the very rich in any area the businessmen and professionals are the most notorious. Second, getting elected even to a school board requires an expenditure that the laboring man cannot afford to make. Third, a person must have the time to do the job. The laboring man who has to make his own repairs on his house, repair his own car, shovel his own walk in winter and manicure his own lawn in the summer—and all of this after working at least a forty-hour week—does not have the time to attend meetings, much less to inform himself about issues that arise there. If he could once get on the board he would discover that no one else is informed either, that being informed is not necessary, and therefore that informing himself would not necessarily take any of his time. But he would still have to take time to attend the meetings, and that time would have to come out of his recreational time. The meetings would decrease the time he could spend bowling, playing softball, and watching the game of the week on television. The working-class woman is as busy as the working-class man. The person who sits on a school board must have time to attend the meetings and to play golf as well.

But the most important reason why members of the working class seldom run for election to a school board is the excellent job that the schooling system, the politicians, and the media have done in creating in them a feeling of their own inadequacy and of awe toward those who are more prosperous than they are. Those who control the schools have made a specific effort to keep working people off the school boards.[15] The worker has been taught that it is not his place to be on the school board. He has been taught that there are others who can do the job better than he can. He has been taught his place and to stay in it, and he has been taught that anyone else in his own class should be able to recognize and accept his place also. He would feel self-conscious and inadequate if by some accident he did get on a committee with people from outside his own class, and he has been taught that others in his class should feel the same way. He feels much more comfortable bowling with the fellows from work, and he has been taught that anyone else in his class should feel the same. He has been taught that even if a member of his own class should have the temerity to run for election to a school board he should vote for a businessman or professional person anyway.

The people who are responsible for the immediate day-to-day operations of the schools are the academic administrators. They include state superintendents of schools, college presidents and vice-presidents, deans, high-school superintendents and principals, and the crowd of functionaries who surround and support them. Like people in student personnel, administrators often do not like and are incapable of serious intellectual discipline* and enjoy the mechanics of administration more than they enjoy the challenge

---

*It is not true that in order to aspire to the position of dean or above a person must have an I.Q. of below ninety. I have known two deans and one vice-president with I.Q.'s of *above one hundred.*

of learning.* Others have tried teaching but have found either that they do not like it or are no good at it or both. Still others go into administrative work because administrators have more power and receive higher salaries than teachers.

Administrators are generally characterized by a lack of imagination[16] and a lack of education.[17] Because of these inadequacies the administrator seldom has any confidence in himself: any confidence he has results from his position and whatever power he wields. For a long time administrators have considered teachers the enemy[18] †—and none-too-bright an enemy at that[19]—but only recently have teachers begun to realize how administrators feel about them. The administrator ordinarily is anxious to follow

---

*What I say about administrators seems to me to be the inescapable conclusion of anyone who reads widely in their own organs, as for example *Educational Record* and *Liberal Education*. Reading them is to enter a world to travel in which sufficient navigational instruments have not yet been invented. But the serious teacher who believes that administrators are interested in the same things he is will find them tremendously enlightening—and disillusioning.

†"Chancellors, presidents, academic vice presidents, provosts, deans, associate deans, assistant deans, assistants to the dean, directors of upper-class core programs, coordinator[s] of lower divisions, academic administrators all, it is time for us to unite against the common foe—the faculty!" "For years the faculty has been hacking away at whatever authority we once exercised." "Let us fight to restore administration to the administrators." Francis H. Horn, "Academic Administrators, Unite!", *College and University Business*, XXX, No. 6 (June 1961), p. 33. Julian Foster takes Horn seriously though he believes that Horn "doubtless" had his "tongue *somewhat* in cheek." Julian Foster,"Power, Authority and Expertise: Administration in a Changing Context," *Liberal Education*, LIV, No. 4 (December 1968), p. 593. My emphasis. The person who speaks tongue-in-cheek, of course, can also be deadly serious, and that is how I read Horn. I think that most people would read him that way. In a private letter to me dated 6 November 1976 Dr. Horn says that when he wrote the editorial he was not "really serious" but that it is "a tongue-in-cheek statement, induced by the growing militancy of the AAUP. . . . I trust that when you quote the material, you won't imply that I was in dead earnest, although the situation is far worse today. Collegiality has indeed disappeared in the face of the confrontation posture created by collective bargaining. Under these circumstances, I can't see any justification for a faculty role in presidential selection—and you may quote me on this." I would argue that collegiality never did exist, that faculties were granted the appearance of power only as long as they did not ask for anything that the elite were not already willing to grant, that that appearance of power of faculties created the myth of collegiality, and that the myth of collegiality disappeared not because of the increased demands of teachers but rather be-

orders and to give them. His two most immediately apparent qualities are a great timidity before those whom he considers his superiors and a feeling of superiority toward and a willingness to
tyrannize over those whom he considers his inferiors.[20] In his view
a superior person is anyone who has more power than he has and
an inferior person is anyone who has less power than he has. His
inferiors include faculty, students, and any administrators who
have less rank and lower salaries than he has himself.

The academic administrator practices his tyranny in a cocoon
of smiles and a flood of words. One of the inalienable rights of the
academic administrator is the right to speak out of both sides of
his mouth. He can say whatever he considers necessary to accomplish the objectives of his overlords. He can try to play students
against faculty and faculty against students. But more than that he
never has to be philosophically consistent. What he says one day
need not have anything to do with what he says the next.*
Because he smiles and professes his helplessness while he presents
his ultimatums to faculties he is tolerated and feared and sometimes even liked. Easily deceived teachers have been known even
to sympathize with administrators.

Administrators consider running a college the same as running a
business, just as their bosses expect them to.[21] Their function is
to turn out the greatest possible number of graduates at the lowest
possible unit cost of production[22] and to guarantee that those
graduates are safe. They make the day-to-day decisions about running the schools. They hire and fire teachers, award and deny
tenure and promotion, and determine salaries. But they do not

---

cause of the increased determination of the elite to guarantee not only
that teachers would be their lackeys but that they would be content to be
lackeys. Unionization and the demand for collective bargaining followed, and
did not precede, the increased aggressiveness of the elite. Collective bargaining
among teachers is defensive rather than offensive.

*The decline of the already low academic standards in teaching programs
has clearly exposed this inconsistency. One often hears the administrator say
that no one should ever fail out of college but that not everyone who graduates from a teaching program should be allowed to teach. He never has to
answer the question of how a teacher can justify passing—and therefore
certifying the knowledge of—someone who knows almost nothing. With a
perfectly straight face he can say that he has not figured that out yet. And he
will never have to figure it out. The teacher, on the other hand, has to make
a judgment. He must either fail some people or else admit that he is certifying
as knowledgeable people who he knows are not. Of course the administrator actually believes, though he would never admit it, that anyone *can*
teach.

make the fundamental academic decisions. These the state legislatures and the boards of trustees make, and administrators merely
follow orders and pass the orders on to the faculties.[23]

The immediate agents for ruining students' minds are the faculties. Like the administrator, the average faculty member is
timid.[24] He often comes from an economic level that is lower than
the one he presently enjoys,[25] and he both fears falling back to the
level of his parents and hopes to increase his standard of living
still further. Often he is a little surprised that he has come as far
as he has, and he knows that the only way to rise still further is
to act as he has acted in the past. He must continue to obey
orders.

The insecure faculty member will do almost anything that a
department chairman or a dean or a vice-president tells him to do.
He will give high grades to make his courses attractive to students.
He will prepare new courses in fields in which he has no background in order to attract students and therefore maintain or increase the student-faculty ratio of his department and division. He
will sit on committees but keep his mouth shut so as not to interfere with the administrators' running the institution any way they
choose. When he sits on a personnel committee he will help to
penalize any member of the faculty who does not willingly float
along with the tide.

Probably nothing in a college better illustrates the insecurity of
the faculty than the various personnel committees. Ordinarily the
committees have to follow formal procedures and consider established criteria, but usually the procedures are elastic enough and
the criteria vague enough to allow the members of the committees
to do just about anything they please. Because the committees
vote secretly no one has to answer to anyone else for anything.

The committees recommend the same sort of person for promotion and the same people for discretionary salary increases year
after year. They reward four categories of people. First, they reward their friends and punish their enemies. Second, they reward
other members of the committee unless one of them is known for
his independence but still has been elected to the committee.*
Third, they reward people who are not on the committee but who

---

*On one occasion when a teacher asked a departmental chairman to ex-
plain the criteria by which the departmental personnel committee decided
whom to recommend for discretionary salary increases the chairman said,
"Well, if you want a recommendation you ought to get yourself elected to
the committee."

they believe can help them or hurt them. They reward senior members of the faculty who might have influence with other faculty and whose favor they want. They vote in favor of the person who seems to have the support of a senior member of the faculty. They vote in favor of departmental chairmen. Fourth, they reward people whose advancement in rank or salary will not make them feel more insecure than they already are. They vote in favor of the person who flatters them and who never says anything disagreeable or dangerous. Most of all they vote for people who they know are mediocre. They reward the people to whom they can feel superior. If there is on the faculty someone who they suspect is a better scholar or teacher than they are they do not want to confirm their own inferiority by recommending a promotion or a discretionary salary increase for him. Especially they do not want to confirm his superiority if he is in the same department that they are in.[26]

Obviously not every teacher goes along with these practices, and obvioulsy others go along with them only reluctantly. But all it takes is a majority.[27]

This does not mean that a good teacher or a good scholar can never get a promotion or what is called a discretionary salary increase. He can, provided that he acts properly. He must wear his humility on his sleeve. He must flatter the other members of the faculty. When he serves on a personnel committee he must have equal praise for all of the members of the faculty unless there is someone who does not ride with the tide. The good teacher must never claim to be a good teacher but rather must talk constantly about his dissatisfaction with his accomplishments in the classroom. The bad teacher, on the other hand, can make any claim he wants for his teaching: he will not frighten anyone. No teacher ever dare suggest that he grades too high, since that will tell his colleagues that he thinks that they grade too high also. The good scholar must not talk much about his research and must never claim to be doing anything out of the ordinary. The bad scholar, though, can talk as much as he wants and make any claim he wants about his scholarship. Again he will not frighten anyone. The good teacher or scholar must, in short, convey the impression that he is trying to do right in all respects but has little hope of success in any respect. He must make it clear that granting him a promotion or a discretionary salary increase will not threaten the emotional security of any of his colleagues. He must be especially careful if by some chance he is both a good teacher *and* a good scholar.

But not everyone dare adopt this tactic. By belittling his own teaching and scholarship the person who is already something of an outsider will only provide ammunition for his enemies. They will be able to say that he admits himself that he is not a good teacher or scholar.

There is no safety anywhere. Even the obsequious person who gains from his obsequiousness cannot be sure of his future. The tone in which he belittles himself must always be just right. He must be serious. He must be *concerned*. He must never appear frivolous about his job. In academia there was once a bad joke about the difference between teaching and merely holding classes. "Some people teach; some hold classes. I hold classes." The point is that it is usually the best teachers who believe that they do not teach much: the bad teacher, expecting little or nothing, is seldom discouraged. But one never hears that joke any more. Everyone knows that his saying it could be used against him. Even the person who appears to be firmly entrenched in the favor of his department dare not say anything light. He never knows when he might be on the outside. Shifts in the political alignment in academia are notorious. The pettiness of the politics of academia is also notorious.[28]

What all of this means is that the primary function of the various personnel committees is to guarantee a steady level of mediocrity uninterrupted by the expression of unacceptable ideas, real teaching, or profound scholarship. When personnel committees were first established they were presented as a device for replacing the autocracy of a single department head, dean, vice-president, or president with the democracy of a system of committees. And they do provide a sort of democracy. But it is a democracy of mediocrity. It is a democracy directed toward guaranteeing that teachers will continue their traditional function of indoctrinating students in the face of the constant danger that an intelligent maverick will suddenly decide to try actually to teach. The judgment of the committees is designed to take some of the onus of disciplining independent or thoughtful faculty members off the administration and thus to weaken the resentment toward the administration by scattering the responsibility for disciplinary decisions among a variety of people.[29]

While it is easy to recognize the responsibility of administrators and faculties for the low state of American education it is often difficult to fault them for it. Both are timid, it is true, and both are insecure. They are avaricious. They are dishonest. Yet they are in a very difficult position. They have become accustomed to a certain standard of living, and they have wives who want new bedroom suites and children whom they want to send to college. They have girlfriends who cost them money. And boards of trustees and state legislatures, representing the interests of the propertied class and therefore of the status quo, are in effect saying to them "Look. We have put you where you are. You will do what we tell you to do or we will put you back where you were. You will say what we tell you to say, and you will keep your campuses quiet, and you will do it at the lowest possible cost to the taxpayer."

Other teachers and administrators willingly indoctrinate students or force others to indoctrinate them not because of their timidity, insecurity, or avariciousness but rather because of their ignorance. A great many teachers and administrators believe that they are doing what they are supposed to be doing. They have, after all, been subjected to the same indoctrination as their students, and they have been subjected to it for a longer time. They have masters' degrees and doctorates. They believe that they are *supposed* to follow orders. They believe that they are *supposed* to say only what someone—the author of a textbook, for example, or a member of a board of regents—tells them to say. They have so thoroughly absorbed the conventional wisdom that they will never want to say or do anything to which even the most conservative capitalist could object. They feel completely free. They believe that everything is okay. They have been taught to believe it, and they believe it also because they have achieved higher positions in life than they ever expected to achieve. Naturally they believe that the system that has proven so beneficial to themselves must be a pretty good one.[30]

Yet, difficult as it sometimes is to blame administrators and faculties for their submission to whatever whim strikes their bosses, they must accept that blame. They do, after all, willingly submit. They are content to be apologists rather than teachers. And for that they must answer for the generations they turn out as thoughtless and as timid as they are themselves. For that they must answer for the minds that will never be used.

Chapter 9

CONTROL

$\mathcal{A}$s long as administrators form a separate clique and do not descend from the faculty there will be an inevitable and insoluble conflict between administrators and the serious teacher. The serious teacher wants to teach, but to the propertied class, whose interests the administrators represent, nothing is more dangerous than education. Probably the most characteristic quality of the educated person is the ability to question his own assumptions. That is the last thing that academic administrators and their propertied bosses want. The primary function of the schooling system is to fix assumptions so firmly in people that they never will doubt them. The object is to make people incapable of thinking. The object is to make people's minds not only useless but also unnecessary. The administrator therefore not only has no interest in education but is positively opposed to it. He does not want good teachers: he wants good indoctrinators. His job is to guarantee the destruction of the largest possible number of minds at the lowest possible cost per mind.[1]

In the battle between administrators and the serious teacher, the administrators have all of the advantages.* In addition to such

---

*It becomes increasingly clear that the only hope for education is the complete unionization of teachers. Whatever good has been preserved in academia is to a great extent the result of the work of the unions, and whatever good

obvious clubs as the power to hire and fire, award and deny tenure, and determine salaries,[2] administrators have other largess to distribute to the meek. One of the most important is the sabbatical leave. Using the threat of the denial of the sabbatical, administrators can control not only the teacher's teaching but also his writing. If the teacher arouses the ire of the administrators he knows that he risks losing his sabbatical. Even if he knows that no sabbatical has ever been denied he knows that there can always be a first time, especially in a period of retrenchment, when the politicians have convinced much of the public that teachers are already getting more than they deserve. Therefore the teacher is likely to tone down both his teaching and his writing. He is likely never to say anything to which an administrator might object. He imposes a self-censorship.

Another device by which administrators control faculties is the insistence on the possession of the doctorate. Historically there are two reasons why the doctorate has been desirable. First, since the primary function of the schooling system is to ruin people's minds it is only logical that the more schooling a person has the more likely it is that his mind will be ruined and the more thoroughly it will be ruined. Only the person whose own mind has been thoroughly ruined can be trusted with the awesome responsibility of ruining the minds of others, and the doctorate attests to the thoroughness of his ruination. Anyone who does not take his job seriously but tries to teach instead is simply eliminated from the profession, usually before he can even get well settled. Historically he was often removed even from the world.[3]

But usually it is not necessary to expel people from the profession. Administrators have adequate tools of intimidation. Usually

---

has been lost is to a great extent the result of the weakness of the unions. Only thorough organization will give teachers the bargaining power to resist the further encroachments of the people who want academia as a whole as well as every individual teacher to reflect perfectly the mindlessness of a factory. Even the partially organized teachers have done a great deal of good. They are especially impressive since they have had to fight not only the administrators but also concerted efforts to discredit them by other teachers who themselves are benefiting from the work of the very unions they attack.

Only through unions will teachers be heard. When "noted educators" gather together to discuss the future of education, the conferences are almost always loaded with administrators, with only a few token professors to create the impression that teachers really do have an influence. See "SUNY Gathers Noted Educators for Conference," *The News* (State University of New York), October 1976, p. 12.

they do not need them but can hold them in reserve. The person with the doctorate, having had his own mind thoroughly ruined, has generally accepted his function of ruining other minds without even knowing he is doing it. He has always thought that he is educating them.

The second reason why the doctorate has been considered necessary for college teachers is that the person who has completed the doctorate can be expected to possess more misinformation than the person who has not. He has had several years to concentrate on the accumulation of the misinformation and misrepresentation that his own mentors have considered important. With good hard work the teacher without the doctorate can gradually and partially make up the deficiency, but he will always be behind the doctorate with equal energy. Thus those teachers with doctorates have the best mastery of the misinformation, slogans, clichés, and misrepresentations that make indoctrination convincing.[4]

In hiring people with doctorates academic administrators sometimes work against the best interests of their propertied-class bosses. While the person with the doctorate very seldom actually becomes a good teacher but usually does perform his expected function of indoctrinating his students he is in a better position to become a good teacher than the person without the doctorate is. This is true not because he has any superior intelligence or ability but rather because of two other factors. First, ordinarily the person with the doctorate will be able to convey more information to his students than the person without the degree can, since he will have studied longer before he started teaching and among the misinformation, slogans, clichés, and misrepresentations that he has picked up there will also be some correct information. If his mentors have been successful with him he will not know what the information means or what to do with it, but once he begins to convey information to his students some of those whose minds have not been completely ruined already will actually begin to think about it. Thus this professor might become a teacher in spite of himself.

Second, with the emphasis on the necessity of having a doctorate, the doctorate provides the security to permit the professor to be a maverick if he wants to be one. It permits him to dare to teach rather than simply to say what he is told to say. Of course it is only seldom that the doctorate represents a commitment to learning and thinking. In most cases it means only that the person who got it wanted the security that it would provide. But there are also those few who not only start out committed to learning and thinking but whose power of resistance is so great that even graduate school does not ruin them. They carry their commitment into the classroom.

Of course the only real requirement for the doctorate is persistence. Almost anyone who has the endurance can get it in the end. For the particularly unimaginative student an infallible device is to write a dissertation so long that no one will read it. If the members of his committee want to refuse him the degree they will have to have some reasons, and therefore they will have to read his dissertation. If it is short these busy and ambitious men might actually read it, discover that it is no good, and refuse him the degree. If it is long they can refuse to read it, award him the degreee, and not have to explain anything to anybody. Thus the person who knows that he cannot achieve even the mediocrity that the profession demands knows also that his one best hope is that his committee will not read his dissertation. He knows that the longer it is the less likely these busy professors who are frantically pushing their own careers will be to read it and the more likely it is that they will award him his degree even though they know as well as he does that he is less than mediocre. Thus he measures his scholarship by the pound.*

Obviously the person with the doctorate is not *necessarily*

---

*From a letter that I received several years ago from a doctoral candidate who had just turned in a dissertation in history:

"Well, its [sic] in— all 15 pounds and 1750 pages of it! When I asked *** ifhe [sic] thought it would get by he said with some surprise that if the second reader—who is probably ***—wanted to throw it out, he would have to read it carefully and make a good case, and who on earth would want to bother to do that! However, I haven't heard, and probably will nothear [sic] for another month, whether or not the reader has wanted to bother. . . .

"After all my efforts, Chapter 3 on ***, the first one you read, is still unreadable, although I hope it is much clearer. I cannot help but agree that it is badly done and that I am simply not ready to put the material in the perspective of the whole paper. The section on *** in Chapter 4 is also still poor, but the deficiency is less important; there I am not trying to do more than summarize what *** and *** have done. It is my hope that the rest of the paper represents a considerably higher level of writing.

"It is not my intention to try to publish any detailed studies from chapters 3 and 4. By the time I have something ready on the *** side, I hope that I will have worked out a more intelligible description of the ***, but I hope also that *** will have published and that I can rely primarily on ***." This person did get the degree.

a better teacher than the person without one. It is only easier for him to be one if he wants to be. The person with only a master's degree can be as committed to learning and thinking as the person with the doctorate. He is more likely to be, in fact, since it is less likely that his mind has been completely ruined. But it takes more courage for a person with only a master's degree to be a good teacher than for a person with a doctorate, since administrators can use the absence of the doctorate as a threat to keep the teacher in line. The person with the doctorate can sometimes teach, while the person without the doctorate can almost never teach. In continuing to hire people with doctorates administrators have got some good teachers in spite of themselves, while if they hired only people with masters' degrees they would get people who would almost never dare to be.

There are two primary reasons why administrators continue to hire people with doctorates. First, the doctorate has been a traditional requirement for teaching in college, and the administrators thoughtlessly continue that tradition. No one has ever accused academic administrators of having any imagination. Second, as colleges expanded more rapidly than the number of people with doctorates during the 1960s the proportion of doctorates in a college became a matter of prestige.

Not only is the doctorate dangerous but it is no longer necessary. The superior ability to indoctrinate that the doctorate represents is no longer worth the risk of hiring people who dare to teach. The increased development of non-academic instruments of indoctrination makes academic indoctrination decreasingly important, and by learning to use the new machines in academia people without doctorates can become as expert at indoctrinating as those with doctorates. Thus the only remaining benefit of having a high proportion of doctorates in a college is the prestige that results from the numbers. But if administrators could guarantee themselves that no learning would occur in their school the satisfaction that they would derive from that condition would more than balance the lost prestige of having few doctorates.

The best thing that academic administrators could do in the interest of their propertied-class bosses, therefore, is to hire only people without doctorates while they continue to emphasize the value of the doctorate. The only risk that they would run in doing this is that the mind of the person without the doctorate is not likely to have been as completely ruined as the mind of the person with the doctorate and he is therefore likely to have retained some enthusiasm for learning and teaching. But that need not be a serious risk. If the administrators keep him so busy conducting classes that he has no time to learn anything his enthusiasm for learning will soon be destroyed. Beyond that, by continuing to emphasize the value of the doctorate the administrators could keep the enthusiasm of these teachers in check by impressing their insecurity on them.[5]

Even now the possession of the doctorate is only officially the highest priority among administrators. The highest actual priority is dullness. Faced with a choice between a dull person without a doctorate and a vigorous person with one, the administrators choose the dull one. They assume that he will be a bad teacher, but they hope that he will be a good indoctrinator. Yet they have not been infallible. They have got some good teachers in spite of themselves. But by carefully sorting people out before hiring them administrators have guaranteed that a high proportion of them are bad teachers but good indoctrinators whether they have doctorates or not.

The threat to eliminate tenure is another device that administrators use to control faculties.[6] In their attack on tenure they deliberately exploit the public's confusion about what tenure actually is. Tenure does not guarantee the incompetent or frivolous professor a lifetime job. Rather it guarantees that once a person has served his probation and his colleagues have found him acceptable he cannot be fired without just cause or financial crisis in his college or university. The financial crisis must be a real and not a contrived one, and if the tenured professor is threatened with termination for his own alleged shortcomings his tenure guarantees him due process, including a hearing with counsel and with the burden of proof on his accusers.

Tenure is inseparably connected with academic freedom. Without tenure there can be no academic freedom since only tenure protects the outspoken teacher from the reprisals of administrators and majorities of faculties who might not like what he says. And academic freedom exists primarily not for teachers but rather for the public as a whole. Freedom of inquiry and freedom to teach are always in the public interest, though the elite do not allow the public to realize this. The public interest is almost inevitably in conflict with the interest of the ruling elite, though the ruling elite identify themselves *as* the public and believe that whatever is in their own interest is also in the interest of the public. Because the elite see faculties doing things that are not in their interest they assume that the faculties are acting against the public interest also, and thus they have become determined to bring teachers directly under their own control. An important step in accomplishing that is to eliminate tenure.

Thus in recent years academic administrators, in the interest of their propertied-class employers, have conducted an intense campaign to blame tenure for declining academic standards. They argue that tenure protects bad teachers and that it makes impossible the flexibility that colleges and universities must have in order to adjust to the changing demands of students. But neither of these arguments is valid. While tenure does sometimes protect the bad teacher it is seldom the bad teacher who needs protecting. Ordinarily he is in no danger of losing his job. Since educating students is not one of the functions of the schooling system the bad teacher, from the standpoint of the people who run the system, can do no harm. In fact he is very useful. Not only does he not interfere with the indoctrination of students but he might even be a good indoctrinator himself. Learning to accept boredom is after all an important part of the indoctrination. By keeping his students bored the bad teacher can also develop in them a contempt for what they think of as learning. The person who needs tenure, who often gets it only by accident, and who would be the first to be fired without it is the occasional good teacher who does excite students and who actually does encourage them to think.

Nor is it necessary to eliminate tenure in order to allow the academic institution to develop flexibility. If the institution is fulfilling its proper function flexibility is not very important and usually is positively evil. Flexibility is, after all, only a device for making the schools more immediately responsive to the demands of the propertied class. There has been too much change already. Since the schooling system should also be an educational system, since colleges and universities should be a part of that educational system, and since the function of an educational system should be to pass on to new generations the learning of the past, there should be no place in colleges and universities for sudden changes in response to temporary fads.[7] The only people who talk about flexibility are either uneducated themselves and therefore have no notion of what education is, are so afraid of state legislatures and boards of trustees that they will do any perverse thing they consider necessary to retain the favor of those they fear, or are administrators who are the natural enemies of education to begin with.

Of course the emphasis on flexibility is only a smokescreen to hide the real motives of administrators and their bosses. Their very emphasis on the preferences of students is hypocritical, since they have never been known to be concerned about students in any other respect. If they had anything to gain from advocating less flexibility rather than more they would be talking about the dangers rather than the merits of innovation and change.

The academic administrators are not attacking tenure in order to provide flexibility, but rather they are advocating flexibility in order to destroy tenure. The destruction of tenure would have two great advantages for them. In the first place it would make teachers easier to control. If every teacher knew that his employer could refuse to renew his contract on one year's notice and without any specific reason he would be constantly on notice that he had better behave himself. He would be constantly aware that he must do nothing to upset the administrators. High on the list of things he must not do would be to teach. He would know that both inside and outside the classroom he would have to be on his guard not to do or say anything that might cause his students to think.

In the second place the abolition of tenure would save money. If each teacher taught for only two, three, or five years at any one school he would never acquire a seniority that would provide him a decent salary. He would start out at ten thousand a year, in five years work himself up to ten thousand five hundred, and in the sixth year start over someplace else at ten thousand again. Administrators, already earning their salaries only if their appropriate function is to operate their institutions to the satisfaction of their propertied-class bosses and positively harmful if colleges are supposed actually to educate, would have all the more money for themselves.

Another device by which administrators control teachers and guarantee the maintenance of a steady mediocrity is their emphasis on extensive publishing. This emphasis guarantees the mediocrity of both teaching and writing. It guarantees the mediocrity of teaching in the first place because if the teacher's primary concern is research and publication he will not have time to learn the things that will make him a dangerous teacher. He will rely on textbooks or other obvious but safe sources. His reading will be confined to his own narrow field. With the great emphasis on publication so much is published within that narrow field that he will not have time to read all of it, much less to read anything outside that field. He will not be likely to learn anything very important. He will accept the intellectual inbreeding that results when, like other scholars in his field, he reads only other scholars in his field.[8]

Second, if after class every day the teacher has to rush back to his writing he will not have time to talk to students, and therefore he will not be likely to say anything that will stir them up. If by some unforeseeable accident he does stir them up he will not have time to pursue their interests with them, and therefore their enthusiasm will die before it becomes dangerous. They will continue to be susceptible to indoctrination.

The emphasis on extensive publication guarantees the mediocrity of publications because if a person must publish rapidly he is able to say only what is already acceptable.[9] If he repeats the myths that people already accept he needs no proof. The statement is itself the proof.[10] If on the other hand he wants to challenge the conventional wisdom he must take time both to discover extensive evidence and to put the evidence in a convincing form. The unimaginative writer therefore can publish much more than the person who tries to think for himself. It takes a long time to prove something that people do not want to believe. Thus the emphasis on extensive publication guarantees that the scholar will neither think seriously enough to develop unacceptable notions nor take time to pursue an unusual idea if by some miracle one should occur to him. The emphasis on extensive publication guarantees the constant production of acceptable propaganda.[11]

In this guaranteeing of scholarly mediocrity and intellectual conformity the scholar's graduate advisor plays an important role long after the novice leaves graduate school. The advisor's first job is to guarantee that in his dissertation the student says nothing that is not acceptable to the rest of the scholarly fraternity. In the doctoral candidate's oral examination his advisor supports him against the irrelevant and ill-natured questions of those on the committee who want to embarrass the candidate and, through him, the advisor. The candidate feels an appreciation and a loyalty to him. The advisor then helps the student find a job, and the new professor's loyalty to his benefactor helps to guarantee that he will say and do nothing that will jeopardize that job and embarrass the person who helped him get it. Then the advisor keeps in touch with his former student. He reads the young scholar's manuscripts and advises him about what he can say and how he can say it. Occasionally he finds it necessary to lecture him gently, then more sternly if the gentleness does no good. Once the student learns to say only the proper things and to say them only in the most proper fashion his advisor helps him to get his articles and books published and for the books helps to find reviewers who will have nice things to say about them. He flatters the young scholar by asking him for information and interpretation and by encouraging his older colleagues to do the same thing. He helps to get his protegé on programs at meetings and conventions. He does, in short, everything he can to push his student's career so long as the student is safe.

Since the advisor does all of this not for the sake of the student but rather to increase his own prestige by having students who advance in the profession it is equally necessary for him to guarantee that no one ever hears from the occasional maverick who says things that established scholars might not like.[12]

The emphasis on extensive publication not only guarantees the mediocrity of teaching and publication but also guarantees that the administrators' control over the college will continue with no threat of effective interference from the faculty. If teachers have to spend their time on research they will not have time to take seriously the work of the multifarious committees through which they are supposed to help run the institution.[13] Thus even if an occasional member of a faculty should like to see his college become an institution of learning he will not have time to make an issue of it. The administrators will be left free to run the school as they please in pursuit of their anti-intellectual aims.[14]

Administrators from time to time develop or adopt other devices that help them to control faculties and to guarantee the maintenance of a consistent mediocrity. An increasingly widespread device is the emphasis on what are called relevant courses. Relevance, of course, is faddish, and fads change. Students are fickle. When a fad expires its relevance fades, and a course that is relevant one year is irrelevant the next. Thus the teacher who wants always to teach relevant courses must constantly teach new ones. He no sooner gets one relevant course organized than he has to start thinking up the next one.

The teacher's constant search for new courses and his regularly plunging into areas only vaguely familiar to him has at least five advantages for administrators and their employers. First, it has divided faculty. It has increased competition among members of departments and sometimes even among members of separate departments to teach courses that they think will draw large numbers of students. Usually only one teacher can teach each course.

That creates resentment and hard feeling in those who lose out in the competition.

Second, the competition to teach the new and relevant courses has increased team-teaching and therefore has speeded the deterioration of teaching. When two or more people want to teach the same course team-teaching solves the problem of competition and therefore alleviates the resentments that otherwise would develop. The assumption is that the teachers will pool their expertise and therefore develop a better course than if only one of them taught it, but since no one is competent to teach the new course the unstated assumption is that pooling the incompetence will somehow transmogrify it into competence.

A very common but not inevitable consequence of team-teaching is that the course has no real point or direction. Like other committees, team-teachers must reach a consensus. Therefore the team-taught course is often only a belaboring of the platitudes on which the teachers can agree. Often in team-taught courses very little learning occurs.* The team-taught course, therefore, seldom presents any threat to the status quo.

The third advantage that the constant invention and discarding of new courses has for administrators is that it keeps teachers insecure. If a teacher teaches a course only once or twice before he is forced to drop it and prepare a new one he never does become competent in it. Not only has he not learned much in graduate school, but he will never learn much while he is teaching, either. He will never be able to make any of his courses into good ones, and he knows it. Not only does he feel inadequate, but he has no hope of ever feeling adequate. He sees no chance of ever thoroughly mastering any field. He sees himself spending the rest of his professional life constantly preparing new courses the value of which he is not convinced himself because he expects never to have the time to make them valuable. He sees himself teaching each relevant course only once or twice and then going on to something else that has temporarily caught the students' fancy. His self-confidence erodes and then disappears. He feels permanently incompetent. He becomes increasingly amenable to the demands of administrators both because his self-esteem steadily declines and because he knows that if he never will be able to do

---

*As in the case of any other generalization, this is something that is not inevitably but rather generally true. Two people who are knowledgeable and congenial no doubt can with experience develop a good course together.

his job the way he knows he should do it he needs all of the friends in positions of power he can get.

Fourth, the constant developing of new courses keeps teachers so busy that they have no time to interfere with the administrators' running the college the way they please even if the teachers do retain enough self-confidence to dare to challenge them. Like the emphasis on publishing, the insistence on the constant plunging into new courses helps administrators to keep the faculty out of their hair.

The fifth result of the emphasis on relevance is the decreased popularity of those courses that are most dangerous to the status quo and the increased popularity of those that support it. History and literature are among the subjects that have suffered the greatest decline. This is no accident. They are among the courses that do not have an immediate appeal to people who do not already know something. Their relevance is not immediately apparent. They require students to get into their heads something to which they can relate other things they learn. The impatience and laziness of students make these courses unappealing.

But the substitution of relevant courses for history and literature is advantageous to administrators and the propertied class whose interests they represent. History and literature are the two subjects that are most dangerous to the status quo. They are the two fields that acquaint students with alternative ways of living, and the propertied class does not want that. People who are aware of alternative ways of living might become less good consumers, and they might even begin to question the very bases of society. They might even begin to question the need for a propertied class. [15]

Just as welcome to administrators and their bosses as the decline of history and literature is the increased popularity of courses that either do not threaten the status quo or else positively reinforce it. Anthropology, sociology, and psychology have become especially popular. Anthropology does reveal alternative ways of living, but they are so remote and primitive that they do not endanger anyone. Sociology is the study of society as it is and does not furnish any comparisons that might cause students to question their own society. The object is to get students to *understand* their society, and with the society as with the wandering spouse he who understands cannot condemn. Psychology is the study of people as they are and reinforces the status quo even more than sociology does: anyone who does not fit the norm is a deviant. There is even a special course for him.

The great increase in very slight and intellectually undemanding relevant courses is possible because the rulers of society do not care what goes on in the classroom as long as no one is learning anything. As long as students are quiescent, as long as faculties are doing a proper job of indoctrinating them, the propertied class and its functionaries will allow the colleges to do literally anything they please. It is only when the colleges appear to be failing in their responsibility of keeping students ignorant and quiescent—as during the protests of the war in Vietnam—that the rulers of society direct their lackeys to investigate what is going on in them and to make appropriate threats against them.[16]

The colleges are allowed to do whatever they please to satisfy students because the propertied class recognizes three very important truths. First, it knows that contented students provide no danger to the status quo and therefore to its position, while frustrated students might analyze not only the courses they do not like but also the whole society. Once a person starts to think there is always the danger that there will be no stopping him. Second, the propertied class knows that any course can be used as a vehicle for indoctrinating students and dulling minds. The very fact that people study the literature of sport means that they are accepting the frivolous as important, that they lack the capacity seriously to scrutinize anything, and that they are doing nothing to develop that ability. Third, the propertied class knows that even if there is an occasional course in which no positive indoctrination goes on it provides no real threat as long as no positive learning goes on in it either. There are plenty of other vehicles of indoctrination so long as the student never learns to analyze them. There are plenty of other vehicles of indoctrination even to neutralize the course in which only a *little* learning occurs. These vehicles include such things as other courses, television programs such as *Mission Impossible* and *Perry Mason*, newspapers and magazines, and commentaries on television news programs.

In the long run teachers who have submitted to the demands for relevance have done themselves more harm than good. While their object was to protect their jobs, they have helped to make themselves irrelevant. Once they accept the administrators' notion that it does not much matter what goes on in the college as long as no one learns anything it is only a short step to the notion that college is not necessary at all. If what the students get in college is only what they can get equally well outside the college the college is no longer necessary. It is only as long as teachers can convince the public that they are doing something that no one else can do and that what they do is important that the public will continue to support them. By acquiescing in the demand that they do in the classroom only what can be done just as well or better outside the classroom the teachers themselves are to a great extent responsible for the increasingly widespread belief that society no longer has any need for them.[17]

Another device that administrators have adopted to help them control the faculty is the course-teacher evaluation. Unless the teacher who knows that his students will formally evaluate him has a great deal of self-confidence he will do whatever he needs to do to get a good evaluation. He will grade high and thus keep his students quiescent and thoughtless. He will make his assignments easy so that his students will not be faced with the unhappy necessity of studying. He will flatter students in their hang-outs. The one thing that he will not do is try to teach better. That would require some additional effort on the part of the students, also, and that might make them less friendly and therefore less generous in their evaluation. It might not, either, but the teacher dare not take the chance.[18]

Similarly administrators have encouraged the seating of students on faculty committees to help control teachers and decrease their influence. The presence of students causes teachers to discuss issues less openly than they otherwise would. They say things that they know will appeal to students and administrators because they know that the students will repeat what they hear. They play to the galleries. Thus the presence of students on faculty committees does more than simply give students a voice there. It allows the administrators to control those committees. And that is what the administrators have in mind.[19]

Faced with the knowledge that anything he says might be held against him, the increasing determination of administrators to manipulate him, the increasing arrogance of students, the constant reminder of his own inadequacy, and the disillusionment of the discovery and the deepening perception that most of the people with whom he will be associating for the rest of his professional life are not much if at all interested in knowledge and learning, the teacher has several alternatives.

He can retreat more and more into his own private world and

treat teaching only as a way of earning a living. If he has a particularly strong ego he can convince himself that no teacher could be expected to be competent under the conditions that now exist.* When he cannot answer a question that comes up in class he can admit that he does not know the answer. Yet even for the self-confident teacher saying "I don't know" all the time can get embarrassing. So he can try to fake his way through his classes. Many teachers are quite successful at faking because the students are so ignorant that they will believe anything that anyone says with confidence. If a student does occasionally read enough to catch the teacher's mistakes the teacher can always claim that the difference is only one of interpretation.

Another defense of the teacher is to feign absent-mindedness. When an embarrassing question comes up he can pretend to know but to have momentarily forgotten the answer. To make this tactic succeed, however, the teacher must also pretend to be absent-minded outside the classroom. He cannot be clear-headed sometimes and absent-minded others. If he carries the trick off skillfully he will acquire a reputation of a brilliant but somewhat eccentric bumbler. Students will affectionately protect him. While one might not relish being known as a bumbler, most people would prefer that to being considered an ignoramus.

Some professors adopt the compromise of becoming the campus characters. Since saying what one thinks and expecting people to listen can be dangerous, professors protect themselves by making certain that no one will ever pay any attention to them. They become actors who get the reputation of being likely to say or do almost anything. They are entertaining, and they are not very dangerous. But there is a limit to the number of characters a campus can absorb, and most professors do not have the sort of personality that enables them to become characters anyway.

A recent refinement of the campus character is the radical clown.[20] The radical clown has an almost uncanny ability to recognize the newest fad in its earliest stages, and he jumps aboard the bandwagon even before it becomes a bandwagon. He has an equally mysterious ability to recognize when a fad is about to fade, and he is always one of the first to jump off the bandwagon, often even before it begins to lose momentum. He considers

---

*In the summer of 1975 a college professor told me that in his view one of the conditions of his employment is that he will not try to teach anybody anything.

himself a leader, though he is always a follower. He always speaks at the top of his voice, though he seldom says the same thing twice. He prides himself on his tough attitude toward administrators, though actually he is terrified of them. While one minute he might be stirring up students, the next minute he might be talking to a dean or a vice-president about how to keep the students calm. Because he is amusing and appears to be friendly, he is often among the most popular teachers.

The radical clown is no more dangerous than the campus character, though he is even more visible. He gets his satisfaction from being the center of attention and by convincing himself that he is in the forefront of every change. But administrators know that he has neither the courage nor the persistence to interfere with their doing as they please. They look upon his buffoonery as a sort of therapy for himself and as a distraction for students.

Most professors simply give in. They censor what they say in order to make it acceptable to those who run the college. They do not say what they think, but others do appear to take them seriously. The result is a sort of perverted success: people appear to take seriously what the teacher himself does not believe.*

---

*In recent years those who control the schools have made classic use of the carrot and the stick in manipulating teachers and others connected with the schools. While they have increased their threats against faculties they have also increased the number of awards for *selected* faculty. These awards include distinguished teaching professorships and distinguished research professorships, both with very high salaries, and smaller monetary awards for excellence in teaching. Now awards for excellence in administration and excellence in librarianship are apparently developing as well. These awards are not designed to improve teaching or professionalism or even to honor excellence but rather are designed to encourage teachers to behave themselves.

The first requirement for the person who would like to receive one of these awards is that he be respectable—that is, that he strive wholeheartedly to achieve the mediocrity of those who do the recommending and selecting. Above all he must not anger anyone by having strong views of his own or by disagreeing vigorously with anyone who might one day review his recommendation for an award. These various awards, therefore, encourage—as they are supposed to encourage—drift.

In order to impress the broadest possible variety of faculty, however, it is necessary that occasionally the people in control of this largess reward the serious teacher or good scholar or real professional. This does not, however, encourage others to aspire to be good teachers or scholars. Rather it encourages the person who is already a good teacher or scholar to believe that if he is only a bit more careful in the future than he has been in the past he too

None of these alternatives is very satisfactory, and among the results of the pressures on professors are alcoholism, ulcers, and colitis. These diseases make teachers all the more vulnerable and therefore all the easier to control. The teacher who has one of them must be tractable not only for his emotional well-being but even for his continued physical existence. Everyone knows that it is alcohol that fuels academia and Lomotil that lubricates it. Alcoholics are especially vulnerable, since they have the least control over their disease. But a teacher with any of these diseases has no choice but to behave himself.

So much for academic freedom. Academic freedom is the teacher's right to say anything he wants to say and to assign any readings he chooses as long as no one pays any attention to what is unacceptable to the propertied class. As long as no one pays any attention to the critical teacher it is in fact useful to have some of them on the faculty. Even radicals are useful. They provide the illusion that people are free to teach as they choose, that academics are indeed interested only in the vigorous pursuit of truth, and that the acceptable wisdom must be the truth, since in this disinterested pursuit more people have chosen it than have arrived at unacceptable views. In ordinary times the protectors of the conventional wisdom take care of the radical to whom students actually listen, as well as the teacher who is *too* radical whether anyone listens to him or not, in the normal course of events.[21] They simply refuse to renew his contract before he acquires tenure. He is an unproductive scholar, a bad teacher, intellectually undisciplined, or simply unsound.[22] In any case he is eliminated.[23] But at a time of extreme crisis, when students might appear to be listening to the unacceptable notions of teachers with tenure as well as of those without, the rulers of society have to take more extreme action. Such a crisis was the protests against the war in Vietnam. The propertied interests responded with concerted intimidation. They retrenched, and they threatened tenure and sabbaticals. They raised tuition. And the intimidation worked.

---

might receive one of these awards. A step at a time, he is supposed to submit.

Occasionally even a radical clown receives one of these awards. That is supposed to prove how tolerant and broad-minded the people who control the awards are and to convince everyone that intellectual freedom actually does exist in the school. And it might have the additional merit of buying off the recipient.

The colleges and universities quieted down. Faculties became timid again.[24] *

One of the conditions that helps to justify the elimination of the really thoughtful person from academia is that in what are called the social studies and the humanities no one has discovered a way to distinguish a genius from a dope. Their external appearance is identical. Both say outrageous things. When conventional academicians hear someone say something outrageous they have no way of determining whether he is a genius speaking from superior insight or a dope speaking from more than ordinary ignorance. In either case they are uncomfortable with what they do not understand, and so they unite to get rid of the speaker. He is fired because he is unsound. The dopes are eliminated, and so are the geniuses. That is as it should be: they are equally dangerous.[25]

---

*It also seems quite likely that to those who control American schools the development of unions among teachers is a crisis that they have to meet with intimidation in order to convince teachers that they were better off without unions. The hard line that the negotiators for the operators often take might be partly designed to cause teachers to believe that their unions are not only ineffective but also positively harmful and that they would be better off trusting to the good will of their employers, as they formerly did. And to some extent the agents of the operators have succeeded. One does sometimes hear a teacher say that the unions have done more harm than good. This device, of course, is a classic tactic that employers have used against unions during the whole history of American labor.

Chapter 10

CHANGE

*A*lmost all of the people who write about American schools assume that they exist to educate and that their not educating represents a failure. They assume that if those who run the schools only knew what is wrong with them they would make appropriate changes.[1]

But the belief that the people who control the schools actually want them to educate anyone represents a profound naivety about why they exist in the first place. The schools are what they are because that is what they are supposed to be. They are doing what they are supposed to do. They exist to reinforce the prevailing economic, social, and political structure.[2] To do that they must destroy people's ability to think as well as their confidence in their own minds. If by some chance a teacher or a department does appear to be a danger to the status quo the teacher can be fired or the department wiped out.[3]

The people who believe that schools could be "an agent for major change" in society[4] are merely whistling in the wind. The people to whom they look for change are the very people who are responsible for the character of the schools as they exist right now.[5]

Of course the people who control the schools do not admit that they want a schooling system that destroys minds and creates insecurities. They cannot be that blatant. Instead they talk about developing good citizens and then define good citizenship in such

131

a way that only a robot can be a good citizen. They continue to talk about quality education and equal opportunity. They continue to blame teachers for not educating in order to hide their own responsibility for the deadening of young minds and to keep the teachers insecure. But when they put thirty-five or forty students in a classroom with one teacher they know that the teacher cannot do much teaching. When they give that teacher five classes a day plus a home-room, periodic noon-duty in the cafeteria, plays to direct or a yearbook to sponsor, dances to chaperon, and cheerleaders to coach, they know that he cannot spend much time preparing his classes. And when they pay him such a low salary that he has to have a second job in order to maintain even a minimum standard of living, when his low salary forces him to make his own repairs on his house and maybe even build it himself, they know that he is going to have neither the time nor the energy to keep up in his field, much less to learn things outside his field that would help him understand his place in society, in history, and in the universe and thus enable him to help his students understand theirs also. When they make it clear that his highest ambition should be to get along they know that he is not going to challenge any of the current wisdom but that he will believe what he is supposed to believe and will tell his students what to believe also, just as he is supposed to do.

Since the schools are performing almost perfectly the functions that they are designed to perform there is little chance that they will change in any significant way. What appears to be change will be constant, but it will not mean anything. There will be new courses, new techniques, and new machines, but they will all be designed to enable the schools to do exactly what they do already but in a more efficient, thorough, economical, and peaceful fashion. Passive students perched before glaring machines in dark rooms will create the illusion of learning.

Yet it is important to consider what the schools could be. It is important to continue to try to make them places where minds are expanded rather than destroyed.

Concern for the student has to start even before he is conceived. Society must make sure that the mother and the child get the sort of food and care that will enable him to start out with a fair chance of being able to learn. It must work out ways of protecting the child from the time he is born until he starts to school. A good place to begin would be to guarantee everyone a job at a decent wage, provide free day-care centers for the children of working mothers, provide free medical care for everyone, provide parents with readily available and free information on diet, child-care, birth control, and home-making, and have trained people readily available to give parents actual instruction without charge.

Once the child starts school teachers and administrators must make sure that he is better off in school than he would be outside it. The first thing the schools must begin to do is to provide the student with the fundamental ability necessary for learning and thinking. That fundamental ability is the ability to use language, the ability to read and write. To do this educationists must first of all re-evaluate the cute gimmicks that the mindless technicians have imposed on them. They must have many more teachers and fewer machines in elementary and secondary schools, and rather than continue to impose machines on teachers they must allow teachers to decide whether and when they want to use the machines.

There are not too many teachers today. Rather there are not enough. There are thousands of devoted but frustrated teachers who know that they are not doing their jobs as they could do them if the emphasis were on education rather than on cost accounting. In elementary schools one teacher for every ten students would not be too many. The teacher could then have some hope of teaching students to read, write, and cipher. For slower students there must be an increased number of special classes with even fewer students in each.

Second, schools must begin to provide students with information. Educationists must rid themselves of the assumption that the school is not the student's primary source of information and that therefore the school's responsibility is not to provide the student with information but rather to teach him to think about the information he gets someplace else. The truth is that while the school is not the student's primary source of information it is virtually his *only* source of information that matters. This is true not because other sources of information do not exist but rather because young people are neither aware of nor interested in those sources. The student does not read newspapers or magazines or books; he does not attend lectures; he does not associate with knowledgeable adults; he does not listen to or watch those few radio programs and television shows from which he might learn something worth knowing. Since the school has given up the job of teaching him how his society works he learns nothing about it at all.

If schools want to turn out informed students they have to start informing them. They must replace the foolishness that goes on in most classrooms with something worthwhile. They must begin to teach students the basic facts about their society so that they will have at least some notion of their surroundings and their place in history. Students must find out such things as how the electoral college works and why it exists, what a stock is and why companies sell stocks, and what laissez faire is and why it has been a popular phrase in American history. The schools must try to get students interested in current events in order that they will know what is happening to their lives. If they want their graduates to know something about their place in society and in the universe they have to start teaching them some science, history, literature, and philosophy. They must get students to begin to think about basic issues of morality and ethics.

The age of silly stories is past. There is no reason why people even in kindergarten cannot enjoy good literature. Surely the fairy tales of Andersen and Grimm are preferable to the fairy tales about George Washington and the cherry tree and Abraham Lincoln's honesty. A little later young people could handle Washington Irving, Willa Cather, Hamlin Garland, and stories from Shakespeare. By the sixth grade they should be reading Shakespeare's plays.

There is plenty of outstanding literature that children could be reading by the time they are twelve years old. Schools discourage them from reading it because great literature deals with human conflicts, and the object of the schools has been to protect young people from those conflicts rather than to acquaint them with them. The object of the schools has been to hide reality from young people by creating the impression that no conflicts exist. They create the impression that everything is just okay. When the students get older either they go through great mental and emotional turmoil when they discover that reality bears no resemblance to what the schools have taught them, or else they never do develop the ability to face reality and therefore are easy prey for evangelistic preachers and demagogic politicians who only lead them further into the mental morass from which they never will have the intellectual resources to enable them to escape.

In addition to literature, students from their earliest years should be learning history rather than myths. They should be saturated with science, mathematics, geography, and economics. From their earliest years in school they should be learning foreign languages. And all the while they should be pushed to the limit of their capacity to work. If their work were clearly important, students would work as hard as athletes play.[6]

As part of becoming acquainted with the past students should be taught the culture of the past. In every school there should be weekly professional or professional-quality performances of plays and serious music. There should be a record player or tape recorder playing serious music for some time every day. Serious music should include not only what is ordinarily called classical music but also the best folk music, country-western, jazz, and musical shows. There should be a large library of art books in color for students to browse through as they please without worrying about soiling them. The paintings could lead naturally into the teaching of mythology and history.

The objection to this learning is that young people are unable to cope with real history, literature, art, science, and mathematics. But we have consistently underestimated the interests and abilities of the very young. The six-year-old is curious about everything. If that curiosity were encouraged and guided rather than discouraged and finally destroyed these young people could learn more before they reach their teens than they do now by the time they finish college. If their curiosity were encouraged rather than destroyed some of them would remain curious all of their lives, and the result would be a gradual but general raising of the political and social sophistication of the entire population. That would make life difficult for the politicians and their bosses, and that would be all to the good.

Junior high schools should be eliminated. There should be six years of elementary school and four years of high school. All students in high school should get exactly the same courses: four years of English, two years of European history and two years of American history, three years of math and three years of science, one year of world geography and one year of American geography, and four years of foreign literature in the original language. That is five courses a year for four years.

Since the function of an educational system is to pass on to each new generation the learning of the past, nothing could be more stupid than allowing students to decide what courses they will take in high school. Nothing could be more stupid than to expect teen-agers to have the maturity and the knowledge to enable them to decide what is good for them to know. Electives make sense only when we are willing to adopt the attitude that not everyone is academically inclined, that the high school must be all things to all people, and that it does not much matter what students learn or, indeed, whether they learn anything at all.[7]

If young people are going to learn anything they must spend their time learning rather than in frivolity. Therefore all interscholastic athletics and other interscholastic competition should be eliminated. Interscholastic competition accomplishes no legitimate function that intramural competition cannot accomplish better and at a much lower cost. By taking money that could be used better for other purposes and by distracting students from more important things interscholastic competition, especially in athletics, is positively destructive. Especially at a time when schools are hard pressed for money and when the American public is becoming increasingly ignorant interscholastic athletics is a frivolity that we can no longer afford.

Other frivolities can be eliminated. The yearbook, the student newspaper, and student government are among the more obvious wastes. Extra-curricular activities should consist of participation in intramural athletics and the arts.

With the elimination of the time-consuming frivolities the students would have more time to read and write. Homework should be heavy and obviously worthwhile. With smaller classes— say four classes a day with ten students each rather than five classes a day with thirty students each—high-school teachers would have time to assign more papers. English teachers and history teachers could coordinate their assignments so that each student could write an essay for each class every second week. By the time he got to college he would be able to read and write his native language.

Many of the people who object to a rigid academic program for all students in high school argue that not all students are academically inclined and that there has to be something for the non-academic ones, too. But while we do know that not all high-school students are academically inclined we do not know how many would be if they had an opportunity to learn rather than only to be bored during their first years in school. The people who run the schools argue that it is democratic to have something for everyone, but nothing could be less democratic than condemning a child at the age of six to the life of a mindless robot existing only to be useful to the owners of the property of the country. These people who claim to be democratic are actually incorrigibly elitist. What they are saying is that most people can never be interested in or understand science, mathematics, art, history, and literature, but what they mean is that they do not *want* most people to be interested in or to understand those things. Occasionally they are completely honest about it. In 1945, a group of American educationists reported their conclusion that high schools should prepare twenty percent of the young people for college, that vocational schools should prepare another twenty percent for skilled occupations, and that communities should provide the remaining sixty percent with "life-adjustment training." Apparently the life-adjustment training would prepare that sixty percent for nothing except poverty, but according to these educationists the young people need it and are entitled to it as American citizens.[8]

What these people are saying is that sixty percent of the population not only cannot use their minds but cannot even aspire to skilled occupations. They are saying that starting at the age of twelve or thirteen sixty percent of the population must be manipulated by "life-adjustment training" to keep them satisfied with their low condition. They are condemning a large proportion of that sixty percent of the population to the status of unskilled laborers and the idle poor. And these are the very people who talk constantly about developing a democratic educational system.

The real democrat thinks differently. The real democrat believes that all or almost all people not only can understand but also can enjoy history, literature, art, science, and mathematics.[9] The real democrat believes that Shakespeare does have something to say to everyone who is not positively retarded. He believes that almost everyone *can* understand what goes on in the economy at least as well as presidential advisors, who ordinarily are both ignorant and dishonest. The real democrat believes that everyone can understand and can be interested in the history of his own country and can live a more satisfying life as a result. The real democrat believes that everyone can be awed and fascinated by the structure of the universe on the one hand and of a flower on the other. The real democrat believes that at the very least everyone must be given a chance to find out whether he can understand and enjoy these things. What this means above all is equality of opportunity. It means that until we can eliminate the ghetto the child from the ghetto must have access to schools and teachers as good as those available to the child in the suburbs. And that means in turn that we must find a new method of financing schools. Financing schools through property taxes is not only inadequate but also is deliberately designed to maintain and expand the inequality of opportunity that already exists.[10]

Since in any legitimate educational system many of the classes that currently occupy the student's time would be eliminated other arrangements would have to made for teaching those things. Free instruction in driving should be readily available not just to young people but to all citizens. All people should have access to free instruction in home economics and in those skills—plumbing, electrical installation, carpentry, mechanics—that are not only handy to know but the knowledge of which also makes life more enjoyable for many. Vocational schools should be readily available and free to anyone who wants to take advantage of them.

Ordinarily the student should graduate from high school at the age of sixteen. He should receive his high-school diploma only after passing a comprehensive examination. No one who fails the exam should be allowed to try again later but should be given a certificate of attendance and have facilities for adult education readily available to him. Having the failures continue in high school would only result in its engaging in remedial work and therefore in the destruction of its academic standards.

After high school every young person should have to work for two years before going on to college. No one can get an adequate understanding of either history or society without having experienced the problems of working for a living and associating with adults.[11] For two years the young person, still living at home, could work for business or government or anyone else who would hire him. To employ those young people who could find jobs no place else the government could re-establish programs such as the Civilian Conservation Corps and the Works Progress Administration. Since turning sixteen-year-olds loose on the economy would increase the available labor supply it could be combined with a lowering of the retirement age to decrease the competition for jobs. With life expectancy for men at 67.4 years and for women at 75.2 years[12] it is inhumane to expect men to work until they are sixty-five. Surely a person deserves to expect more than two and a half years of leisure after working hard all of his life. Given the technological development and the wealth of the United States, with full use of productive capacity and with an appropriate distribution of wealth retirement at fifty-five should be reasonable.

A second way of making room for young people on the labor market is to shorten the work week. A week of thirty hours for everyone should be reasonable. As the economy matures hours could be shortened further. If the schooling system were an educational system it would provide people with the intellectual resources that would enable them to enjoy the additional leisure time.

No one can argue that the country cannot afford all of this. If the economic system cannot provide a decent life for everyone it becomes all the more important to redistribute what wealth does exist in order that the excessive consumption of some does not deprive others of educational opportunity and a few years of worry-free leisure.[13]

At the age of eighteen several alternatives should be open for the young person. First, he could take a permanent job. Second, he could go one or two years to a vocational school in order to learn a skill. Third, he could go to college. Fourth, he could just bum around for a while. But before any of these alternatives becomes a real one we have to increase the respect we have for manual labor. No one should go to college just because it is the thing to do, but it will remain the thing to do until the young person can believe that he can lead a respectable life without going to college. For many of the people who consider college an alternative today it is really no alternative at all. Because they have been taught to consider themselves failures if they do not go to college they really have no choice in the matter. So they go to college, are not very good at academic pursuits, and hate it. They become teachers and pass their hatred for learning on to their students for forty-three years.

Colleges should admit only those students who, after having had plenty of opportunity under the reformed elementary and secondary educational system, have demonstrated an aptitude for and an interest in the academic. No special programs for the educationally deprived would be necessary. There would be no educationally deprived. For the first three years the student should study the same subjects he studied in high school, but on a more sophisticated level. Since he would already have learned to read and write there would be no necessity for the vulgarity of English composition for freshmen. Nothing could be more grotesque than the condition that now exists. After the high-school graduate has been exposed for twelve or thirteen years to the American schooling system the first thing the college has to do is try to teach him to write his own language. Of course it is impossible: by the time he graduates from high school he has learned to hate his language and has come to believe that the ability to say and write what he means is a luxury contemptible in the man of action and the woman of charm.[14]

The second great vulgarity, the survey course in history, could also be eliminated. Since students would already have learned some history in the elementary and secondary schools they could study shorter periods in depth. Similarly in science and mathematics the courses could be taught in depth rather than on the superficial level now required in order to get anyone to understand anything at all. Since students would be able to read when they enter college, the third and fourth great vulgarities, the lecture system and the textbook, could be eliminated. Students could read widely and then discuss what they read. Classes could meet once a week rather than three times: meeting three times a week is only a device for making it easier for students to stand the boredom of the lectures by spreading them out over the whole week anyway. In mathematics and the sciences all or almost all of the courses could be laboratory courses.

In the general education of the first three years of college every student should take exactly the same courses. He should get three years of history, three years of literature, two years of foreign literature in the original language, a year of the history of art, a year and a half of mathematics, a year and a half of science, a year of philosophy, and a semester each of anthropology, sociology, political theory, and economics. During his freshman year every student should have one additional course: a two-semester course in the history of education, beginning with the Greeks but not limited to the so-called Western World. This course should concentrate on educational practices rather than on educational theories.

As in the high school, there should be no place for electives during the student's first three years in college. The college student is no more able than the high-school student to determine what he should know.[15] At a time of financial crisis in colleges the elimination of electives during the student's first three years would also have the practical advantage of allowing colleges to plan their courses and make better use of their faculties. The number of students taking specific courses would not fluctuate from year to year, and colleges could then achieve the "steady-state staffing" that administrators pretend to want but probably do not.[16]

In his fourth year the student should concentrate on his major. During this year he might take a maximum of four electives out of his ten courses. For prospective teachers all teacher-training programs should be eliminated.[17] * Saturating the student with

---

*Any schools that do want to retain special programs for prospective teachers would do well to investigate the program in secondary social studies at Cortland under the direction of Professors Roger Sipher, Harry Dahlheimer, and Sanford Gutman.

knowledge of his subject would make a much better teacher than courses in educational methods: the teacher has to learn to teach once he finds himself dumped on his own in the classroom anyway.[18]

Students should have no voice in determining the curriculum[19] or in evaluating teachers. Since the proper function of education continues to be to acquaint each new generation with the learning of the past, those people who are already best-educated are the ones who should decide what students should learn and who should evaluate their colleagues. The student's function in the educational system should be to learn. He has no basis for judging *what* he should learn or who should teach him. That should be left to those who are educated themselves.

The willingness of administrators and some teachers to accept formal student evaluations and membership of students on policy committees results from three factors. First, it results from a false view of the relationship between the students and the school. Often one hears that the college exists for the students. Of course it does not. All schools exist for all people.

Neither is it accurate to say that schools exist for society. In two ways that statement creates confusion. First, it implies that the function of the school should be to mold the student to fill a role that those in authority have chosen for him. The function of the school should be, rather, to provide the student with the sort of liberal education that would enable him to find his own place in the world.

Second, saying that the school exists for society creates a false distinction between the student and society. The student is a part of society. The school exists for him and for everyone else, also.

The school should exist for everyone equally. It should exist for the student and the non-student alike. What the student learns in college is just as important to the person who does not go to college as to the student himself. Both should benefit from the experience of the one. The mechanic should benefit from the experience of the college graduate just as the college graduate benefits from the experience of the mechanic. Going to college should result in the student's having a more interesting and intellectually exciting life than he would have had without it, just as the person who wants to be a mechanic should have a more interesting and intellectually exciting life by not going to college. But the primary purpose of going to college should never be the selfish one of enabling the student to lead a more interesting and intellectually exciting life. The primary purpose of his being in school should be to make him into a human being with a broad vision. It should be to enable him to help others to eat better, to live better, and to lead more interesting and intellectually exciting lives themselves. Education should provide the student with alternatives, but it should also help him to help provide alternatives for others.

At present colleges exist for the benefit of the propertied class. Administrators know that. But to keep the students quiescent in their egotism and to make them more receptive to indoctrination administrators continue to insist that schools exist for the students. It makes the students feel good to believe it, and it makes no real difference to the administrators. They continue to run the schools the way their bosses tell them to.

The willingness to accept formal student evaluations and the membership of students on faculty committees results in the second place from the administrators' recognition that it does not really matter what goes on in the classroom as long as the students are peaceful and do not learn anything. Since the primary function of the college is to indoctrinate as many students as possible as thoroughly as possible at the lowest possible unit cost of production, deciding what should go on in the classroom and evaluating what does go on there requires no special knowledge or expertise. Students can do it as well as anyone. They can in fact do it much better than someone who might actually consider knowledge, learning, and thinking important. They can best judge whether what they hear in the classroom and read for a course agrees with their previous indoctrination. That is how they judge whether a teacher knows what he is talking about and whether he assigns legitimate readings. They can best judge whether the course makes them feel optimistic or pessimistic. That is how they judge the depth of a course. They can best judge whether other students would like to take the course. That is how they tell administrators whether the teacher is earning his money. They can best judge what new courses students would like to take and what old courses can be eliminated. That his how they help administrators decide how to service the largest possible number of students with the smallest possible faculty.

The willingness to accept formal student evaluations and the membership of students on faculty committees results in the third place from the desire of administrators to keep the students out of their own hair and to get the assistance of students in harassing the faculty. Occasionally an administrator will admit that he wants students on committees not because of their expertise but because of their lack of it, not because he believes that they are qualified to make judgments but because he knows they are not.[20] Allowing students to harass faculty members and keeping them occupied in such safe activities as administering course-teacher evaluations, sitting on faculty committees, and planning homecomings keeps the students from noticing the waste involved in the plush offices of administrators or the large number of administrators who perform functions that half as many could perform twice as well.

Just as all influence of students on academic organization and policy should be eliminated, so also should the influence of administrators and other non-teaching personnel. Administrators should administer: they have no legitimate role in making academic decisions.[21] They should administer the educational policies that faculties establish.[22] The number of administrators and other non-teaching personnel should also be sharply reduced.[23] Only faculty members should be eligible for those jobs,[24] and no one should spend more than three years in a non-teaching position without going back to teaching for at least three years. That should include college and university presidents.

The reduction of the number of administrators should be accomplished by having them go back to teaching after a year or two of re-education. Probably an appropriate plan would be to require one year of re-education for every year a person has spent in administration. This should not result in the retrenchment of the less senior members of the departments to which the administrators return, since in colleges as well as in elementary, junior high, and high schools there are now too few teachers rather than too many. The reduction in the number of other non-teaching personnel should be accomplished through attrition rather than through firing or lay-off, since once a person has committed up to three years and more to an institution the institution has a moral obligation to him that transcends the necessity of reducing numbers. But still only teachers should vote on academic issues. An academic issue is almost anything that involves the college or university.

All professors should be required to teach. Neither the public through its taxes nor students through their tuition should be expected to support either the sinecure of the research professorship in which the professor does no teaching at all or the prestigious chair in which the professor teaches only a seminar or two each year and spends the rest of his time on his own research. The rulers of society allow these positions to exist to begin with only to provide places for people who have proven their loyalty to the propertied class. The person who gets such a position ordinarily is an older professor who during his long career has never said or written anything to which the elite might object but has been prolific in the production of propaganda. Occasionally he might be a relatively young professor who has already written enough to prove that he is safe and to allow the elite to predict his future usefulness. If he does have to teach an occasional course he is not expected to spend much time on it: his job is to produce propaganda full-time. Neither students nor taxpayers should have to support such positions, though if wealthy people want to endow such sinecures that is up to them. It would be better, though, if they had no connection with public institutions.

No graduate student should be thrown into the classroom on his own. Professors should teach their own courses, and graduate students should receive enough support to enable them to concentrate on their own learning. Surely the freshman deserves better than to be placed in the hands of other students whose own learning has really barely begun.

As in the high school, all of the expensive and time-consuming frivolities should be eliminated. Intramurals should replace intercollegiate athletics;[25] a weekly information sheet should replace the student newspaper; the yearbook should be dropped without a substitute. There should be no such thing as student government. Private social committees could exist to sponsor dances and other activities, but they should have no official status and should receive no financial assistance from the college.

As in the high school, there should be regular professional or at least professional-quality performances of serious music and plays. Guest lecturers chosen by the faculty should appear once a week. The criterion for choosing the guest lecturer should be that he has something to say that students could not hear any other way. Under the present system by which the students choose their guest lecturers the only necessary qualification is notoriety. The students will invite a person to the campus only if they already know what he is going to say. The only requirement that they apply in deciding to invite a person to speak on the campus, therefore, is that there is no reason to invite him.

All credit for living and for courses offered on television should be eliminated. At the same time the number of extension courses, in which the teacher does meet the students face to face at least once a week, should be increased and should be free. The student should not have to be enrolled in any specific course of study in order to take the courses he wants, but he should be required to have the prerequisite courses that would enable him actually to learn something in the extension courses and to keep up with the rest of the class without holding it back. The emphasis should be on learning rather than on getting a degree.

Grading should be much tougher than it is. The same standards should apply to extension courses as to conventional courses. What many students lack is not the ability or the desire to learn but rather the incentive to learn. The question is how to provide the incentive. Initially there is only one incentive that will over-come the students' inertia. That is the presence of grades. If teachers could grade harder they could teach more. Until the student experiences the pleasure of learning his motivation must be external. If teachers could use grades to force students to work harder four things would happen. First, some students would de-cide that the college degree is not worth the work it would require and therefore either would not enter college or else would drop out once they did enter. Second, many who still would enter col-lege would fail out. Third, many would work hard only because of the pressure of grades and would graduate without ever discovering the pleasure of learning even though they would learn more than they do under the present low standards. Fourth, some students who start out working hard only because of the pressure of grades would discover the pleasure of learning and then would work hard because they enjoy it. For them the pressure of grades would disappear because if they worked hard to learn the grades would come naturally. These are the students who are being cheated under the present low academic standards.

While grades should serve the positive function of encouraging students to work and of reflecting the quality of work they do, they are not now serving either of those functions. Grades are so high that no one has to work very hard, and they do not in any way reflect how little students learn. And there is no possibility that individual teachers will begin to grade honestly, since giving high grades for little or no accomplishment is necessary for the professor to get students to take his courses and therefore to pro-vide for his unprofessional security. Even those teachers who grade harder than others do not grade as hard as they should. Their classes are already small, and if they graded as hard as they should they would have no students at all.

Three alternatives exist, though none is likely to be implemented. First, the faculty of each college could decide that each teacher should aim for a certain proportion of each grade each semester: say five percent A's and failures, twenty percent B's and D's, and fifty percent C's. To prevent injustice any teacher could depart slightly from the proportion in any one semester, but over the years he would be expected to hit it pretty close. Since all teachers would be grading approximately alike no teacher would feel the necessity of grading high in order to entice students into his courses. If he did feel the necessity he would not dare do it anyway. For the teacher the change would not be as great as it appears at first glance: all teachers grade pretty much alike now, but very high. Under this system they would still grade pretty much alike, but their grades would reflect approximately the quality of work students are doing. If students get better and work harder the proportion of high grades could increase. In upper-level courses, in which one would expect most of the students to be able to do acceptable work, the percentages could be different from those applied to introductory courses. They could be, say, ten percent A, thirty percent B, and sixty percent C. Having to give a high proportion of C's would encourage the teacher also to give D's and failures to those who deserve them. A great advantage of adopting this policy would be that in order to entice students into their courses teachers would be forced to adopt the revolutionary strategy of teaching more rather than teaching less.

In a profession that adores notoriety this plan would also have the advantage that the first college to adopt it would become famous overnight. Incidentally, of course, it would also become a much better school, but many teachers who would not adopt the system to improve the college would be happy to adopt it for the sake of the notoriety that it would create for them.

The second possibility is that a system something like this might be imposed on the colleges from the outside.

If either of these things were to happen the first reaction of many teachers would be to cry that their academic freedom is being violated. But academic freedom is the freedom to teach. It guarantees the teacher that neither the readings he assigns nor what he says in the classroom will be censored. It has nothing to do with the establishing of purely mechanical administrative procedures such as grading systems. If the system were established, however, academic freedom would include the teacher's right to determine which students get which grades.

However they do it, colleges should establish grading patterns for teachers to follow. Even a pattern of twenty percent A's, sixty percent B's, and twenty percent C's, with no D's or failures, would provide protection for the serious teacher. He could grade according to the pattern without feeling dishonest. No one could have any doubt about what his grades mean. Under the present system the serious teacher is doubly penalized. In the first place, students do not take his courses. In the second place his colleagues argue that if his students get such low grades he must not be teaching very much. They use their own high grading to prove that they are superior teachers. All a bad teacher has to do to become a good one is to raise the grade of each of his students a letter or two.

The third possibility is to eliminate grades altogether and at the end of each semester award each student a satisfactory or an unsatisfactory in each of his courses only for the purpose of determining whether he will stay in school. Any student who receives two or more unsatisfactories in any one semester or who accumulates more than four unsatisfactories during his four years in college would be dismissed without the possibility of readmission. If he cannot do properly what students are supposed to do there is no reason for him to continue to waste everyone's time.

Then after his four years of college but before he receives his degree the student would have to pass an examination administered by an agent from outside the college.[26] The college could not examine its own students, since it would have to pass unqualified students in order to make itself look good. The examination could not be administered by people from another college, since that would result in back-scratching. Those who would do the examining would be tempted to pass everyone, since they would expect reciprocal leniency. Right now professors from one college evaluate the graduate programs of other colleges, and very seldom do they give any of them a bad report. Every evaluator knows that the graduate program of his department will be evaluated too, and he does not want to risk upsetting anyone who might end up in a position to seek revenge. So everyone admires everyone else.

The problem with subjecting every student to an examination by a neutral party before he receives his degree is that the examination would be very difficult to administer. It would probably be impossible to make it an essay exam, since the public probably would not be willing to pay the salaries of the large crew of readers that would be necessary. If the public wanted its college graduates to be educated, though, it would be well worth the price.[27]

But even a multiple-choice exercise would be an improvement over the system that exists now. It would at least test approximately the amount of information the student has accumulated, and it would test the accuracy of his information, though it would not test in any meaningful way his ability to analyze it. But accumulation of information is, after all, the first step: no one has ever been known to think about anything without having something to think about. The passing score could be made high enough to compensate for any successful guessing the student might be able to do. Prospective teachers should be required to achieve a higher score than would be required simply to graduate. The exam could replace the Graduate Record Exam and Law Board Exam, and the graduate schools and law schools could establish the scores they would require for admission.

Temporarily under this changed system a smaller proportion of young people would go to college than do now, though the average high-school graduate would know more than the average college graduate does today. As elementary, junior high, and high schools began to educate students and as students began to go to college to learn rather than to prepare for specific jobs the number of college students might increase again. But temporarily there might be more rooms in dormitories than there are students to fill them. That could be turned into an advantage.

One of the serious flaws in the American system of raising its youth is that they seldom have a chance to associate with adults. Until they get through high school they associate only with those adults—parents, teachers, bosses in part-time jobs—who are in positions of authority over them. They never have to learn to live *with* adults or to be adults themselves. At a time when they should already be adults they are not, and at a time therefore when they need more than ever to live with adults we send them off to college to live in an even more infantile atmosphere. They live in dormitories, where they have even fewer associations with adults than they had before. Because they are eighteen years old and have no one to whom to compare themselves except others as childish as they are they consider themselves mature. To prove their maturity they seek the companionship of the only older people—their teachers—to whom they have any access at all. But they meet the teachers on their own terms—in the student hang-outs—rather than on adult terms. The teachers with whom they associate in the bars that cater to students are usually the least mature people on the faculty: the very fact that they find the social company of students exciting or interesting—or even to-erable—proves that. Thus the association of teachers and students in student hang-outs has the effect not of maturing the students but rather of further juvenilizing the already immature members of the faculty.

The dormitories provide a readily available means of enabling students to associate with mature people and others who would provide them with a more realistic view of the world than their association only with their own kind does. There should be enough dormitories that no more than half the residents are students. Elderly people should live in the dormitories with them. The elderly would provide not only an example of maturity but also a stabilizing influence on the transient young residents. They could be not only examples but also counsellors and friends. Since they would be the permanent residents of the dormitories the students would be expected to meet their standards of conduct. The dormitories might even become quiet enough to allow students to study in them.

But it is necessary for students to associate also with other people who are ordinarily hidden from their view. Dormitories would be excellent homes for the mobile physically handicapped. Students would benefit from living in daily contact with the blind, the deaf, the crippled, and the maimed. It would be a humanizing experience for them. It would make them more tolerant and understanding.

But there are also the mentally handicapped. Every dormitory should include a proportion of the self-supporting or partially self-supporting mentally retarded.*

All activities on the campus should be free to all of these people. More than that, in order to encourage other adults as well as people from all economic and social classes to mix with students all activities on campus should be free to everyone. Gradu-

---

*It is not true, as one person has suggested, that either the students or the mentally retarded would have to wear badges in order to distinguish them from each other. Since the introduction of co-educational dormitories the students are the ones with the silly-looking grins.

ally students might get over their arrogance and their discourtesy to those whom they consider their inferiors. Gradually they might come to realize that they are only fortunate rather than outstanding.

Finally, all public education must be free. Students who have the ability, the inclination, and the energy should be able to go to college and to graduate school or professional school regardless of the economic position of their parents. They should get their books, supplies, rooms, and meals without charge. Beyond that they should get a few dollars a week in spending money. Before we dismiss this as ridiculous we ought to remember that if we can do it for athletes we should be able to do it for scholars. When it becomes as important to society to have good teachers and sufficient highly qualified doctors, lawyers, engineers, and other professionals as it is to have good professional football and basketball players the society will discover ways to raise the money necessary to educate them. Whether or not a young person can hope to become a doctor or a dentist or to earn his doctorate should not depend on anything as haphazard as the amount of money he has. It should depend only on his ability and his willingness to work. When it becomes evident that he lacks either of these qualities his financial support should be revoked. Continuing in school should depend on learning rather than on such irrelevant qualities as wealth or family.*

Of course we need not be determinists to despair of ever making the schooling system an educational system. The society is cor-

---

*Student loans are potentially a real disaster for young people. While the loans do make college training possible for some people who without the loans would not be able to go to college, the result almost certainly will be to bring those people even more completely under the control of those who run the society than they would be without degrees. Students who graduate with debts of three or four thousand dollars are going to need jobs even more desperately than those without the debts. A young couple starting out with combined debts of six or eight or ten thousand dollars is really going to be behind the eight ball. They will *have* to behave themselves so that they can get their debts paid off and begin to think about having a family or buying a house. Even if their income is higher than it would have been if they had not gone to college—a possibility that is by no means certain, even if they can find jobs—the difference very often will not balance the cost of going to college, especially since instead of paying off the debts the young people could have been using the money to develop equity in homes or other property. There seems no doubt that the loans will make people easier to control, first by allowing them to go to college to begin with and second by putting them deeply in debt.

rupt, and the corrupt schooling system reflects that corruption.[28] Change in the schooling system will come only with change in society, and there is no evidence that Americans want real change. In their profound historical and political naivety[29] they lack the understanding that is the first prerequisite for accomplishing change. The schools have made them what they are, and what they are guarantees that the schools will also continue to be what *they* are. The only people who can bring about change are the economic and political elite, and they do not want it. The system as it is pleases them too well: they are, after all, the ones who created it.

Notes to Chapter 1

1. Ewald B. Nyquist, "Postsecondary Education: Nontraditional Approaches," *Today's Education: Journal of the National Educational Association*, LXIII, No. 4 (November-December 1974), p. 64.

2. Stanley Aronowitz, *False Promises: The Shaping of American Working Class Consciousness* (New York, 1973), p. 399.

3. American Historical Association *Newsletter*, XII, No. 8 (November 1974), p. 13.

4. "... there is a cognitive socialization process taking place whereby we learn what to learn and how to learn not to learn about that which falls outside certain parameters." Robert Morgart and Gregory Mihalik, "On What Isn't Learned in School: Schools, Social Science and the Laying On of an Anti-Labor Ideology," Paper presented to American Educational Studies Association, 2 November 1974, Manuscript Copy, p. 11.

5. For an example of the naive idealization of students see Ronald Segal, *The Struggle Against History* (Bantam edition; New York, 1973), pp. 29-39.

6. Percentage of Public and Non-Public High School Graduates Entering Four-Year Degree-Granting Institutions Within and Outside New York State

1964	41.0%
1965	38.0
1966	35.0
1967	39.0
1968	40.1
1969	40.5
1970	41.5
1971	40.2
1972	38.7
1973	38.8

Source: Distribution of High School Graduates and College-Going Rate, New York, Fall, 1971 (The University of the State of New York and the State Education Department Information Center on Education), pp. 2, 3; ibid., Fall 1972, pp. 2, 3; ibid., Fall 1973, pp. 2, 3, 5.

7. Percentage of Public and Non-Public High School Graduates in the United States Entering Institutions of Higher Education on a Full- or Part-Time Basis in Programs Creditable Toward a Bachelor's Degree

Fall 1963	53.6%
Fall 1965	52.5
Fall 1967	60.3
Fall 1969	61.5
Fall 1971	57.8

Source: Private letter from Mr. John J. Stiglmeier, Director, Information Center on Education, the University of the State of New York and the State Education Department, 24 January 1975. For the decline of seven percent from 1968 to 1974, see Chester E. Finn, Jr. and Terry W. Hartle, "The Chancy Health of Higher Education," *The New Republic*, 12 June 1976, p. 13.

8. New York *Times*, 16 December 1973, p. 1; Annegret Harnischfeger and David E. Wiley, *Achievement Test Score Decline: Do We Need to Worry?* (Chicago, 1975), p. 131; Albert Shanker, "Where We Stand," New York *Times*, 14 March 1976, IV, 9. See also Syracuse *Herald American*, 23 March 1975, p. 25; Malcolm G. Scully, "Fewer Score High on the College Boards," *The Chronicle of Higher Education*, X, No. 2 (3 March 1975), pp. 1, 7.

9. New York *Times*, 16 December 1973, p. 1; Scully, "Fewer Score High on the College Boards," p. 7.

10. Scully, "Fewer Score High on the College Boards," p. 7.

11. Cortland *Standard*, 17 November 1975, p. 2.

12. Paul A. Baran and Paul M. Sweezy, *Monopoly Capital: An Essay on the American Economic and Social Order* (Penguin edition; Harmondsworth, Middlesex, 1968), p. 311.

13. What is true of colleges is also true of high schools. Robert Maynard Hutchins, *The Higher Learning in America* (New Haven, 1936), p. 11.

14. CBS Morning News, 16 May 1975.

15. ". . . the advancement of blue-collar youngsters is unlikely, for the quality of schooling now being experienced is inadequate to the challenge of social opportunities. Blue-collar children may spend increasingly more years in school, but high-quality educational content and not time alone influences postschool achievement." Arthur B. Shostak, *Blue-Collar Life* (New York: Random House, Inc., 1969), pp. 274-275.

16. After pointing out that because young people comprise an important market advertisers have flattered them as the greatest generation ever, Wilson Bryan Key also points out that what the young people see on television is a very carefully edited version of reality that does not even remotely resemble the real thing. Wilson Bryan Key, *Subliminal Seduction: Ad Media's Manipulation of A Not So Innocent America* (Englewood Cliffs, N.J., 1973), pp. 71-73.

17. "Nor is this framework of fairness conducive to questioning the arguments presented [by spokesmen for each side of an issue], or exposing the

weakness or superiority of one or another side in a controversy. For even to appear to favor one side might be construed as an unfair presentation by network executives who closely monitor the news. Quite inadvertently, the fairness standards encourage rhetoric and even demagoguery, at least to the degree that spokesmen in a controversy are aware that their arguments are not likely to be questioned. Moreover, the networks' vulnerability to government regulation—which includes antitrust action as well as the FCC—requires a firm policy of neutrality in the view of key network executives. This entails recruiting correspondents without fixed views on political subjects, frequently rotating those who cover sensitive subjects, and not encouraging them—if only by not making sufficient time or resources available—to attempt to resolve controversial issues in favor of one side or another by conducting their own investigations. In a very real sense, then, the network policies of fairness and neutrality limit, if not define, the style of journalism on network news." Edward J. Epstein, *News from Nowhere: Television and the News* (Vintage edition; New York: Random House, Inc., 1974), pp. 264-265.

18. AHA *Newsletter*, IX, No. 2 (May 1973), p. 26. Emphasis added.

Notes to Chapter 2

1. Since the inadequacy of the schools and the ignorance of high-school graduates has always been apparent to people who look at the schools objectively, the comparison of today's high-school graduates with those of earlier decades becomes all the more difficult. For the ignorance of high-school graduates in the 1950s, see the appropriate items in Note 1 of Chapter 7.

"Argentinian writer and poet Jorge Luis Borges says his recent U.S. speaking tour has shown him that American college students are 'extraordinarily ignorant.'

" 'They (students) read only what they must to pass exams, what the professors choose. Otherwise, they are totally dedicated to television, to baseball and to football.'

"Borges, 77, who is blind, said America has lost the literary tradition that produced such writers as Emerson, Frost, Melville, and Thoreau." Cortland *Standard*, 7 June 1976, p. 24. (AP Newsfeatures).

2. When a historian can say "But then, history never is much help." one wonders why he does not correct his original mistake of getting into the wrong field in the first place. Michael Zuckerman in "Recasting American Historical Consciousness," a review of William Appleman Williams, *America Confronts a Revolutionary World: 1776-1976, The Nation*, 11 September 1976, p. 216.

3. Hutchins, *The Higher Learning in America*, pp. 89-90. ". . . the general distribution requirements presently in use at most colleges and universities should be abandoned and a real 'general education' curriculum adopted in their place. The new program in liberal studies should not use lectures to inculcate facts, for society is increasingly characterized by information obsolescence. Rather, it should stress development of certain transferable skills and abilities to enable students to design and implement analytic-action projects. All students, regardless of major, should take the liberal education program. It should form the basis for and be universally applicable to all majors and disciplines." William F. Sturner, "An Analytic-Action Model for Liberal Education," *Educational Record*, LIV, No. 2 (Spring

1973), p. 155. What this obtuse language appears to mean, so far as we can make it out, is that since information becomes obsolete there is no need to accumulate it at all. What the author never explains is how people can analyze anything without information.

4. Students appear to find it very easy to rationalize or deny the existence of their illiteracy. Almost any teacher who gives essay exams hears students explain their low grades by saying He just doesn't like the way I write.

5. Lucy B. Golsan, "Wasting Black Minds," *The Progressive*, September 1976, pp. 29-32.

6. In spite of this there are people who believe that the schools should not try to teach everyone to read. See A. H. Lauchner, "How Can the Junior High School Curriculum Be Improved?," *Bulletin* of the National Association of Secondary-School Principals, March 1951, pp. 299-300, quoted in Mortimer Smith, *The Diminished Mind: A Study of Planned Mediocrity in Our Public Schools* (Chicago, 1954), pp. 36-37.

7. William James, *The Principles of Psychology* (2 vols.; New York, 1890), II, 325-371; Edward B. Titchener, *A Text-book of Psychology* (New York, 1923), pp. 521-525; Howard C. Warren, *Human Psychology* (Boston, 1919), pp. 314-329.

8. Cortland *Standard*, 17 November 1975, p. 2; Gene I. Maeroff, "Rise in Remedial Work Taxing Colleges," New York *Times*, 7 March 1976, p. 1.

9. Recently there has developed an apparent concern about the illiteracy of college students. See for example Roger B. Smith, "Why Can't College Students Write?," *The News* (State University of New York), Summer 1976, p. 3. But probably we ought not take that apparent concern very seriously. During the years of rapid expansion the colleges did not worry about their graduates' illiteracy. Now, when colleges need all the students they can get, there seems little chance that administrators will allow teachers either to put the necessary pressure on students to get them to improve their use of language or to fail those students who do not read and write on what should be a college level. There is no certainty, either, that teachers will *want* to put the pressure on the students in the face of the students' fierce resistance to learning to express themselves or that the teachers, in the face of already decreasing enrollments, retrenchment, and competition for students, will be willing to fail those students who are incompetent with language.

Another thing to remember is that by the time the student starts college he often expresses himself so badly that even when he could learn to express himself it would take all or almost all of his time. Many are so far behind that they could never catch up.

Something else that we ought to keep in mind is that the apparent concern of college faculties and administrators about the illiteracy of students might be only an effort to turn the wrath of the rulers of society away from themselves and against the elementary, junior high, and high schools. It is in those schools, after all, that the students have failed to learn to express themselves. But teachers there are not permitted to teach students to write, either.

All of these are things that Gene Lyons apparently does not realize. In his attack on college English professors for not teaching students to write he fails to recognize either how far behind the students are when they get to college or the pressures on teachers not to put pressure on students and not to fail those students who do not measure up. See Gene Lyons, "The Higher

Illiteracy," *Harper's*, September 1976, pp. 33-40. Rather than to attack college English departments for not teaching students to write it would seem to make a lot better sense to criticize the people who organize the elementary, junior high, and high schools in such a way as to guarantee that the teachers there will not be able to teach students to use language properly.

Notes to Chapter 3

1. Standards appear to be even lower today than in the 1930s and the 1950s, when Robert Maynard Hutchins and James Bryant Conant wrote. Hutchins, *The Higher Learning in America*, pp. 37-38; James Bryant Conant, *The American High School Today: A First Report to Interested Citizens* (New York, 1959), p. 6.

2. Alexander Gerschenkron, "The Legacies of Evil," *Daedalus*, CIII, No. 4 (Fall 1974), pp. 44-49.

3. "Among our better educators and almost all faculty, there is a consensus that grades are, at best, meaningless, and more likely, harmful to real education." Carl Davidson, "University Reform Revisited," *Educational Record*, XLVIII, No. 1 (Winter 1967), p. 9. See also George Mannello, "Grades Must Go!," ibid., L, No. 3 (Summer 1969), pp. 305-308; Robert A. Feldmesser, "The Positive Functions of Grades," ibid., LIII, No. 1 (Winter 1972), pp. 66-72; Louis Troyer, "Grades Have Gone: What Then?," *Liberal Education*, LVI, No. 4 (December 1970), pp. 542-556.

4. Richard M. Gold, Anne Reilly, Robert Silberman, and Robert Lehr, "Academic Achievement Declines Under Pass-Fail Grading," *The Journal of Experimental Education*, XXXIX, No. 3 (Spring 1971), pp. 17-21.

5. Howard S. Becker, Blanche Geer, and Everett C. Hughes, *Making the Grade: The Academic Side of College Life* (New York, 1968).

6. For the high proportion of high grades even at what are supposed to be respectable colleges, see Syracuse *Herald American*, 23 March 1975, p. 25; Washington *Post*, 1 March 1975, p. A15; University of Alaska, Anchorage, Survey of Grades, 1973-1974, courtesy of Philip Swarr, Director of Institutional Research, Cortland; Malcolm G. Scully, "Inflated Grades Worrying More and More Colleges," *The Chronicle of Higher Education*, X, No. 13 (19 May 1975), p. 1; Office of Institutional Planning, Cortland, Reports No. 23, 31, 40. See also Michael Routh, "Grade Inflation—Big Disappointment," *The Press* (Cortland College), 12 March 1976, p. 7; Steven M. Cahn and Patricia Kitcher, "There's No Percentage in College Grades," *The Chronicle of Higher Education*, XIII, No. 4 (27 September 1976), p. 19.

7. "During the past decade, many institutions, including some of our most honored ones, admitted many more graduate students than they could decently train. . . . Some of our finest departments became so overwhelmed that they were in danger of turning into diploma mills." Alonzo L. Hamby, in AHA *Newsletter*, IX, No. 4 (September 1971), pp. 25-26.

8. Allan Bloom, "The Failure of the University," *Daedalus*, CIII, No. 4 (Fall 1974), p. 65; Richard A. Lester, "The Fallacies of Numerical Goals," *Educational Record*, LVII, No. 1 (Winter 1976), pp. 58-64.

9. For a long time there has been an apparent concern about improving teaching on the college level in the United States. See for example Dexter

Perkins, "We Shall Gladly Teach," *The American Historical Review*, LXII, No. 2 (January 1957), pp. 291-309. But ordinarily that concern has been only apparent. It has been neither deep enough nor broad enough to prevent the deterioration of teaching in colleges and universities.

Notes to Chapter 4

1. I have a reference for this, but I do not include it because I do not want to embarrass anyone.

2. There *are* exceptions. In preparing this book I have received patient assistance from Philip Swarr, Director of Institutional Research, Cortland; Thomas Syracuse, Director of Admissions, Cortland; and David Lewis, Admissions Counselor, Cortland. I take this occasion to thank them. Obviously there are other exceptions as well.

3. Many of these students are really seriously concerned about the issues they raise and are conscientiously determined to reform the world in their own image. The only thing they lack is the humility of ignorance. Others are simply erratic. A few years ago when I was returning from the first departmental meeting of the fall a student whom I had had in class and who I believe had graduated the previous spring fell into step beside me and told me that he wanted to see me right away about my grading because I graded too tough and was unfair to students. I told him to come in any time, but he never appeared.

4. "Conscious of the power of student opinion, . . . [teachers] too frequently court student popularity at the expense of academic integrity." Howard V. Evans, "The Liberal Arts College in an Age of Increasing Nihilism," *Liberal Education*, LVI, No. 3 (October 1970), p. 396.

5. Hutchins, *The Higher Learning in America*, p. 40.

6. For a start, see Daniel H. Perlman, "New Tools and Techniques in University Administration," *Educational Record*, LV, No. 1 (Winter 1974), pp. 34-42. Perlman has a bibliography in his footnote on page 35. See also Sandi E. Cooper, "A Research Proposal," AHA *Newsletter*, XIV, No. 1 (January 1976), p. 7.

7. Here I use the terms *community college, junior college,* and *two-year college* interchangeably, although I realize that some people make distinctions among them. For our purposes here they are identical.

8. Information from Thomas Syracuse, Director of Admissions, Cortland.

9. In the fall of 1974 one four-year college and one University Center of the State University of New York would accept *any* graduate of a community college in the state. The four-year college is Brockport and the University Center is Stony Brook. Information from Thomas Syracuse, Director of Admissions, Cortland.

10. Becker, Geer, and Hughes, *Making the Grade*, pp. 94-98.

11. Hutchins, *The Higher Learning in America*, pp. 18-19.

12. Maeroff, "Rise in Remedial Work Taxing Colleges," p. 1.

13. Two of the three people who are written up in the story on the Special Talents Program at Geneseo, for example, are athletes. "Geneseo Admits Students for 'Special Talents'," *The News* (State University of New York), October 1976, p. 6.

Notes to Chapter 5

1. Lewis B. Mayhew and James R. Glenn, Jr., "College and University Presidents: Roles in Transition," *Liberal Education*, LXI, No. 3 (October 1975), pp. 299-308; Cooper, "A Research Proposal," p. 7.

2. One of the discouraging things about the recent writings on the future of colleges and universities is the widespread acceptance among both faculty and administrators that the student is supreme, that the institution must adjust to the faddish interests of the students. See for example John W. Gillis, "Academic Staff Reductions in Response to Financial Exigency," *Liberal Education*, LVII, No. 3 (October 1971), pp. 367-368; Robert H. Maier and James W. Kolka, "Retrenchment—A Primer," ibid., LIX, No. 4 (December 1973), pp. 433-441; Willard F. Enteman, "Tenure at Union College," ibid., LX, No. 4 (December 1974), p. 461; David G. Brown, "Criteria for Pruning Programs," *Educational Record*, LI, No. 4 (Fall 1970), pp. 405-409; Joanne M. Sprenger and Raymond E. Schultz, "Staff Reduction Policies," *College Management*, IX, No. 5 (May 1974), p. 36.

3. Already in 1974 Brown University was getting disillusioned with "innovation" and was getting back to the "old curriculum." Robert Reinhold, "Brown University Trend: Back to the Old Curriculum," New York *Times*, 24 February 1974, I, 1. On the silliness of relevance see Bloom, "The Failure of the University," pp. 58-63; Leonard Kriegel, "Expendable CUNY: End of a Free University," *The New Republic*, 2 October 1976, p. 19.

4. "As a student once suggested to me, people will start demanding three hours credit for being born." Joel H. Spring, *Education and the Rise of the Corporate State* (Boston: Beacon Press, 1972), p. 153.

5. AHA *Newsletter*, VII, No. 1 (October 1968), pp. 13-15.

6. Ibid., XII, No. 9 (December 1974), p. 6. Emphasis in original.

7. Ibid., VII, No. 2 (December 1968), p. 43.

8. Ibid., XIII, No. 3 (March 1975), p. 4.

9. Ibid., VI, No. 3 (February 1968), pp. 10-14. The thrust of most of the suggestions for teaching history is that the person making the suggestion is the greatest history teacher ever and that all the problems of teaching history would be solved if everyone would only do exactly what he does. See especially Robert A. Waller, "An Historical Skills Approach in the U.S. History Survey," ibid., XIV, No. 1 (January 1976), pp. 4, 5, 7.

10. Cortland *Standard*, 19 December 1974, p. 7. (AP Newsfeatures).

11. AHA *Newsletter*, XII, No. 9, p. 5. Emphasis added.

12. Ibid., XIII, No. 3, p. 4.

13. Michael Lodwick and Thomas Fiehrer, "Undoing History: or, Clio Clobbered," ibid., XIII, No. 5 (May/June 1975), pp. 4-5.

14. Ibid., XIII, No. 8 (November 1975), pp. 11-12.

15. Ibid., XIII, No. 5, p. 5.

16. Ibid., p. 6.

17. Ibid., XII, No. 9, p. 6.

18. ". . . a discussion of slavery without a consideration of the exploitation of other labourers tends to obscure fundamental issues. . . . The basis of the problem is exploitation: the gross injustice which acquisitive society always inflicts on those who have nothing to offer but their body's labour." J. H. Plumb, "Slavery, Race and the Poor," in *In the Light of History* (Boston:

Houghton Mifflin Co., 1973), p. 110. ". . . a study of slavery, disengaged from the general history of the exploitation of labour, has inherent dangers, leading to a false emphasis and to a too simplified causation." Ibid., p. 113.

The result of studying Black History or Women's History might be similar to one result of my fifth-grade geography. Studying the United States, we started with New England. A map of the New England states made Maine look pretty big. A map of the southwest made Texas look bigger than the other southwestern states. But Texas did not dwarf the other southwestern states as much as Maine dwarfed the other New England states, and it took me a long time to understand why people could say that Texas was the biggest state in the union.

19. Borough of Manhattan Community College, *Catalog*, 1975-1976, pp. 183, 185, 187, 191.

20. Alfred University, *Catalog*, 1974-1975, pp. 29A, 30A, 31A.

21. For "relevance" in high schools, see Merrill Sheils, Elaine Sciolino, and Mary Lord, "Bunk as History," *Newsweek*, 10 November 1975, pp. 84-86.

Note to Chapter 6

1. "We are what we pretend to be, so we must be careful about what we pretend to be." Kurt Vonnegut, Jr., Introduction to *Mother Night* (Avon edition; New York, 1967), p. v. "And men will commonly believe and live up to those things which they habitually profess. That is the meaning of auto-suggestion." Thorstein Veblen, *Absentee Ownership and Business Enterprise in Recent Times: The Case of America* (Beacon edition; Boston, 1967), p. 427. Quoted by permission of the Viking Press, Inc. ". . . men and women come to believe in the truths which they profess, on whatever ground, provided only that they continue stubbornly to profess them." Ibid., p. 164. See also ibid., p. 428. Of course the unscrupulous teacher can also penalize the student who does not agree with him in an essay, but the very fact that he encourages the student to organize his material for himself means for the serious teacher that he has no desire to control the student's mind.

Notes to Chapter 7

1. A. Harry Passow, "The American High School: Beleaguered Institution," *The Nation*, 14 December 1974, pp. 623-626; Shostak, *Blue-Collar Life*, pp. 142-144, 149-152, 274-275; Charles Silberman, *Crisis in the Classroom: The Remaking of American Education* (New York, 1970); Conant, *The American High School Today*, pp. 23, 39-40, all of Section III; Andrew Levison, *The Working-Class Majority* (New York, 1974), pp. 118-122; Arthur E. Bestor, *Educational Wastelands: The Retreat from Learning in Our Public Schools* (Urbana, Ill., 1953); Arthur E. Bestor, "Anti-Intellectualism in the Schools," *The New Republic*, 19 January 1953, pp. 11-13; Arthur E. Bestor, *The Restoration of Learning* (New York, 1955); Albert Lynd, *Quackery in the Public Schools* (Boston, 1950); Admiral H. G. Rickover, *Education and Freedom* (New York, 1959); Smith, *The Diminished Mind;* C. Winfield Scott, Clyde M. Hill, and Hobert W. Burns, eds., *The Great Debate: Our Schools in Crisis* (Englewood Cliffs, N.J., 1959); C. Winfield Scott and Clyde M. Hill, eds., *Public Education Under Criticism* (New York, 1954). Conant, always

the diplomat, tries to make things appear to be pretty good even while he criticizes the schools. For examples of his pulling his punches, see Conant, *The American High School Today*, pp. 22, 40.

2. Michael Katz, *Class, Bureaucracy, and Schools: The Illusion of Educational Change in America* (New York, 1971), pp. 31-32, 33, 141; Ruth Miller Elson, *Guardians of Tradition: American Schoolbooks of the Nineteenth Century* (Lincoln, Neb., 1964), p. 1. See also William H. Whyte, Jr., *The Organization Man* (Anchor edition; Garden City, N. Y., 1956), p. 428; Talcott Parsons, "The School Class as a Social System," *Harvard Educational Review*, XXIX, No. 4 (Fall, 1959), pp. 297-318.

3. Cortland *Standard*, 7 June 1975, p. 3.

4. CBS Evening News, 24 July 1975.

5. Robert D. Hess and Judith V. Torney, *The Development of Political Attitudes in Children* (Chicago, 1967), pp. 105-108, 110, 217-218; Howard K. Beale, *Are American Teachers Free? An Analysis of Restraints upon the Freedom of Teaching in American Schools* (New York, 1936); Spring, *Education and the Rise of the Corporate State*, pp. 75, 76, 83-84, 103, 107, 110, 111-112, 118; Murray B. Levin, *Political Hysteria in America: The Democratic Capacity for Repression* (New York, 1971), p. 69. ". . . the young are taught to believe what their elders profess to believe. This indoctrination of the young by undeviating habituation in word and deed, precept and example . . . should logically bring grave consequences in the way of an accentuated nationalist bias in the incoming generation. It is something like drill in the manual of arms, both in respect of the mental qualities involved and in respect of the automatic responses induced in persons subjected to it. The resulting action-pattern of national animation runs on much the same lines as the habitual use of the Paternoster and Rosary, and carries the like uncritical assurance of well-doing." Veblen, *Absentee Ownership*, p. 427. See also Note 19 below.

6. At one time one of the functions of the schooling system was thought to be to facilitate social mobility. If that was ever true it is no longer true. Patricia Cayo Sexton, *Education and Income: Inequalities of Opportunities in Our Public Schools* (New York, 1961). More probably the school never did facilitate social mobility, except insofar as it drained potential leaders away from their natural groups, but rather helped to solidify the inequalities already existing in society. Colin Greer, *The Great School Legend: A Revisionist Interpretation of American Public Education* (Compass edition; New York, 1973), pp. 46, 54, 55, 59, 63, 73, 75, 105. Wilson Bryan Key points out that the schooling of students of journalism is a "super-automatic, high-speed brainwashing" that prepares them to accept "any rationalization necessary to justify the status quo." Key, *Subliminal Seduction*, p. 191.

7. Joseph Stocker, "Compulsory Free Enterprise: Brainwashing the Classrooms," *The Nation*, 17 December 1973, pp. 653-655; "Free Enterprise in the Schools," ibid., 19 April 1975, p. 453.

8. Willard Waller, *The Sociology of Teaching* (reprinted New York, 1961), pp. 33-35, 35-36; Hess and Torney, *The Development of Political Attitudes in Children*, p. 218. "The distinguished historian, John Bach McMaster, expressed a common view when in 1898 he declared that history should be so taught as to convince students that as a people we had been animated by the highest and noblest ideals of humanity, and that there was no land 'where

the people are so prosperous, so happy, so intelligent, so bent on doing what is just and right as the people of the United States.' " Merle Curti, *The Social Ideas of American Educators* (New York: Charles Scribner's Sons, 1935), p. 251, quoting from *Fourth Yearbook of the National Herbart Society*, 1898, pp. 29-30. "Bancroft, in 1887, conversing with the present writer, freely admitted that, when speaking of felons among our settlers, he had been very economical in dispensing the truths he had discovered. Having a handful, he had opened only his little finger. He wrote too early to expect that American eyes could bear the light of full disclosures." James Davie Butler, "British Convicts Shipped to American Colonies," *The American Historical Review*, II, No. 1 (October 1896), pp. 12-13. In 1949 Conyers Read, calling on American historians to "accept and endorse such controls as are essential for the preservation of our way of life," invited them to suppress inconvenient facts by reminding them that they "must realize that not everything which takes place in the laboratory is appropriate for broadcasting at the street corners." Conyers Read, "The Social Responsibilities of the Historian," *The American Historical Review*, LV, No. 2 (January 1950), p. 284. See also Sexton, *Education and Income*, pp. 233-234. For the deliberate falsification of the real world in graduate schools of economics, see John Kenneth Galbraith's review of Robert Lekachman, *Economists at Bay: Why the Experts Will Never Solve Your Problems*, *The New Republic*, 6 March 1976, pp. 22-23.

9. Morgart and Mihalik, "On What Isn't Learned in School," p. 12.

10. Vincent P. Lannie, "Common School Movement," in *The Encyclopedia of Education*, II, 312-320; Randall Collins, "Functional and Conflict Theories of Educational Stratification," *American Sociological Review*, XXXVI, No. 6 (December 1971), p. 1011; Curti, *The Social Ideas of American Educators*, Chapter 2 and p. 206; Frank Tracy Carlton, *Economic Influence upon Educational Progress in the United States* (Madison, Wis., 1908, reprinted New York, 1965), Chapter 4; Sidney L. Jackson, *America's Struggle for Free Schools: Social Tension and Education in New England and New York, 1827-42* (Washington, D.C., 1941), Chapter 9; Michael B. Katz, *The Irony of Early School Reform: Educational Innovation in Mid-Nineteenth Century Massachusetts* (Cambridge, Mass., 1968), pp. 33, 43-45, 46-47; Katz, *Class, Bureaucracy, and Schools*, p. 58; Greer, *The Great School Legend*, pp. 16-17.

11. Peter P. De Boer, "Compulsory Attendance," in *The Encyclopedia of Education*, II, 376; Curti, *The Social Ideas of American Educators*, Chapters 6 and 7, especially pp. 218, 220-221, 255; Lawrence A. Cremin, *The Transformation of the School* (New York, 1961), pp. 127-128; Greer, *The Great School Legend*, p. 18; Spring, *Education and the Rise of the Corporate State*, pp. 62-63.

12. Katz, *Class, Bureaucracy, and Schools*, passim, but especially pp. xviii, xxiii-xxiv, 9, 33, 48, 52, 94, 106, 108-109, 110, 116, 121, 122, 125; Elson, *Guardians of Tradition*, pp. 1, 9, and Chapter 12; Curti, *The Social Ideas of American Educators*, pp. 85, 190, 199, 278, 330, 563, 577, 577-578; Greer, *The Great School Legend*, p. 56.

13. Katz, *Class, Bureaucracy, and Schools*, pp. 33, 48, 68-70, 94; Jack London and Robert Wenkert, "Obstacles to Blue-Collar Participation in Adult Education," In Arthur B. Shostak and William Gomberg, eds., *Blue-*

Collar World: Studies of the American Worker (Englewood Cliffs, N.J., 1964), pp. 450-451; Craig Haney and Philip G. Zimbardo, "The Blackboard Penitentiary: It's Tough to Tell a High School from a Prison," *Psychology Today*, IX, No. 1 (June 1975), pp. 26, 29, 30; Silberman, *Crisis in the Classroom*, Chapter 4 and pp. 323-324; Waller, *The Sociology of Teaching*, pp. 43-47; John Dewey, "Education as Engineering," *The New Republic*, 20 September 1922, p. 91; Hutchins, *The Higher Learning in America*, pp. 11-12.

14. Robert A. Gordon and James E. Howell, *Higher Education for Business* (New York, 1959), p. 121.

15. Parsons, "The School Class as a Social System," pp. 298, 304, 307, 310, 316, 318; Jean Floud and A. H. Halsey, "Education and Social Structure: Theories and Methods," *Harvard Educational Review*, XXIX, No. 4 (Fall 1959), pp. 289, 290, 291, 292, 293, 294, 296; Hess and Torney, *The Development of Political Attitudes in Children*, p. 1 and passim; Emile Durkheim, *Education and Sociology*, trans. Sherwood D. Fox (Glencoe, Ill., 1956), pp. 71, 124; Levison, *The Working-Class Majority*, p. 120; Spring, *Education and the Rise of the Corporate State*, pp. 104, 108, 124, 148, 149. For indoctrination that is called still something else, such as "Personal-Social Adjustment," see Whyte, *The Organization Man*, pp. 104-105. Or it might be called "Family Living." Ibid., p. 432.

16. Katz, *Class, Bureaucracy, and Schools*, p. 11; Silberman, *Crisis in the Classroom*, p. 324. One of the things that the writers on socialization have not adequately emphasized is that the student is taught to get along well only with those who have power over him. He is taught to tolerate them only to make life more pleasant—and more profitable—for them, and, by ingratiating himself with them, for himself. See Spring, *Education and the Rise of the Corporate State*, Chapter 6, "The Comprehensive High School and Socialization." Spring apparently does not realize the extent to which people resent the very people with whom they appear to be getting along, even when they are acting on the same team as the others. That is why the molders of public attitudes have had to create the mystic idea of the team to begin with. They know that every member of the team resents every other member and that no one wants to do anything that will result in credit for anyone but himself. So he does it for the team. If he does not receive the credit he thinks he deserves it is not some other individual who is stealing his credit but rather the team that gets it because it deserves it. But the person who really gets the credit is the coach.

17. "In many underpriviledged schools, the I.Q. steadily falls the longer ... [the children] go to school." Paul Goodman, *Compulsory Mis-Education* (Vintage edition; New York: Random House, Inc., 1966), p. 26. See also Katz, *Class, Bureaucracy, and Schools*, p. 140; Jonathan Kozol, *Death at an Early Age: The Destruction of the Hearts and Minds of Negro Children in the Boston Public Schools* (Boston, 1967); Spring, *Education and the Rise of the Corporate State*, p. 153; Baran and Sweezy, *Monopoly Capital*, p. 308; Sexton, *Education and Income*, pp. 67-69.

18. Curti, *The Social Ideas of American Educators*, p. 310.

19. "Tentative Flow Chart of the Social Studies Program," in *Social Studies: Tentative Syllabus, Grade 12—Advanced Placement*, produced by University of the State of New York, State Education Department, Bureau of Curriculum Development (Albany, 1967), pp. x-xvi. According to this Tenta-

tive Flow Chart developing patriotism is an important part of kindergarten and grades one through three. Then in grade four "The total program of this year is aimed at building patriotism." Then, in grade five, the student studies "Patriotic citizenship." An important device for building patriotism during all of these years is the celebration of "the usual holidays and festivals." Apparently the people who develop the curriculum believe that after six years the attitudes of the students will be pretty well set and pretty safe, since after the fifth grade they do not consider it necessary to make the building of patriotism explicit. The conclusion that young minds are effectively ruined by the time the students reach the age of eleven or twelve agrees with the evidence supplied by Hess and Torney, though those authors do not put it this way. Hess and Torney, *The Development of Political Attitudes in Children*, pp. 1-92, passim.

20. "The plain fact is that men's minds are built, as has been often said, in water-tight compartments." William James, *The Varieties of Religious Experience: A Study in Human Nature* (Modern Library edition; New York, n.d.), p. 330. Bronislaw Malinowski points out that in "civilized" as well as in "savage" life the law of logical contradition does not apply to belief. A person can hold two beliefs that contradict each other and can ignore obvious inferences that are unpalatable to him. Bronislaw Malinowski, "Baloma; the Spirits of the Dead in the Trobriand Islands," in *Magic, Science and Religion and Other Essays* (Anchor edition; Garden City, N.Y., 1954), p. 220.

21. Durkheim, *Education and Sociology*, pp. 72, 87, 122, 123, 125; Katz, *Class, Bureaucracy, and Schools*, p. 46; Spring, *Education and the Rise of the Corporate State*, pp. 2, 46. See also Douglas F. Dowd, *The Twisted Dream: Capitalist Development in the United States Since 1776* (Cambridge, Mass., 1974), p. 145.

22. Greer, *The Great School Legend*, p. 5. Montgomery County, Maryland, High School Student Alliance to Board of Education: "From what we know to be true as full-time students it is quite safe to say that the public schools have critically negative and absolutely destructive effects on human beings and their curiosity, natural desire to learn, confidence, individuality, creativity, freedom of thought, and self-respect." Quoted in Erwin Knoll, "Five Crises in Public Education," *The Progressive*, December 1972, p. 24. Reprinted by permission. Copyright © 1972, The Progressive, Inc.

23. The evidence indicates that students become more rather than less like each other during their four years of college. Nevitt Sanford, "Higher Education as a Social Problem," citing P. E. Jacob, *Changing Values in College* (New York, 1957), in Nevitt Sanford, ed., *The American College: A Psychological and Social Interpretation of the Higher Learning* (New York, 1962), p. 13.

24. Collins, "Functional and Conflict Theories of Educational Stratification," pp. 1010-1011; Dowd, *The Twisted Dream*, pp. 128-129.

25. Curti, *The Social Ideas of American Educators*, pp. 112, 113, 263, 418, 563; Katz, *Class, Bureaucracy, and Schools*, p. 32; Cremin, *The Transformation of the School*, Chapter 2; Raymond E. Callahan, *Education and the Cult of Efficiency: A Study of the Social Forces That Have Shaped the Administration of the Public Schools* (Chicago, 1962), pp. 8n., 13-14, 58, 227-228; Spring, *Education and the Rise of the Corporate State*, pp. 1, 13, 18, 19, 22, 43, 44-45, 46, 55, 56, 57, 60, 61, 97, 121-122, 124, 148, 166.

Ivan Illich: ". . . the primary purpose of the school system is social control for a corporate state, and for an economy which has as its goal the efficient production and the disciplined consumption of growing amounts of goods and services." Foreword to Spring, *Education and the Rise of the Corporate State*, p. x. ". . . a number of high-ticketed executives took the floor to say the liberal arts colleges were important to them, that they sought liberal arts graduates for employment, and that they would continue to support the colleges as a sound investment so long as the colleges turned out men they could use." John Ciardi, "Democratically Speaking," *Saturday Review*, 24 March 1962, p. 31. "Colleges and universities are not churches, clinics, nor even parents. They are devices by which a limited number of skills, insights, and points of view are communicated to the young in the belief that possession of these somehow aids the individual to become a more skilled worker." Lewis B. Mayhew, "A Rendering of Accounts," in G. Kerry Smith, ed., *Stress and Campus Response* (San Francisco: Jossey-Bass, Inc., 1968), p. 154. See also Durkheim, *Education and Sociology*, p. 122.

26. Whyte, *The Organization Man*, p. 305.

27. Silberman, *Crisis in the Classroom*, pp. 323-324; Hutchins, *The Higher Learning in America*, pp. 11-12; Katz, *Class, Bureaucracy, and Schools*, pp. 33, 48, 69-70, 94; London and Wenkert, "Obstacles to Blue-Collar Participation in Adult Education," pp. 450-451; Haney and Zimbardo, "The Blackboard Penitentiary," pp. 26, 29, 30; Waller, *The Sociology of Teaching*, pp. 43-47.

28. Harry L. Miller, "Liberal Adult Education," in Malcolm S. Knowles, ed., *Handbook of Adult Education in the United States* (Chicago, 1960), p. 510, quoted in London and Wenkert, "Obstacles to Blue-Collar Participation in Adult Education," p. 446.

29. For a recognition that the business elite control both the media and the universities, see Key, *Subliminal Seduction*, p. 192.

30. Whyte, *The Organization Man*, p. 214; Curti, *The Social Ideas of American Educators*, pp. 563, 577.

31. Herbert J. Gans, *More Equality* (New York, 1973), Chapter 4, "The Positive Functions of Poverty and Inequality."

32. Greer, *The Great School Legend*, p. 116. The schools are not and never have been permitted to teach students anything about the condition of labor. Spring, *Education and the Rise of the Corporate State*, p. 144; Morgart and Mihalik, "On What Isn't Learned in School," passim. ". . . analysis tends to lead, not to national self-approval and euphoric self-confidence, but to criticism and doubt." J. H. Plumb, "Plantation Power," in *In the Light of History*, p. 115.

33. Max Weber, *The Protestant Ethic and the Spirit of Capitalism*, trans. Talcott Parsons (Lyceum edition; New York, 1958); R. H. Tawney, *Religion and the Rise of Capitalism* (reprinted Gloucester, Mass., 1962).

34. Today more than ever before the teacher's " '*unquestioned obedience* is the first rule of efficient service.' The teacher must remember that her relation to her superiors was 'entirely analogous to that in . . . the army, navy, governmental departments, great business enterprises.' " Curti, *The Social Ideas of American Educators*, p. 231. Curti's quotes are from William Chandler Bagley, *Classroom Management* (New York, 1907), pp. 262, 265. Emphasis and ellipsis in Curti. An almost identical quote from Bagley's

edition of 1910 appears in Callahan, *Education and the Cult of Efficiency*, p. 7. John Dewey pointed out long ago that the schools reward docility, that the most docile students become teachers, and that naturally they will readily follow orders. Dewey, "Education as Engineering," p.91.

35. Richard Hofstadter, *Academic Freedom in the Age of the College* (Columbia Paperback edition; New York, 1961), p. 63n.

36. On 1 August 1976 at the conclusion of the summer Olympics in Mont-real ABC showed the American Gold Medal Winners, one after another on the winners' stand as they were when they received their medals, with Ray Charles' version of "America" as the accompanying music. Twice Jim McKay mentioned that there was a princess and a night-club bouncer in the compe-tition and that the bouncer won a medal while the princess did not.

37. In the spring of 1976 the State Board of Regents of New York ad-mitted that the schools do not even train adequately when it ruled that begin-ning in 1979 students will not receive their high-school diplomas until they can read on a ninth-grade level and have a minimum skill in mathematics. The object is not to guarantee that the students will be able to think but rather to guarantee that they will possess "the basic skills needed to function as adults in the modern world." Cortland *Standard*, 27 March 1976, p. 1. Of course the object here is to make the students more useful to the people who control the American economy. The ability to read on the ninth-grade level will allow the students to read directions and fill out forms but will not enable them to read well enough to enjoy it or to pick up any information that might be dangerous to the position of the propertied class. So once again the dissatisfaction with the schools is not that they do not educate but rather that they do not train. "Albert A. Briggs, superintendent of Chicago School District No. 9, has kicked up a fuss by decreeing that sixth-graders must be able to read in order to qualify for an elementary school diploma." *The Progressive*, June 1976, p. 11. Reprinted by permission. Copyright © 1976, The Progressive, Inc.

38. Collins, "Functional and Conflict Theories of Educational Stratifica-tion," p. 1010. See also Spring, *Education and the Rise of the Corporate State*, pp. 31-32, 46, 125.

39. For the meaninglessness of competencies, see Malcolm G. Scully, "No Grades, No Credits, But 40 'Competence Units'," *The Chronicle of Higher Education*, IX, No. 18 (3 February 1975), p. 5.

40. Erik Barnouw, "So You Think TV Is Hot Stuff? Just You Wait," *Smithsonian*, VII, No. 4 (July 1976), p. 82.

41. Wilson Bryan Key points out that while as an educational device tele-vision is a disaster, it is a superb tool for training and has enormous and devastating potential for conditioning and brainwashing people and for destroying individualism. Key, *Subliminal Seduction*, p. 69.

42. One of the advantages of competency-based schooling is that if stu-dents spend all of their time learning such things as filling out tax returns, comparison shopping, balancing check books, buying insurance, and filling out applications for jobs (Larry Margasak, " 'Skill List' for Pennsylvania Students," Cortland *Standard*, 16 July 1976, p. 12), they will have no time to learn to read beyond the level necessary to accomplish those things. They will not have time to become interested in great literature or any of the other liberal arts. In college I had a course that was supposed to be principles of

economics but in which we learned to fill out income tax forms and heard guest lecturers talk about such things as social security and running a grocery store. But I did not learn any economics. When I started teaching I did not know what the futures market is.

43. The people who advocate the elimination of the schools ought to reflect that without schools the propertied class would simply devise other means of accomplishing what the schools presently accomplish. On abolishing schools, see John Holt, *Instead of Education: Ways to Help People Do Things Better* (New York, 1976); Ivan Illich, *Deschooling Society* (New York, 1970); Alan Gartner, Colin Greer, and Frank Riessman, eds., *After Deschooling, What?* (New York, 1973).

A fair proportion of the forty-four undergraduate teachers in the State University of New York who were honored for excellence and innovation in teaching for 1975-76 received their awards for experimental projects in the use of the media and therefore in the end their projects should make teachers less necessary. "University Honors 44 Undergraduate Teachers," *The News* (State University of New York), March 1976, p. 2. See also Barnouw, "So You Think TV Is Hot Stuff?," pp. 79, 80, 83.

44. Haney and Zimbardo, "The Blackboard Penitentiary," p. 106. "If knowledge is power, asked . . . [the Reverend B. O. Peers in the nineteenth century], how can the unsuspected ascendency of the rich be more effectually secured than by putting off the poor . . . with the present of a poor education?" Curti, *The Social Ideas of American Educators*, p. 95.

45. "At the end of twelve months I returned to Texas, ill, deep in debt, and without the degree. . . . There should be a moral here, but the only one I can find is this: Don't take an original idea into a graduate school." Walter Prescott Webb, "History as High Adventure," *The American Historical Review*, LXIV, No. 2 (January 1959), p. 271. "Without design, I was now on the way to becoming a western historian. I was excellently prepared because I had never had a course in that field, and therefore could view it without preconceived notions or borrowed points of view." Ibid., p. 272. "The brute fact of the situation is that as presently ordered the American graduate schools are not preparing the kind of historians that the future will need. Instruction in these institutions, save in rare and isolated instances, tends to sublimate, almost to suppress, rather than to arouse or invigorate qualities of imaginative and creative thinking." Carl Bridenbaugh, "The Great Mutation," ibid., LXVIII, No. 2 (January 1963), p. 328.

In addition to the survey of American history I teach American colonial history, American constitutional history, and the history of American labor. It seems significant to me that the course in which I have the least confidence is the American colonial, which was my major field for both the M.A. and the Ph.D. In neither the labor nor the constitutional have I ever had a formal course. I do not think that the confidence in the labor and the constitutional is the confidence of ignorance, since by now I have read approximately as much in those two fields as in the colonial. The point is that in the colonial I was reading things that really are not very good. That is not entirely the fault of my teachers, since until recently American colonial historians were among the least imaginative, most conventional, and most conservative of any historians I have read. But the main point remains: training in a field is designed to perpetuate conventional interpretations rather than to inspire curiosity. When those conventional interpretations no longer hold up, the teacher has a difficult time finding a context into which he can fit what he knows.

46. See Appendix.

47. Hutchins, *The Higher Learning in America*, pp. 14, 15-16.

48. Spring, *Education and the Rise of the Corporate State*, pp. 97, 103, 104, 111, 118, 119, 121-122, 124, 125.

49. Sara Burstall, *Impressions of American Education in 1908* (New York, 1909), pp. 290-291; Katz, *Class, Bureaucracy, and Schools*, p. 68; Callahan, *Education and the Cult of Efficiency*, passim, but especially pp. 15, 151, 152, 165, 176. Students, however, are not only the product of the schooling system: they are also the market. William H. Bergquist, "Responding to the Future through Curricular Reform," *Liberal Education*, LXII, No. 2 (May 1976), p. 236; Paul S. Hugstad, "The Marketing Concept in Higher Education: A Caveat," ibid., LXI, No. 4 (December 1975), pp. 504-512.

50. Richard Parker, *The Myth of the Middle Class: Notes on Affluence and Equality* (Harper Colophon edition; New York, 1974), p. 179; Gans, *More Equality*, p. 107; Joseph A. Pechman and Benjamin A. Okner, *Who Bears the Tax Burden?* (Washington, D.C., 1974), pp. 10, 64; Joseph A. Pechman, "The Rich, the Poor, and the Taxes They Pay," *The Public Interest*, No. 17 (Fall 1969), pp. 21-43, especially pp. 33, 43; Philip M. Stern, *The Rape of the Taxpayer* (New York, 1973), pp. 16-17, 23-25. See also TRB, "Infernal Revenue," *The New Republic*, 6 April 1974, p.4.

51. Greer, *The Great School Legend*, p. 152.

52. Whyte, *The Organization Man*, pp. 214, 220, 234-235, 236, 264, 428.

Notes to Chapter 8

1. Katz, *Class, Bureaucracy, and Schools*, p. 41; Haney and Zimbardo, "The Blackboard Penitentiary," p. 106; Greer, *The Great School Legend*, pp. 125, 138, 139.

2. Some writers appear to believe that academic institutions exist apart from the propertied class and can do almost anything they want to do, even to the extent of reforming themselves in directions not beneficial to that class. See for example Stephen R. Graubard, "Thoughts on Higher Educational Purposes and Goals: A Memorandum," *Daedalus*, CIII, No. 4 (Fall 1974), p. 5. Of course they cannot. They can introduce changes only within the context of their functions in society. On the issues that really matter, faculties and administrators are really quite helpless.

Fred Hechinger does a reasonably good job of distributing the responsibility for the absence of education in universities between administrators and faculties, but still he overestimates the real power of the faculties. Until recently faculties had the appearance of power, but they have never had any real power. They could make decisions only as long as those decisions were acceptable to the people who control the schools. That is what Hechinger appears not to understand. He also overestimates the ability of students to decide academic issues. Fred Hechinger, "Student Targets: Professors are Next," *Change in Higher Education*, I, No. 1 (January-February 1969), pp. 36-40.

3. C. Wright Mills, *The Power Elite* (New York, 1956); G. William Domhoff, *Who Rules America?* (Englewood Cliffs, N.J., 1967); Gabriel Kolko,

Wealth and Power in America: An Analysis of Social Class and Income Distribution (New York, 1962).

4. Marilyn Bender, *The Beautiful People* (New York, 1967).

5. Ferdinand Lundberg, *The Rich and the Super-Rich: A Study in the Power of Money Today* (New York, 1968).

6. According to Bronislaw Malinowski, myth is used to account for extraordinary privileges, duties, social inequalities, and burdens of rank. Bronislaw Malinowski, "Magic, Science and Religion," in *Magic, Science and Religion and Other Essays*, p. 84. For more on the functions of myth, see Bronislaw Malinowski, "Myth in Primitive Psychology," in ibid., pp. 97, 101.

7. "The Myth of Influence," *The Nation*, 2 November 1974, pp. 420-421; "The Rockefeller Issue," ibid., 21 December 1974, pp. 643-644; "Rockefeller on the Stand," *The New Republic*, 5 October 1974, p. 5; "Rockefeller and the Congress," ibid., 2 November 1974, pp. 5-7; "Rockefeller," ibid., 21 December 1974, p. 9; *Time*, 7 October 1974, pp. 29-30; 16 December 1974, pp. 26-27. See also "Rocky's the One," *The New Republic*, 31 August 1974, pp. 7-8.

8. Curti, *The Social Ideas of American Educators*, p. 157.

9. Edward Pessen, ed., *Three Centuries of Social Mobility in America* (Lexington, Mass., 1974); Katz, *Class, Bureaucracy, and Schools*, p. xxiii. See also Seymour Martin Lipset and Reinhard Bendix, *Social Mobility in Industrial Society* (Berkeley, Calif., 1959). For a typical statement of the myth of social mobility and the corresponding myth that classes do not exist in the United States by a man who accepts the myths, see Alfred L. Hall-Quest, Foreword to Howard David Langford, *Education and the Social Conflict* (New York, 1936), p. xvi.

10. "Far from being objects of pity, workers, according to this [unidentified] writer, ate better food than the wealthy, slept more soundly, sweetly, and unbrokenly, suffered less from changes of temperature, and pursued occupations 'more favorable to morals, and quite as much so to healthy intellectual development.' He denounced [Seth] Luther for insinuating that capitalists calculatingly monopolized education for the training of drones, vampires, and young men who 'spend their time in patching up the present state of things and lord it over others.' " Curti, *The Social Ideas of American Educators*, p. 93. Curti refers to *American Annals of Education and Instruction*, III (June 1833), pp. 255, 258-259.

11. Spring, *Education and the Rise of the Corporate State*, p. 130.

12. Lightner Witmer, *The Nearing Case: The Limitation of Academic Freedom at the University of Pennsylvania by Act of the Board of Trustees, June 14, 1915* (New York, 1915); David Danelski, *A Supreme Court Justice is Appointed* (New York, 1964), pp. 16-17, 100-107.

13. Lee Stephenson, "Our Kept Universities," *The Progressive*, March 1973, pp. 46-49. Chicago *Journal*, 1895: "The duty of a professor who accepts the money of a university for his work is to teach the established truth, not to engage in the 'pursuit of truth.' " Quoted in John Kenneth Galbraith, Introduction to Thorstein Veblen, *The Theory of the Leisure Class* (Boston: Houghton Mifflin Co., 1973), p. xix. "More typical [than educational writers who believed that teachers should encourage independent inquiry] was Jacob Abbott, who thought that a teacher was employed for specific purposes—the interpretation of the will of his employers—and that he therefore had no

right to wander away from that purpose. The limitations of this conception may be inferred from the fact that while Abbott thought a teacher in a republic might explain and commend the principles and blessings of a republican government, he would not be justified in doing so under a monarchy—in other words, he could lead his students only to accept, not to question, the existing order." Curti, *The Social Ideas of American Educators*, p. 61. Curti refers to Jacob Abbott's *The Teacher, Moral Influences Employed in the Instruction and Government of the Young* (New York, 1856), p. 178. See also Curti, *The Social Ideas of American Educators*, p. 566.

14. Spring, *Education and the Rise of the Corporate State*, pp. 128-130, 130-132; Knoll, "Five Crises in Public Education," p. 24; Sexton, *Education and Income*, pp. 234-237.

15. Spring, *Education and the Rise of the Corporate State*, pp. 86-87, 89, 131-132.

16. The lack of imagination and the parochialism of administrators is indicated by Eldon L. Johnson's statement that "The use of complex organization most distinguishes civilized man from primitive man. . . ." Eldon L. Johnson, "Education: Cutting Edge for Social Change," *Educational Record*, XLIX, No. 4 (Fall 1968), p. 360. While what are called primitive societies might be technologically less complex than what are called civilized societies, anyone who has read even a little anthropology would recognize that technically primitive societies often have very complex social organizations.

On administrators of primary and secondary schools, see Callahan, *Education and the Cult of Efficiency*, passim.

17. "Education is too important a business to be left to deans. The deanly condition is the condition of ignorance camouflaged by secretaries, charts, IBM cards, and statistics, but ignorance none the less. That ignorance is occupational. Let a good man be trapped into a dean's swivel chair and his inhumane ignorance grows upon him as a condition of his employment. The only real difference between the arrogant and the apologetic deans is that the apologetic ones know to what extent their work drains them of mentality. How can one leave educational decision to men who lack the time to read a book?" Ciardi, "Democratically Speaking," p. 31.

Many people have seen the lack of education among future high-school administrators for some time. Whyte, *The Organization Man*, pp. 91, 91-92, 92n., 109, 110; Smith, *The Diminished Mind*, pp. 87, 87-88, 88; Harold L. Clapp, "The Stranglehold on Education," *Bulletin* of the American Association of University Professors, XXXV, No. 2 (Summer 1949), p. 341; Lynd, *Quackery in the Public Schools*, p. 164n.; Baran and Sweezy, *Monopoly Capital*, pp. 315, 317. The people who control colleges come from the same schools from which those who control the elementary and secondary schools come. But the anti-intellectualism of the people who run American schools is not something that has developed since World War II. See Thorstein Veblen, *The Higher Learning in America: A Memorandum on the Conduct of Universities by Business Men* (American Century edition; New York, 1957). *The Higher Learning* was first published in 1918. See also Hutchins, *The Higher Learning in America*, p. 52.

18. The whole tone of Charles W. Lindahl's "Reaffirmation of Administrative Authority" is that the faculty is the enemy of administrators. Charles W. Lindahl, "Reaffirmation of Administrative Authority," *Liberal Education*,

LVIII, No. 4 (December 1972), pp. 524-532. ". . . the goals of administrators are closer to those of the students than those of the faculty." Ibid., p. 528. Lindahl cites Mayhew, "A Rendering of Accounts," p. 155, and John Searle, personal conversation. "The students comprise one 'estate,' the faculty another, and the trustees and their representatives, the officers of administration, still another." Ellis L. Phillips, Jr., "Toward More Effective Administration in Higher Education," *Educational Record*, XLVII, No. 2 (Spring 1966), p. 160.

19. "Faculty tend to be debaters, not decision-makers. As a class, they are disposed to philosophize, scrutinize and analyze but have proved to be poor problem-solvers." Lindahl, "Reaffirmation of Administrative Authority," p. 528. For a none-too-subtly contemptuous view of teachers, see Edward A. Dougherty, "Should Faculty Be Considered Well-Educated Individuals?," *Liberal Education*, LX, No. 4 (December 1974), pp. 521-530. Although he never comes straight out and says it, Dougherty argues by implication that faculties are not well educated but says that "We should not underestimate the ability of our faculty to become well-educated individuals." Ibid., p. 529. Presumably teachers will become well educated under the direction of administrators who, like Dougherty, have doctorates in higher education. Ibid., p. 559. Dougherty's argument is part of a pitch for "faculty development," one of the new catch-phrases in higher schooling. Although no one knows for sure what faculty development would entail, what we have heard about it so far indicates that it would be simply another device for placing teachers still more directly at the mercy of the administrators and to provide an additional means of accomplishing the flexibility that would enable the colleges and the universities to respond more immediately to the demands of the business class. On faculty development, see Richard P. Vaughan, "Teaching the Teachers," ibid., LV, No. 3 (October 1969), pp. 417-420; Warren Bryan Martin, "Faculty Development as Human Development," ibid., LXI, No. 2 (May 1975), pp. 187-196.

While we no doubt should discount part of Gail Thain Parker's intemperance as the result of her frustrations at Bennington, what she says probably is fairly representative of what the average administrator thinks of teachers. Gail Thain Parker, "While Alma Mater Burns," *The Atlantic*, September 1976, pp. 39-47.

No realistic and objective person with the doctorate would object to being called uneducated provided that the speaker includes himself among the uneducated. What he objects to is the administrator's calling him uneducated with the arrogant implication that only administrators are educated and that teachers must be re-educated under the direction of the administrators. We have all been through the same anti-intellectual schooling system, and the better a person manages to educate himself in spite of that system or after he leaves it the better he will realize how much his schooling has cheated him. It hardly behooves administrators, whose academic programs have often been even less intellectually respectable than those of the rest of us, to call teachers uneducated. Very often the difference between the administrator and the teacher is, in fact, that the teacher knows enough to recognize his ignorance, while the administrator is too ignorant to recognize his. This is often true even of administrators who have been teachers, since the education of the serious teacher continues all of his life, while the education of the teacher who becomes an administrator often stops the day he becomes an administrator.

20. If anyone doubts this let him spend a week reading the organs of the administrators. The items listed in Note 22 below would be a good place to start. According to Gail Thain Parker not only is administration alienating but one of the functions of the administrator is to encourage other people's alienation. Parker, "While Alma Mater Burns," p. 42.

21. Stephenson, "Our Kept Universities," p. 47; Callahan, *Education and the Cult of Efficiency*, passim.

22. Paul Lauter, "Retrenchment—What the Managers are Doing," Manuscript Copy, pp. 5-6; Maier and Kolka, "Retrenchment—A Primer," pp. 435-441; Sprenger and Schultz, "Staff Reduction Policies," pp. 23, 36; Gillis, "Academic Staff Reductions in Response to Financial Exigency," p. 367; Brown, "Criteria for Pruning Programs," pp. 407, 409; John P. Minahan, "Administrative Cost Accounting: Whose Cost and Whose Accounting?," *The Journal of Higher Education*, XLV, No. 1 (January 1974), pp. 38-47. See also Jack Magarrell, "Some Top Universities Retrenching," *The Chronicle of Higher Education*, IX, No. 18 (3 February 1975), p. 3. For an approach that could hardly be more wrong-headed, see Stephen A. Hoenack and Alfred L. Norman, "Incentives and Resource Allocation in Universities," *The Journal of Higher Education*, XLV, No. 1 (January 1974), pp. 21-37. What all of the cost-accounting advocates illustrate is a cynical manipulation of faculty. David G. Brown, in "Criteria for Pruning Programs," is particularly cynical. For a humorous criticism of the treatment of the university as a system to be managed, see W. David Maxwell, "Number Numbness," *Liberal Education*, LIX, No. 4 (December 1973), pp. 405-416. The anonymous administrator who wrote "Confessions of an Academic Administrator" *(The New Republic*, 27 July and 3 August 1974, pp. 18-19) either is an exception or is fooling himself.

23. Even someone as perceptive as Michael Katz can make the mistake of believing that in universities the faculties make the academic decisions. Katz, *Class, Bureaucracy, and Schools*, p. 131.

24. Bloom, "The Failure of the University," p. 64.

25. Sexton, *Education and Income*, pp. 193-194.

26. Bronislaw Malinowski notes that man gets as much satisfaction from thwarting others as from advancing himself. Malinowski, "Magic, Science and Religion," p. 85. Paul Radin points out that in modern as well as in aboriginal societies no man can rise above the theory of exchange value of his society. Anyone who substitutes his own absolute values for the "negotiating value" of his society is stigmatized as anti-social. If a man wants to get along he must always be willing to negotiate, to give something in return. Paul Radin, *Primitive Religion: Its Nature and Origin* (Dover edition; New York, 1957), pp. 182-183.

27. For personnel committees, see Parker, "While Alma Mater Burns," p. 40.

28. There are several academic novels that any prospective teacher should read. From them he will get a far better idea of what goes on in academia than he can get from all of the so-called scholarly books ever written on schooling. Some of these are more than academic novels, but their settings are academic. Kingsley Amis, *Lucky Jim* (1953); Kingsley Amis, *One Fat English-*

man (1963); Pamela Hansford Johnson, *Night and Silence Who Is Here?* (1962); Mary McCarthy, *The Groves of Academe* (1952); John Barth, *End of the Road* (1958); Bernard Malamud, *A New Life* (1961); Virgil Scott, *The Hickory Stick* (1948). During the early 1960s the novels of C. P. Snow were a popular fad, but those I read are not very impressive. It might or might not be significant that many of the same people who were impressed with Snow were also impressed with Ian Fleming.

29. Lauter, "Retrenchment—What the Managers Are Doing," pp. 7-9; Maier and Kolka, "Retrenchment—A Primer," pp. 435-437; Sprenger and Schultz, "Staff Reduction Policies," p. 23; Gillis, "Academic Staff Reductions in Response to Financial Exigency," pp. 371, 375-376; Brown, "Criteria for Pruning Programs," pp. 407-408. Faculty participation in dismissal "will militate against any subsequent allegations of arbitrariness or bad faith . . . [and] will add greatly to faculty morale. . . ." Jordan E. Kurland, "Reducing Faculty Positions: Considerations of Sound Academic Practice," *Liberal Education*, LVIII, No. 2 (May 1972), p. 305.

30. See Dowd, *The Twisted Dream*, p. 253. What Malinowski says about native informants also explains why some scholars see only a part of the world. No one deliberately tries to deceive anyone. He simply ignores what he does not want to see. He does not wash his dirty linen in public. Bronislaw Malinowski, *The Sexual Life of Savages* (Harvest edition; New York, 1929), p. 506.

Notes to Chapter 9

1. One of the most impressive things about reading the organs of the administrators is the extent to which they are concerned with the most recent fads and the mechanics of administration and the slight concern they show for liberal education. I have not counted, but certainly there are far more articles on such things as interests and values of students, curricular changes to meet "student needs," relevance, admissions, "faculty development," accountability, evaluation of teachers, new approaches to teaching, "efficiency," and problems of administrators than on liberal education. See for example the tables of contents of *Liberal Education* for the past five or ten years. *Educational Record* appears to be even less interested in education than *Liberal Education* is. In 1964 *Liberal Education* did devote an entire issue to "Reflections on the Role of Liberal Education." *Liberal Education*, L, No. 2 (May 1964). And in 1969 *Educational Record* had a series of four articles in a section headed "Liberal Education in the Complex University." *Educational Record*, L, No. 1 (Winter 1969), pp. 78-100.

The administrators appear to believe that an education is whatever a student wants and is measured by his getting a degree of some sort at the same time that they believe that the quality of an education is determined by its usefulness to the people who run society. They show little interest in liberal education, except when by implication they condemn it when they write about making the schools more useful to society. When they do consider directly what they call liberal education they sometimes redefine it out of all recognition. See Sturner, "An Analytic-Action Model for Liberal Education," pp. 154-158; Franklin W. Wallin, "Educational Implications of the Limits to Growth: Colleges as Instruments for a Great Transition," *Liberal Education*, LXII, No. 2 (May 1976), pp. 133-142. More often they exhibit a talent for laborious obfuscation that amounts almost to genius. See John W. Gustad, "Prologomena to Revision of the Curriculum," ibid., LVII, No. 3 (October 1971), pp. 324-336; David L. McKenna and Charles J. Ping, "The Forgotten American and the Response of Liberal Arts," ibid., LVI, No. 2 (May 1970), pp. 258-269. Some teachers exhibit the same talent. See for example Maxwell H. Goldberg, "Vocational Training, Career Orientation, and Liberal Education," ibid., LXI, No. 3 (October 1975), pp. 309-318. Occasionally however even an administrator writes a perceptive article. See Bernard S. Adams, "Liberal Education and the 'New Vocationalism'," ibid., pp. 339-348. Probably the best one I have found is Father Theodore M. Hesburgh's "Resurrection for Higher Education," *Educational Record*, LII, No. 1 (Winter 1972), pp. 5-11.

One of the most revealing ideas to come out of recent discussion of the liberal arts is to make the study of the humanities an *extra-curricular* academic activity. Garry D. Hays and C. Robert Haywood, "Liberal Education at Southwestern: An Interdisciplinary Approach," ibid., LIII, No. 4 (December 1967), pp. 526-539, especially p. 527.

2. A story that was reported to me as true illustrates the willingness of administrators to use raw power to get agreement. When a teacher was coming up for tenure a high-ranking administrator called him into his office and reminded him that it might not be a good idea to disagree with the administrators as often as he had been doing at a time when the administrators were about to make that decision. The teacher said that he could not be bothered with such concerns, that he would say what he had to say, and that he would either get tenure or not. He did get tenure. But he is a part of a small minority. Most untenured teachers in such a position would take the hint and keep their mouths shut. They would not *know* whether they would get tenure, and they would not take any chances. Administrators know that. Once a person gets tenure they can always hold promotions and potential salary increases over his head.

3. Richard Hofstadter and Walter P. Metzger, *The Development of Academic Freedom in the United States* (New York, 1955).

4. An increasing number of people are becoming increasingly impressed with the ignorance of people with doctorates. The convict knows more about penology than the criminologist; the pauper more about poverty and the prostitute more about prostitution than the sociologist; the bureaucrat more about government than the political scientist; the laborer and the businessman more about the economy than the economist; the explorer more about geography than the geographer; and the octogenarian more about history than the historian. Yet none of these knowledgeable people is hired to teach the young. The reason is that the object of schooling is not to teach but to praise and condemn. The rulers of society have to be sure that those who do the praising and the condemning are "sound," as they would say, and it is the doctorate that certifies them as sound.

Social science professors can have some freedom of inquiry because "their intellectual horizon is bounded by the same limits of commonplace insight and preconceptions as are the prevailing opinions of the conservative middle class. That is to say, a large and aggressive mediocrity is the prime qualification for a leader of science in these lines, if his leadership is to gain academic authentication." Veblen, *The Higher Learning in America*, pp. 135-136.

Quoted by permission of The Viking Press, Inc. These professors create and live in a world much like the Greek world of the early Christian era. "The world of the time was a world . . . which had created an artificial type of life, and which was too artificial to be able to recognize its own artificiality—a world whose schools, instead of being the laboratories of the knowledge of the future, were forges in which the chains of the present were fashioned from the knowledge of the past." Edwin Hatch, *The Influence of Greek Ideas on Christianity* (New York: Harper and Row, 1957), p. 49. "New improvements in learning are seldom adopted in colleges until admitted everywhere else." Oliver Goldsmith, *An Enquiry into the Present State of Polite Learning in Europe*, quoted in *Poems and Plays*, ed. Sir Sydney Roberts (Everyman's edition; New York, 1910), p. vi.

For the innocence, superficiality, and inconsistency of a professor of economics, a professor of political science, and a professor of urban values—whatever that is—see Robert K. Heimann, ed., *The American Revolution: Three Views* (New York, 1975).

The narrowness of people with doctorates and the bad teaching that goes on in colleges are things that even graduate departments have begun to recognize during the past ten years. For this recognition among historians, for example, see Lawrence Stone, "A Multidisciplinary Seminar for Graduate Training," AHA *Newsletter*, VI, No. 5 (June 1968), pp. 12-15; Russell Major, "A Doctoral Program for College Teachers," ibid., VII, No. 2 (December 1968), pp. 36-40; Les K. Adler, et al., "The Graduate Student as an Educator," ibid., VII, No. 5 (June 1969), pp. 30-32; W. Warren Wagar, "A Historian's Report from Bloomington," ibid., VIII, No. 2 (December 1969), pp. 11-14; Henry Bausum and Myron Marty, eds., "Teaching History Today," ibid., XIII, No. 4 (April 1975), p. 6; Richard H. Brown and Glenn Linden, "Faculty Development Program at Stony Brook: An AHA Report," ibid., XIII, No. 6 (September 1975), pp. 5, 16, 18; Edwin Fenton, "The Doctor of Arts Degree in History: A Report from Carnegie-Mellon University," ibid., XIII, No. 7 (October 1975), pp. 9-11; Norman A. Graebner, "Observations on University Teaching and Research," ibid., XIII, No. 9 (December 1975), pp. 5-7. See also David F. Musto, "NIMH Survey of Graduate Programs in History," ibid., VII, No. 4 (April 1969), pp. 15-18.

5. There is already some evidence that administrators are beginning to do this. In recent years in hiring new teachers they have begun to offer salaries so low that no one who already has a job will accept them. At the same time they list as a qualification "the doctorate or near." With the apparent excess of people with doctorates over jobs available for them the short-term result of this policy might be to increase the proportion of doctorates on teaching staffs but to keep them intimidated into behaving themselves so that they can keep the jobs and eventually receive a living wage. But it seems likely that the long-term result of this policy might be to discourage people from completing their doctorates and thus make people with doctorates scarce. Thus teaching jobs might increasingly be filled by people who will not have their doctorates, who will be so busy that they will not be able to finish them, and who will be so underpaid that they will have to behave themselves in order to hang on. They will hang on until they are denied tenure, when they will be replaced by others exactly like themselves and who will have to behave themselves also.

6. For the discussion of tenure, see Commission on Academic Tenure in Higher Education, *Faculty Tenure: A Report and Recommendations* (San Francisco, 1973); John Perry Miller, "Tenure: Bulwark of Academic Freedom and Brake on Change," *Educational Record*, LI, No. 3 (Summer 1970), pp. 241-245; Frederick H. Jackson and Robin S. Wilson, "Toward a New System of Academic Tenure," ibid., LII, No. 4 (Fall 1971), pp. 338-342; Robert K. Carr, "The Uneasy Future of Academic Tenure," ibid., LIII, No. 2 (Spring 1972), pp. 119-127; W. Todd Furniss, "Steady-State Staffing: Issues for 1974," ibid., LV, No. 2 (Spring 1974), pp. 87-95; Richard R. West, "Tenure Quotas and Financial Flexibility in Colleges and Universities," ibid., pp. 96-100; William R. Keast, "The Commission on Academic Tenure in Higher Education: A Preview of the Report," *Liberal Education*, LIX, No. 2 (May 1973), pp. 194-201; David D. Dill, "Tenure Quotas: Their Impact and an Alternative," ibid., LX, No. 4 (December 1974), pp. 467-477; Edward D. Eddy and Richard L. Morrill, "Living With Tenure Without Quotas," ibid., LXI, No. 3 (October 1975), pp. 399-417; Enteman, "Tenure at Union College," pp. 461-466; Brown, "Criteria for Pruning Programs," p. 409; Gillis, "Academic Staff Reductions in Response to Financial Exigency," pp. 369-370; "Academic Freedom and Tenure, 1940 Statement of Principles, Proposed Interpretive Comments," *AAUP Bulletin*, LIX, No. 1 (March 1970), pp. 26-29; "1976 Recommended Institutional Regulations on Academic Freedom and Tenure," ibid., LXII, No. 2 (August 1976), pp. 184-191; "Academic Tenure at Harvard University," ibid., LVIII, No. 1 (March 1972), pp. 62-68; Kingman Brewster, Jr., "On Tenure," ibid., LVIII, No. 4 (December 1972), pp. 381-383; W. J. Kilgore, "Reviewing Tenure," ibid., LIX, No. 3 (September 1973), pp. 339-345; Walter Adams, "The State of Higher Education: Myths and Realities," ibid., LX, No. 2 (June 1974), pp. 119-125.

7. Hutchins, *The Higher Learning in America*, p. 66.

8. I once had a European history professor say to me, "Yeah, Ellefson, I know you read a lot, but you read too much outside your own field." "What I wanted to be was a writer, and I wanted to write, not for the few but for the many, never for the specialist who doesn't read much anyway." Webb, "History as High Adventure," p. 268.

9. "A popular author must, in a thoroughgoing way, take the accepted maxims for granted. He must suppress any whimsical fancy for applying the Socratic elenchus [refutation] or any other engine of criticism, scepticism, or verification, to those sentiments or current precepts of morals, that may in truth be very equivocal and may be much neglected in practice, but which the public opinion of his time requires to be treated in theory and in literature as if they had been cherished and held sacred *semper, ubique, et ab omnibus* [at all times, everywhere, and by all]." John Viscount Morley, *Critical Miscellanies* (London: Macmillan and Co., 1923), p. 236.

10. "From the initial accusation to the final judicial hearing, the procedure followed in the witch cases reminds us at every stage that men seldom seek a high degree of proof for what they already believe to be true." Keith Thomas, *Religion and the Decline of Magic* (New York: Charles Scribner's Sons, 1971), p. 551.

11. "An ill-informed writer may state almost any propositions he pleases, with the certainty of finding listeners; a well-informed writer may state propositions which are as demonstrably true as any historical proposition can

be, with the certainty of being contradicted." Hatch, *The Influence of Greek Ideas on Christianity*, p. 15.

12. Of course the people who plan conferences similarly must do whatever they can to guarantee that no one on any program will say anything unconventional. For the conservatism and fear of controversy of historians at their professional meetings, see Arthur I. Waskow, "Radicals, Conservatives, and History: 1969," AHA *Newsletter*, VIII, No. 3 (February 1970), pp. 25-30; John K. Fairbank, Howard Zinn, Carl Landauer, Linda Grant De Pauw, and Boyd C. Shafer, "Professional Comment and Controversy," ibid., VIII, No. 5 (June 1970), pp. 14-23.

13. Thorstein Veblen speaks of "the many committees-for-the-sifting-of-sawdust into which the facutly of a well-administered university is organized. These committees being, in effect if not in intention, designed chiefly to keep the faculty talking while the bureaucratic machine goes on its way under the guidance of the executive and his personal counsellors and lieutenants." Veblen, *The Higher Learning in America*, p. 186. Later: ". . . the faculties have become deliberative bodies charged with the power to talk." Ibid., p. 206. See also ibid., p. 120n.

14. This is not to say that research and writing are not important. Probably the person who engages in a regular program of research can be a better teacher than the one who does not. He is learning new things, and he is immersed in his field. The problem is that the pressure to publish extensively makes it impossible for the teacher actually to teach. He cannot take time to organize and reorganize his courses; he cannot take time to read anything that is not directly related to his research; and he cannot take time to talk to students. For the controversy over the pressure to publish, see William Van O'Connor, "Publishing and Professionalism in English Departments," *College English*, XXIII, No. 1 (October 1961), pp. 1-5; Donald H. Reiman, "Research Revisited: Scholarship and the Fine Art of Teaching," in ibid., pp. 10-14; Lester Hurt, "Publish *and* Perish," in ibid., pp. 5-10; Jacques Barzun, "The Cults of 'Research' and 'Creativity'," *Harper's Magazine*, October 1960, pp. 69-74; John William Ward, "Cleric or Critic? The Intellectual in the University," *The American Scholar*, XXXV, No. 1 (Winter 1965-1966), pp. 101-113; Noel Perrin, "Publish and Perish—1984," *Publications of the Modern Language Association of America*, LXXXI, No. 7 (December 1966), p. A-4, reprinted from *The New Yorker*, 4 December 1965, p. 205; Richard L. Means, "Research Versus Teaching: Is There a Genuine Conflict?," *Liberal Education*, LIV, No. 2 (May 1968), pp. 238-244; Geoffrey Pill, "Publication and Professional Integrity," ibid., LIX, No. 3 (October 1973), pp. 349-356; Steven B. Sample, "Inherent Conflict Between Research and Education," *Educational Record*, LIII, No. 1 (Winter 1972), pp. 17-22; John Harold Wilson and Robin Scott Wilson, "The Teaching-Research Controversy," ibid., LIII, No. 4 (Fall 1972), pp. 321-326.

Ordinarily the value of conventional research and publication is not something that scholars talk about. It does not bear serious scrutiny, and therefore scholars simply assume its value. It must have value: it gets them promoted.

For satires of historians and scholars, see Cervantes, *Don Quixote* (Modern Library edition; New York, 1930), pp. 462, 492, 502, 503, 554, 584-585, 597, 598-599, 668, 846, 900; Henry Fielding, *The History of the Life of the Late Mr. Jonathan Wild the Great* (Everyman's edition; New York, 1932), pp. 64n., 164n.; Henry Fielding, *The History of Tom Jones, A Foundling* (Watford, Hertfordshire, n.d.), pp. 376, 377-378; Rabelais, *Works* (London, 1954), pp. 176, 177. For Thorstein Veblen on research and publications, see *The Higher Learning in America*, pp. 63-64, 78, 80-81, 99-100, 125-126, 131, and *The Theory of the Leisure Class*, p. 382.

15. It seems significant that in the spring of 1976 Ewald B. Nyquist refused to renew the registration of the doctoral programs in history and English at Albany. Private letter from Mr. Alvin P. Lierheimer, Associate Commissioner for Higher Education, New York State Education Department, 30 July 1976.

16. State University Federation of Teachers, Cortland Chapter, Legislative Memo No. 1 (7 April 1971); Legislative Memo No. 2 (13 April 1971); Federation of Teachers, Cortland Chapter, *Newsletter* No. 15 (19 April 1971); No. 16 (28 April 1971); No. 18 (12 May 1971); III, No. 2 (12 October 1972); III, No. 5 (9 April 1973); United University Professions, Cortland Chapter, *Unity News*, I, No. 4 (13 November 1973); I, No. 5 (n.d.); II, No. 5 (12 February 1975); New York State Federation of Teachers, *Teacher News*, II, No. 8 (April 1971).

17. Key, *Subliminal Seduction*, p. 190.

18. Michael A. Faia, "How—and Why—to Cheat on Student Course Evaluations," *Liberal Education*, LXII, No. 1 (March 1976), pp. 113-119. Howard V. Evans calls published course-teacher evaluations a subtle form of intimidation. Evans, "The Liberal Arts College in an Age of Increasing Nihilism," pp. 395-396.

19. James D. Koerner could hardly have guessed less accurately when he said that "the one thing that is clear in the contemporary scene is that classroom teachers, one way or another, are going to demand and get a much enhanced role in the making of school policy in America." Koerner, *Who Controls American Education?*, p. 45.

Of course the pressure of other members of the faculty is also important in controlling those who really want to teach, but I have considered that sufficiently in Chapter 8 in my discussion of personnel committees.

20. I first heard this term used by Professor Frank Ray of the History Department at Cortland.

21. For the refusal of the History Department at Yale to approve Herbert Aptheker, one of the most prominent Communist scholars in the United States, to teach a seminar on "W. E. B. Du Bois: His Life and Thought" in the spring of 1976, see Organization of American Historians, *Newsletter*, IV, No. 1 (July 1976), pp. 3-6.

22. ". . . the first prerequisite of a historian is a sound social philosophy." Read "The Social Responsibilities of the Historian," p. 285. "One can afford to be dull, if one has good friends at court, but one cannot afford to be unorthodox, at least not when the merits of democracy are in question." Ibid., p. 282. For democracy read the United States.

23. What Richard Hofstadter calls restraint by recruitment is still probably the chief device for guaranteeing that teachers will have acceptable views. During the eighteenth century those who controlled the schools guaranteed the conformity of teachers by making sure that they had the proper views before they ever got the jobs. Hofstadter, *Academic Freedom in the Age of the College*, p. 155.

24. Daniel C. Spitzer, "Ph.D.—The New Migrant," *The Progressive*, September 1976, pp. 25-28.

25. Sometimes a person who says particularly silly things can acquire the reputation of being especially subtle or of having an outstanding sense of humor. When I was in graduate school I said a lot of really dumb things. Because I was fairly quiet I did not say enough to enable most of the other students to realize how dumb I was. While some students no doubt did recognize my ignorance, among others I got the reputation of being very wise or of having a subtle sense of humor. Occasionally some time after I had said something particularly foolish a student would explain that it had taken him a while to catch on to my joke or that my point was a very good one but so subtle that it had taken him a while to see it. By that time, of course, I had recognized my own dumbness. Of course this sort of thing can happen only because graduate students do not have enough information to recognize ignorance when they see it and because they are so insecure that they dare not allow anyone else to think that they fail to recognize a joke or an especially subtle point. The same thing has happened on occasion even in more recent years, with teachers rather than graduate students turning my foolishness into subtlety or a sense of humor.

Notes to Chapter 10

1. Conant, *The American High School Today*, p. 1; Bestor, *Educational Wastelands*, Chapter 1; Silberman, *Crisis in the Classroom*, p. vii; Cameron P. West, "The First Priority for Faculty," *Liberal Education*, LVII, No. 4 (December 1971), pp. 521-528. See all of the references in Note 1 of Chapter 7. Among the more realistic writers are Michael Katz, in *Class, Bureaucracy, and Schools;* Colin Greer, in *The Great School Legend;* and Joel H. Spring, in *Education and the Rise of the Corporate State.* Even a person who deliberately tries would find it difficult to be more naive than Arthur Bestor when he says that schools exist to teach the power to think. Bestor, *Educational Wastelands*, p. 10. But not only is Bestor naive. He is also ignorant of the history of the American schooling system. He can say that "Many vital needs of men cannot be satisfied except through the extensive and rigorous application of intellectual means. No agency but the school can provide the systematic, disciplined intellectual training required. This is, and always has been, the primary, indispensible function of the school." Bestor, "Anti-Intellectualism in the Schools," p. 11. Reprinted by permission of *The New Republic.* Copyright © 1953, The New Republic, Inc. That, of course, is nonsense. For an equally nonsensical view of the function of the schools just after the American Revolution, see Kenneth B. Clark, Foreword to Sexton, *Education and Income*, p. vii. For a long list of suggestions for changing the schools, which the author believes are "reasonable . . . under present circumstances," see Sexton, *Education and Income*, pp. 253-287. The quote is from p. 266.

2. Dewey, "Education as Engineering," p. 89.

3. Richard Schauffler, "Criminology at Berkeley: Resisting Academic Repression," *Crime and Social Justice*, 1 (Spring-Summer 1974), pp. 58-61; Richard Schauffler and Michael Hannigan, "Criminology at Berkeley: Resisting Academic Repression, Part II," ibid., 2 (Fall-Winter 1974), pp. 42-45.

4. Greer, *The Great School Legend*, p. 154; John W. Gardner, "Universities as Designers of the Future," *Educational Record*, XLVIII, No. 4 (Fall 1967),

pp. 315-319. Eldon L. Johnson makes the real condition obvious. Colleges and universities might be the "cutting edge for social change," but the cutting will be directed by people outside those institutions. Johnson appears to believe that that is as it should be. Johnson, "Education: Cutting Edge for Social Change," pp. 359-365. The same thing is true of Franklin W. Wallin's "Educational Implications of the Limits to Growth: Colleges as Instruments for a Great Transition," passim.

5. There is always an apparent concern about what goes on in the academic institutions of the country. *Daedalus* recently devoted two issues to what is called higher education in the United States. *American Higher Education: Toward an Uncertain Future, Daedalus,* CIII, No. 4 (Fall 1974); CIV, No. 1 (Winter 1975).

6. Though they could not expect to enjoy every minute. See Durkheim, *Education and Sociology,* p. 87.

7. Hutchins, *The Higher Learning in America,* pp. 70-71.

8. Bestor, *Educational Wastelands,* p. 82.

9. According to George Weber, editor of publications of the Council for Basic Education, everyone except the most severely retarded is educable. John Egerton, "Back to Basics," *The Progressive,* September 1976, p. 24.

10. Knoll, "Five Crises in Public Education," p. 21. While the United States has plenty of wealth to provide good education and training for all of the young people in the country, the federal system of government guarantees that the schools will never have sufficient money to make that good education and training a reality.

A federal system of government is one in which the functions of government are divided among levels of government—local, state, national. In at least two ways the federal system guarantees that there will never be sufficient money to support adequately either education or other social services. First, as the central government increases its expenditures for such things as weapons, space shuttles, and other boondoggles for business a decreasing proportion of the total wealth of the country is available for more important purposes. As the central government increases its taxes it leaves less money for state and local governments. Second, the states and local governments are unable to tax adequately the wealth that does exist. They are unable to tax the great corporations, since as soon as the officials of a state or a locality suggest that they might increase taxes on corporations the corporations threaten to move to states or localities with more friendly officials. Thus the politicians who dared to try to tax corporations would not only not increase the income of the state or locality but also could be held responsible for the loss of jobs that would result from the departure of the corporations. And that is exactly why the leaders of the business world adore the federal system. It guarantees that the state and local governments will be responsible for functions that they will not have the resources to perform and therefore that those functions will not be performed at all. Some leaders of business do believe that they want good education and training, but what is really important to them is maintaining a system that guarantees that they will not have to pay their fair share of taxes and that therefore guarantees the continued inadequacy of education and training and other social services.

The only solution for this dilemma is the central government's absorption of the functions historically reserved for the states. Logic as well as common sense dictates that ultimately the states should be abolished and be replaced by half a dozen or so administrative districts. Of course there is almost no chance that that will ever happen. The people who benefit from the present system are the people in control, and they are not going to permit any change that would destroy their advantageous position.

11. Paul Goodman has suggested something such as this. Goodman, *Compulsory Mis-Education*, pp. 124-126. See also Steven Muller, "The Case for Universal National Service," *Educational Record*, LII, No. 1 (Winter 1971), pp. 17-22.

12. *Statistical Abstract of the United States* (1974), p. 58.

13. R. H. Tawney, *The Acquisitive Society* (Harvest edition; New York, n.d.), p. 84.

14. There exists also the notion that if the ability to communicate ever does become necessary a person can find someone else to do the communicating for him. When I was teaching in the high school of a small city in Wisconsin many of the senior boys told me that it was not necessary for them to write correctly because they would have secretaries who would turn their language into correct English. Although most of them were so ignorant that they could realistically aspire to nothing economically higher than manual labor or at best a foreman's job, their schooling had misled them into believing that they could expect to become executives in some of the industries in that pretty little class-ridden one-horse town. It never occurred to these ambitious young men that since they could speak no better than they could write any secretary would have a difficult time understanding them well enough to turn *any*thing they said into understandable English, and it never occurred to them either that since they could not read any better than they could write they would have a very difficult time discovering the things executives must know and on which the ideas of the executive are based. Nor did it occur to them that they simply belonged to the wrong economic class to begin with and that the schooling system in the city was designed to keep them in their place. The schooling system accomplished this through busywork, athletics, and flattery.

Premarital sex also helped to keep the lower economic class in its place. More than twenty years before the sexual "emancipation" of the young, the people in this town appeared to have a very relaxed attitude toward premarital sex. The result was that what appeared to be a large number of girls became pregnant and had to get married. The result of this in turn was that the young man whose ambitions were frustrated but who would not have accomplished them in any case now had to blame his own carelessness rather than his lack of real opportunity. Whether the wealthy class knew what it was doing and did it deliberately I do not know, but the result was the same either way. And whether the rate of pregnancy among teen-aged girls was higher in this town than in many others I do not know either. We thought it was at the time, but it is possible that the same phenomenon exists in many cities, and for the same reasons.

15. Hutchins, *The Higher Learning in America*, pp. 70-71; Hofstadter, *Academic Freedom in the Age of the College*, p. 227.

16. Furniss, "Steady-State Staffing," pp. 87-95.

17. On the graduate level all courses in educational administration and student personnel should be eliminated. To expect people who have wasted

their time studying plumbing and toilet paper to know what education is all about is naive. See Callahan, *Education and the Cult of Efficiency*, Chapters 8 and 9. Similarly, to consider the student's personal and psychological problems a legitimate concern of the college is nonsense. Often his personal and psychological problems are the result of his academic problems, and the student has no more right to publicly supported counselling than anyone else has. The counselling offices on college campuses should be eliminated, and free counselling should be made readily available to *all* people.

18. Hutchins, *The Higher Learning in America*, pp. 33-58.

19. Ibid., p. 70. A few years ago, about two weeks after classes began in the fall, a male freshman began to talk to one of my colleagues and me about reforming the curriculum of the college. Having been on campus for an entire two weeks he was obviously an expert. Later he became active in student government, and the last I knew he was in Albany, on some sort of administrative internship, I think, no doubt applying his twenty-two-year-old expertise to the whole state system.

20. "If the university wishes to contract for programs *un*related to the interests and needs of undergraduate students, it should place undergraduates on the committees making the ranking decisions." Brown, "Criteria for Pruning Programs," p. 408. Emphasis added.

21. For a recognition of the importance of the participation of faculties in making academic decisions as well as a recognition that faculties have been allowed too little voice in those decisions, see Bertram H. Davis, "The Faculty and Institutional Policy," *Educational Record*, XLVII, No. 2 (Spring 1966), pp. 185-191. John Ciardi speaks of "the fungi of that administrative blight that has marked the face of . . . American colleges, a blight whose simple disaster is the fact that college policy has passed almost entirely from the hands of the faculty into those of the administration." Ciardi, "Democratically Speaking," p. 31.

22. "Our colleges will be measurably better the day deans become the clerical servants of the faculty." Ciardi, "Democratically Speaking," p. 31.

23. Even people who think they think seriously about education often fear teachers more than they fear administrators. Koerner, *Who Controls American Education?*, p. 43.

24. See Hofstadter, *Academic Freedom in the Age of the College*, pp. 234-238, and Donald C. Darnton, "A Case for the Faculty-Administrator," *Educational Record*, LI, No. 2 (Spring 1970), pp. 154-158.

The unwillingness of professors to make decisions that Gail Thain Parker complains about (Parker, "While Alma Mater Burns," pp. 39-47) results— insofar as the complaint is not exaggerated—in the first place from the insecurity of professors at a time when the elite have decided that colleges and universities are not as useful to them as they once were and therefore are less necessary than they were and in the second place from the teachers' recognition that administrators pay attention to them only when it suits the purposes of the administrators and that faculty committees are designed to take some of the onus of making tough decisions off the administrators. ". . . responsibility is impossible without power. . . ." Tawney, *The Acquisitive Society*, p. 128. If trustees or state legislatures would say to faculties "Okay, here is how much money is available. You decide how to use it." faculties would be willing to thrash it out. But they could not thrash it out every year.

They would have to have stable budgets. The fluctuation of the budgets for schools, making new decisions necessary every year, is probably the one thing that makes administrators appear most necessary and therefore justifies, in the minds of those who do not know any better as well as those who want administrators to run the schools to begin with, most of their power. It is not outrageous to suggest that with stable budgets faculties could run colleges and universities better than administrators do, since many of the decisions that administrators make should not have to be made at all. One of the things that administrators are going to discover if they ever achieve the steady-state staffing that they say they want is that the university in steady-state will make most administrators unnecessary. It might be because they recognize this that they emphasize "faculty development" as much as they do. Without anything else to keep them busy they will be able to keep themselves occupied harassing teachers through the constant creation of new faculty-development programs. Faculty-development programs have unlimited possibilities: there is no limit to the ways that administrators can devise to harass faculties.

25. ". . . college sports come in for an ever increasing attention and take an increasingly prominent and voluminous place in the university's life; as do also other politely blameless ways and means of dissipation, such as fraternities, clubs, exhibitions, and the extensive range of extra-scholastic traffic known as 'student activities.' " Veblen, *The Higher Learning in America*, pp. 74-75. To compete for students "it is well . . . [for a college] to promote a complete and varied line of scholastic accessories, in the way of athletics, clubs, fraternities, 'student activities,' and similar devices of politely blameless dissipation." Ibid., p. 87.

26. Paul Goodman has suggested something such as this. Goodman, *Compulsory Mis-Education*, pp. 127-130.

27. In other countries the essay exam in used. Koerner, *Who Controls American Education?*, p. 47.

28. Durkheim, *Education and Sociology*, p. 94; Curti, *The Social Ideas of American Educators*, p. 424.

29. Paul Conkin says that the American electorate is appallingly ignorant about economics and appallingly immature philosophically. Paul Conkin, *The New Deal* (New York, 1967), p. 106.

Appendix

I must point out that my own Ph.D. advisor did not do most of these things. He left me pretty well alone. But not all of the members of my committee were so generous. One of my fields was English history from 1485 to 1914. I did all of the work through readings, and I concentrated on the Tudors and the Stuarts. During my oral examination the professor of English history spent about twenty-five minutes—one-fifth of two hours—asking me questions he knew I could not answer, and I spent twenty-five minutes saying "I don't know." Once he made a mistake. He asked a question that I could answer by tracing the history from the time of the Tudors, and when I began to do that he interrupted and said, "Yeah, Ellefson, I know you want to get back to the Tudors and Stuarts, but let's stick to the nineteenth century." When the two hours were up the committee kept me waiting for twenty minutes while it talked, and long after I had given up hope of passing, my advisor appeared, told me I had passed, and ushered me back into the room. There the rest of the committee, all smiles—including the professor of English history—congratulated me heartily. The professor of English history did manage to get the rest of the committee to accept what he hoped would be the humiliating condition that I attend the seminar he was conducting that semester on England in the nineteenth century.

I think that the professor of English history acted as he did for three reasons. First, all through graduate school I was cocky, and he was determined to take me down a notch while he still had a chance. Second, there was a vicious political battle going on in the history department at the time. By humiliating me he could indirectly humiliate my advisor. Third, I had humiliated him in front of ten or twelve students by causing him to admit that he had not read a book he had claimed to have read. In a readings course that he conducted in his home he commented that *The Elizabethan House of Commons* is only a rewrite of one of the volumes of *Elizabeth I and Her Parliaments.* My job, I thought, was to explain what it really is. That is what I did. He needed to get back at me.

The indifference of professors in graduate school also wears the student down and might be deliberately designed for that purpose. The greater the importance of the exercise on which the professors show their indifference, the greater the effect on the graduate student should be. And probably the most important exercise that the graduate student goes through is his written exam. At Maryland in 1963 four fields were required for a doctorate in history. The student took the exam in two parts, called the preliminary exam and the comprehensive exam. I was scheduled to take my preliminary exam on a Tuesday and a Thursday. Since I could not sleep anyway, I got up earlier than usual on Tuesday and went to the history department. I got there before anyone else. The secretary came in on time. Finally the professor whose exam I was supposed to take came in. He said good morning and disappeared into his office. I waited. Suddenly he came bursting out of his office, according to the secretary, and said "*I* know why Ellefson is here so early. He's supposed to take his exam today." He called me into his office and told me, very apologetically, that he had not had time to make up the exam but that I should go ahead and take the other exam as scheduled on Thursday. In the meantime he would make up the exam, and I could pick it up on Friday evening, take it home, and write it over the weekend. I took the other exam on Thursday, but when I went back to the history office late on Friday afternoon the first professor told me, very apologetically, that he still had not had time to make up the exam but that if I would come back on Monday he would have it ready and I could take it home and write it on Monday evening and Tuesday morning. When I appeared at the office late on Monday the professor did have the exam ready. I took it home, and I had written for about three hours when I had a visitor. When he discovered what I was doing he left almost immediately, but since I could not recover my concentration I decided to finish the exam in the morning. In the morning I read it over and decided to hand it in as it was. I decided that if I did not pass I would protest the whole mess.

About a year later I was ready for my comprehensive exam, which would cover the two remaining fields. I thought that I had arranged to take the exam in one week, on Monday and Wednesday, with the oral exam on Friday, but the week before that my advisor informed me that on one field I would have to take two exams. One of these would be made up by the professor under whom I had studied and the other by a professor whom I barely knew. Of course I agreed. So I would take the written exam on Monday, Wednesday, and Friday with the oral exam on the following Monday. On Monday morning I got to the history department early again. Finally the chairman arrived. Remembering what had happened a year earlier I told him why I was there. He had bad news for me. The professor whose exam I was to take that day had not turned it in yet. Ellefson: Maybe I could take one of the others. Chairman: Well, unfortunately, that's not possible. Neither of them has turned in an exam, either. But he did call the first professor, who rushed in and while I waited outside his office made out an exam for me. The other two professors had more time and did have their exams ready on schedule. On Monday I did take the oral exam, and the professor who had had to rush to make up the exam spent his twenty to twenty-five minutes keeping me saying "I don't know."